For Colleen

In solidarity for
the work you do

THE SPIRIT OF FREEDOM

Jun 2003

# THE SPIRIT OF FREEDOM

*South African Leaders on Religion and Politics*

CHARLES VILLA-VICENCIO

With a Foreword by Thomas G. Karis

Interviews with Neville Alexander,
Ray Alexander, Franz Auerbach, Cheryl Carolus,
Frank Chikane, Sheena Duncan,
Ela Gandhi, Nadine Gordimer, Chris Hani,
Trevor Huddleston, Nelson Mandela,
Govan Mbeki, Fatima Meer, Stanley Mogoba,
Ruth Mompati, Itumeleng Mosala,
Beyers Naudé, Ebrahim Rasool,
Albertina Sisulu, Joe Slovo, Desmond Tutu

UNIVERSITY OF CALIFORNIA PRESS
Berkeley      Los Angeles      London

This book is a print-on-demand volume. It is manufactured using toner in place of ink. Type and images may be less sharp than the same material seen in traditionally printed University of California Press editions.

University of California Press
Berkeley and Los Angeles, California

University of California Press, Ltd.
London, England

© 1996 by
The Regents of the University of California

Originally published by Skotaville Publishers, Johannesburg, South Africa

**Library of Congress Cataloging-in-Publication Data**

Villa-Vicencio, Charles.
    The spirit of freedom : South African leaders on religion and
politics / Charles Villa-Vicencio ; with a foreword by Thomas Karis.
       p.   cm. — (Perspectives on South Africa ; 52)
    Includes bibliographical references.
    ISBN 0-520-20044-6 (alk. paper). — ISBN 0-520-20045-4 (pbk. : alk. paper)
    1.  Religion and politics—South Africa.  2.  South Africa—
Religion—20th century.  3.  South Africa—Politics and
government—1989–  4.  South Africa—Politics and government—20th
century.  5.  Political activists—South Africa—Interviews.
I. Title.  II. Series.
BL2470.S6V55   1996
291.1'77'0968—dc20                              95-20361
                                                 CIP

Printed in the United States of America

# CONTENTS

MAPS

# South Africa, pre-1994

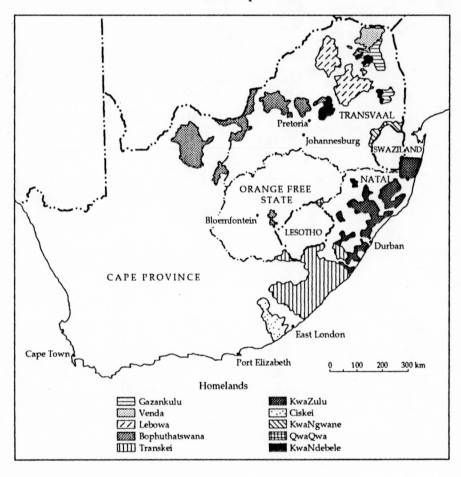

Pretoria

Johannesburg

TRANSVAAL

SWAZILAND

NATAL

ORANGE FREE
STATE

Bloemfontein

LESOTHO

Durban

CAPE PROVINCE

East London

Cape Town

Port Elizabeth

0    100    200    300 km

## Homelands

| | |
|---|---|
| Gazankulu | KwaZulu |
| Venda | Ciskei |
| Lebowa | KwaNgwane |
| Bophuthatswana | QwaQwa |
| Transkei | KwaNdebele |

## South Africa, post-1994

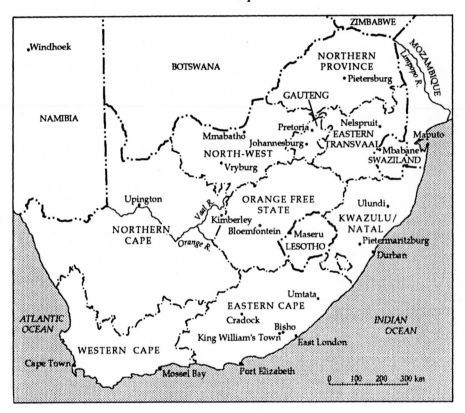

# FOREWORD

Charles Villa-Vicencio has written an extraordinary book, inquiring into the politics, religion, and values of twenty-one leading opponents of apartheid. All twenty-one share a spirit of hope and optimism for democracy in South Africa. "Hope," says Archbishop Trevor Huddleston, one of the twenty-one, is theologically the knowledge that God's righteousness will prevail whereas optimism is transitory. Although their perceptions of God vary widely, all believe in the coming of a righteous, or right-minded, South Africa. Six are atheists, eight are professed Christians, three are close to Christianity, one is a religious Jew, two are Muslims, and one is a Hindu; but all share a common moral vision of a new South Africa. After years of opposition to a powerful and brutal regime, they foresaw— in 1992 or early 1993 when they were interviewed by Villa-Vicencio — the transition process with varying degrees of optimism and pessimism; yet no one predicted the celebratory and peaceful spirit of the election days of April 26–29, 1994, and the breadth of reconciliation that has followed.

South Africa has been riven by centuries of racial conflict and cruel oppression; but as the election returns came in, Nelson Mandela, the future president and one of the subjects of this book, declared that "a small miracle" had occurred. He raised a glass "to celebrate the birth of democracy" in a calm and tolerant atmosphere and commended the security forces for "the sterling work done." The African National Congress (ANC) had won a landslide electoral victory, and South Africa had experienced revolution by consent. The right-wing newspaper *The Citizen* praised Mandela as "a president of the people for the people" who would begin a "healing process that will make us one nation in one country." There appeared to be no precedent for the peaceful relinquishing of power to an oppressed racial majority by a militarily undefeated regime.

Both believers and unbelievers may well ask how South Africa arrived at such a consummation. By the end of the 1980s the National

Many passages in this foreword are taken from Thomas G. Karis, " 'A Small Miracle' Continues: South Africa, 1994–1999," in *The Round Table: The Commonwealth Journal of International Affairs*, April 1995.

Party regime attained a clarity of vision that had previously been clouded by ideology and wishful thinking. In order to maintain the viability of an economy whose interdependence had been growing for more than a century and to secure stability, there was no alternative to dealing with credible black leaders. Internal and external pressures had combined: the resurgence of the African National Congress, a mass protest movement that could not be subdued, the regime's loss of confidence in reform, the withdrawal of confidence by foreign banks, an economic crisis, the enactment of American sanctions over President Reagan's veto, and the withdrawal of the Soviet Union from southern Africa.

The ANC also saw the future with new clarity. Its armed struggle, begun symbolically in 1961, was at a stalemate, and rhetoric about the seizure of power was empty. Founded in 1912, the ANC had come to embody a South African nationalism of all races, ethnic groups, and classes, and its leadership, not only at the top but in layers throughout the country, was predominantly pragmatic. In September 1985 leading businessmen met with ANC leaders in Zambia. Two months later the Minister of Justice met Mandela, who was in a hospital and beginning his twenty-fourth year of life imprisonment. This was the first in a long series of many private meetings, culminating in a meeting with President P. W. Botha at his residence in mid-1989. In a memorandum, Mandela set the tone for all that followed: reconciliation between the government and the ANC could be achieved "only if both parties are willing to compromise."

In an epochal speech of February 2, 1990, Frederik de Klerk, the new president, announced the unbanning of the ANC, the Communist Party, and other organizations. Shortly afterward, he released Mandela from prison. During the more than four years that followed, the negotiation process suffered so many setbacks amid spasms of violence in some parts of the country that the task at times seemed doomed. Perhaps political leaders had to endure these travails and face the specter of failure before their reserves of pragmatism could be tapped. South Africa was lucky to be led by Mandela and de Klerk, yet the key was the realism of a wide range of leaders who recognized their common interests and the perils of no compromise. A complex structure of multilateral negotiations was created, accompanied by bilateral negotiations between the government and the ANC and between either major party and parties who were boycotting the formal arena. Four pragmatic turning points were highlights of the period leading up to the election.

*De Klerk and the Nationalists.* De Klerk had hoped to forge an anti-ANC coalition that included the preeminent Zulu chief, Mangosuthu Buthelezi. In September 1992, nearly two-thirds of the way through the negotiation process, he gave up such hopes and entered into deal-making with the ANC. De Klerk was responding to a combination of pressures: a breakdown in negotiations, Mandela's belief that de Klerk was personally involved in undercover "third force" violence (never expressly established), and mass strikes and demonstrations. These were partly in protest against killings by Buthelezi's followers aided by the police. De Klerk accepted constitution-making by an elected constitutional assembly rather than by an unelected multiparty conference. He also accepted other ANC demands, including definitive movement toward a political settlement.

*Slovo and the Communists.* Shortly after the understanding with de Klerk, Joe Slovo — chair of the Communist Party and a leading member of the ANC, a folk hero among the youth, and one of the subjects of this book — argued that election would achieve nothing but political office. As an exemplar of pragmatism during the transition, he proposed that assurances including job security should be given to members of the police, armed forces, and civil service, and that the constitution should entrench power-sharing in a government of national unity for five years or more. Slovo had the support of Chris Hani (also a subject of this book), the Party's general secretary and the ANC's most popular leader after Mandela. The ANC accepted the analysis, opening the way for renewed negotiations. On April 10, 1993, a tragic and dangerous moment occurred when Hani was assassinated by a right-wing extremist whose ringleader was a Conservative Party leader. Slovo himself died of cancer in January 1995.

*Viljoen and the Right Wing.* Generals and religious leaders have played unifying leadership roles at critical times in the Afrikaner community. General Constand Viljoen, an admired former chief of the defense force, and other generals came out of retirement to unite, within an Afrikaner Volksfront, twenty-one groups who demanded self-determination. Viljoen finally abandoned any notion of separate territorial sovereignty and rejected violent strategies, privately dismissing the neo-Nazi Afrikaner Resistance Movement as a nuisance. Significant opposition to violence also came from the main branch of the Dutch Reformed Church (DRC), which categorically opposed the right wing's strategy of boycotting negotiations in 1993 and threatening war. Shortly before the election, Viljoen split the right wing by registering a new party, the Freedom Front, and leading it into the election after Mandela and de Klerk endorsed the establishment of a Volkstaat Council to study the feasibility of a semiautonomous state.

*Buthelezi and the Inkatha Freedom Party.* Furious about being marginalized by the de Klerk–Mandela understanding of September 1992, Buthelezi became more than ever disposed to act as a spoiler. As a shrewd politician, he was winning concessions by making demands from outside the negotiating forum. In making common cause with racist whites and African "homeland" collaborators, however, he was self-defeating. His intransigent refusal to participate in the election became the despair of some of his closest advisers. If any miracle occurred, it was the breakthrough of Buthelezi's pragmatism a week before the election when even he realized that he had overplayed his hand and faced isolation if he did not participate.

South Africa's first universal election — a liberation election, widely accepted as substantially free and fair despite some fraud, maladministration, and "no-go" areas during the campaign — produced South Africa's first government of popular legitimacy. An interim constitution to last for five years went into effect, approved by a vote of 237 to 45 in the joint white, "Coloured," and Indian parliamentary houses of the old regime. Remarkably, the document described itself as "a historic bridge between the past of a deeply divided society characterized by strife, conflict, untold suffering and injustice, and a future founded on the recognition of human rights, democracy and peaceful co-existence."

These high hopes are being pursued in 1995 in a new and complex era in which the relative simplicities of the struggle against apartheid have given way to the politics of competing interests. The contest for power is constrained to some extent by a commitment to consensus within a government of national unity that is proportionally representative of Parliament. Two parliamentary houses, the National Assembly and the Senate, occasionally sit jointly as a Constitutional Assembly to draft the permanent constitution. At the same time, politicians of the ANC, the National Party (now nonracial and talking of rewinning power), and others are girding for local elections in late 1995 and the critical general election due in 1999.

During negotiations, the National Party proposed that the cabinet should reach decisions by a two-thirds vote, but at the end they gave in and agreed to settle for a constitutional admonition: the cabinet should function in "the consensus-seeking spirit underlying the concept of a government of national unity." In that spirit, parliamentary minorities are entitled to proportional representation in the cabinet if they win at least 5 percent of the vote for the National Assembly. Cabinet decision-making, however, is not subject to veto. Four of the leaders featured in the historical review just described became members of the cabinet: Mandela, who was elected as president by the National Assembly; de Klerk, who is the second deputy president after Thabo Mbeki of the ANC (the son of Govan Mbeki, one of the subjects of this book); Buthelezi, who was brought into the fold as Minister of Home Affairs; and Slovo, as Minister of Housing.

The National Assembly, whose 400 members were elected from a party list according to proportional representation, is dominated by 252 members of the ANC. The National Party has 82 members; the Zulu-based Inkatha Freedom Party, 43. Of the sixteen other parties who participated in the election, only four won seats in the National Assembly: the Freedom Front, nine; the liberal and primarily white Democratic Party, seven; the radically nationalist Pan Africanist Congress, five; and the inconsequential African Christian Democratic Party, two. Three members of the National Assembly are in this book: Ela Gandhi, Ruth Mompati, and Albertina Sisulu.

Also in this book is Govan Mbeki, who had been in prison with Mandela and is the deputy president of the Senate. This ninety-member body gives equal representation to nine provinces. Its composition reflects a compromise favored by the Inkatha Freedom Party and other regionally based parties. At the election for the National Assembly, voters also marked a separate ballot for provincial legislatures, thus being able to give different weight to national and provincial concerns. The legislatures have selected senators in proportion to party strength. Two of the nine, those of the Western Cape and KwaZulu/Natal, were won narrowly by the National Party and the Inkatha Freedom Party, respectively.

For Americans, accustomed to a Constitution with a Bill of Rights and a Supreme Court that can declare legislative action unconstitutional, South Africa has undergone fundamental change. The parliamentary sovereignty of the past has been replaced by constitutional supremacy implemented by a powerful Constitutional Court. The new Court can exercise judicial review comparable to that in the United States. Even the Constitutional Assembly is subject to the

Court in drafting the permanent constitution. It must comply with thirty-four constitutional principles in the interim constitution, including universally accepted human rights.

By winning the election, the ANC won state power — or at least a "launching pad," according to Slovo. ANC leaders see their party as uniquely anchored in a broad social movement. As a liberation movement being transformed into a political party, it must work out relationships between the ANC inside the structures of government and the ANC outside. The mission outside is to mobilize mass support and to bring it to bear on the ANC inside. Although the two ANCs are structurally separate, at the leadership level the wearing of two hats makes for substantial integration. A further complication is the fact that the ANC functions as the head of an alliance that includes the South African Communist Party and the Congress of South African Trade Unions (COSATU), but the ANC alone was on the ballot. COSATU is the largest trade union federation with over 1,300,000 members. Linked to the tripartite alliance is the South African National Civic Organization, representing a large number of civic associations.

The alliance constitutes a new center in South African politics. The ANC's Reconstruction and Development Program (RDP) was formulated with the participation of COSATU, and the Communist Party and has won the support of major representatives of business. It favors a mixed economy with a stronger emphasis on the private sector than the public sector and a commitment to fiscal restraint and macroeconomic stability. The RDP declares that the first priority is to "begin" to meet basic needs. "No political democracy can survive and flourish," it maintains, "if the mass of our people remain in poverty, without land, without tangible prospects for a better life." The expectations of the poor are great, but Mandela did not promise radical change overnight. One can expect continued understanding and patience among Africans so long as they see that change is beginning. In addition to the creation of jobs, the RDP sets out programs that it claims are achievable in five years: "to distribute a substantial amount of land to landless people, build over one million houses, provide clean water and sanitation to all, electrify 2.5 million new homes, and provide access for all to affordable health care and telecommunications."

Itemizing achievable aims does not begin to suggest the problems the ANC faces in dealing with social disintegration, family breakdown, and the emergence of an African underclass in areas where unemployment is over 40 percent. The ANC must not only appeal to some six million workers who are unemployed and unorganized, but it must also call for restraint on the part of employed and organized workers. Alec Erwin, a veteran trade unionist, member of the Communist Party, and deputy minister of finance, has urged that employed workers must be instilled with a readiness to refrain from demanding exorbitant pay increases, which would unsettle the "macro balance," let inflation loose, and be irresponsible to the working class as a whole.

A common theme in this book is a passionate concern for the poor and the dispossessed — "the least among us." The twenty-one people interviewed share "many common values," Villa-Vicencio observes, and are part of "a broad and heterogeneous democratic tradition." He avoids as simplistic any effort to place the people he has selected into partisan categories. Nevertheless, differences in political orientation exist, and their strength is indicated by the election.

About 63 percent of the popular vote supported ANC candidates in the national election. Of Villa-Vicencio's twenty-one subjects, twelve are (or were) members of the ANC. Of the twelve, six are (or were) also members of the Communist Party: Slovo, Hani, Mbeki, and Ray Alexander, all of them veterans; Ela Gandhi, who joined recently; and Cheryl Carolus, a young and rising star, who was elected as deputy secretary-general of the ANC in December 1994. ANC members who do not belong to the Party are Mandela, Ruth Mompati, Albertina Sisulu, Fatima Meer, Ebrahim Rasool, and Nadine Gordimer. Among ANC women, Mompati was one of the most important in exile and Sisulu one of the most highly respected inside the country. Meer was distinguished as a stalwart of the women's movement and as an academic. Rasool represents the evolution of a young man from the principled but politically sectarian New Unity Movement to black consciousness and then to the United Democratic Front (UDF), in effect a surrogate for the ANC. Gordimer played a unique role as an internationally acclaimed writer in the years before she could join the legal ANC.

In relation to a movement like the ANC, one may be a dues-paying member, or publicly known as a member, or strongly sympathetic and associated with it. Dr. Beyers Naudé, for example, is a pro-ANC nonmember who was included in the ANC's eleven-person delegation to the first round of talks with the government in 1990. (The two women in the delegation were Ruth Mompati and Cheryl Carolus.) Naudé is a legendary religious leader who was attacked as a traitor to Afrikanerdom when he gave up a high position in the Dutch Reformed Church for ecumenical antiapartheid activity and was placed under ban. Frank Chikane, another religious leader, was involved with the ANC underground but resigned from a UDF-aligned organization when he became general secretary of the South African Council of Churches, since his role was to promote the unity of all political organizations. When the government moved to crush the political opposition in the mid-1980s, Archbishop Desmond Tutu spoke vigorously for many who had been silenced. But he has no political ambition, and he and his fellow bishops have prohibited Anglican priests from belonging to political parties. Two others in Villa-Vicencio's book are nonpartisan independents who are sympathetic to the ANC: Sheena Duncan, of the Black Sash, and Franz Auerbach, a religious and activist Jew. Trevor Huddleston, a British citizen, may be considered an honorary member of the ANC.

What is the relationship of Communists to the ANC? Individual Communists and former Communists are, indeed, key players in the new government, but it does not follow that the Party itself has much importance. Since 1969 the relationship has been so symbiotic, with dual membership and agreement on short-term goals, that the Party has virtually lost any separate identity as a working-class vanguard. Since legalization in 1990, the ANC as an all-class movement has largely absorbed Communist energies. Seeking to become a mass party, the Party claims over 65,000 members but is short of funds. Its future role, if any, is under continuing debate. Some internal critics deplore "the gradual abandonment of Marxist-Leninist principles." Impatience and radical militancy are bound to rise in South Africa, but their main source is unlikely to be the Communist Party.

Historically the Party has been the earliest and most important proponent of nonracialism. Influenced by the Party, the ANC counts whites among its important members. Opinion polls estimate that no more than 3 percent of white voters support the ANC, but this is a substantial number and a growing one. An ANC branch in the conservative city of Pretoria, for example, has about 350 to 400 white members, at least three-fourths of them Afrikaners.

Three other political orientations — the Pan Africanist Congress (PAC), the Workers' Organization for Socialist Action (WOSA), and the Azanian People's Organization (AZAPO) — appear in this book. The PAC is only touched upon in the conversation with Bishop Stanley Mogoba; he was imprisoned in the early 1960s for

PAC activity. Formed in 1959 and banned the following year, the PAC opposed the ANC's Freedom Charter, which proclaimed that South Africa belonged "to all who live in it, black and white." In exile, it was never able to surmount internecine quarrels. During the election campaign, its policies were confused and sometimes contradictory, and it lacked leadership, organization, and money. Despite its radical rhetoric and potential mass appeal, the PAC won only 1.25 percent of the votes for the National Assembly, or 5 out of 400 seats. Mogoba has not been a member for some time, but despite his past opposition to sanctions, PAC leaders as well as others listen to Mogoba with respect.

Neville Alexander, chair of WOSA, is a highly regarded intellectual with a Trotskyist background who was imprisoned for ten years. He and thirty-four others ran in the election as candidates of the Workers' List Party, which rejected "the idea of a Government of National Unity that includes the racists." Their aim is the formation of a "Mass Workers' Party," and they place a higher priority on political education than on electoral politics. Despite public funding, the party received only one-fiftieth of 1 percent of the vote; receipt of one-fourth of 1 percent would have won the Party one seat in the National Assembly.

Itumeleng Mosala, former president of AZAPO, is a theologian and academic colleague of Villa-Vicencio's. After much debate, the all-black AZAPO decided not to participate in a "flawed" election, but individual members were allowed to vote if they wished. (Some may have voted for the Trotskyist "Workers International to Rebuild the Fourth International [S. A.]" party.) AZAPO is a socialist group with roots in the black consciousness movement. It claims thousands of members, mostly Africans, mainly students, some workers and rural chiefs. It also appeals to intellectuals and professionals, some of whom are in corporate positions.

The beliefs and actions of these men and women are part of an emerging culture that is important in South Africa's future. Will it be one of tolerance, pluralism, nonracism, nonsexism, and majority-rule democracy in which minority rights are protected? Will the new South Africa achieve its aim of building national unity while encouraging diversity? This book goes far to encourage optimism that such a South Africa is in the making. The country is fortunate that religion is a force for reconciliation, not division. Unlike the situation in some other countries, interethnic conflict is of little importance in national politics, although conflict among Zulus continues to bedevil Buthelezi's KwaZulu / Natal. Pragmatic and able leaders who recognize common interests have become experienced in negotiation and compromise. Working together to oppose apartheid, especially in the 1970s and 1980s, has bolstered the sense of national unity and involved many in strong and independent organs of civil society.

The twenty-one individuals in this book are broadly representative of a pantheon of heroes and martyrs who are no longer living. Steve Biko, Bram Fischer, Robert Sobukwe, Ruth First, Griffiths Mxenge, Zeph Mothopeng, Matthew Goniwe, and Neil Aggett, for example, are names in "an emerging common memory," which Villa-Vicencio describes as essential in shaping national identity. Among others of historic importance, whom Mandela has praised as religious people and leaders of the ANC, are Rev. John Dube, Canon James Calata, Chief Albert Lutuli, and Professor Z. K. Matthews. The twenty-one are also broadly representative of thousands, many still youthful, who took part in the liberation struggle and are now influential in politics, trade unions, business, and civil society. Still others who "suffered, fought and bled" remain unsung.

A major theme in these pages is the extent of fundamental agreement. There is much evidence for Villa-Vicencio's suggestion that "context and shared experience" — the struggle against racial oppression — might be more important than religions and philosophies. "My values and my life," says Mandela, "have been shaped by the circumstances and the history that I have lived through." Mutual respect is a related theme. Although there is severe criticism of the institutional church and the complacency of churchgoers who supported the status quo, Slovo, Hani, and Mbeki — all atheists — are filled with admiration for religious people, for example, Chikane, Tutu, and Naudé. They are praised by Mandela (a Christian) for having been "in the forefront of our struggle." In turn, Chikane pays tribute to the atheists and agnostics who fought against evil. Chris Hani, according to Tutu, "has done more for justice than most Christians." And at the funeral service for Joe Slovo, South Africa's Chief Rabbi, Cyril Harris, praised Slovo for fighting for individual dignity while religious people kept silent.

The extent to which radicals of various hues have had a religious upbringing is remarkable, and the continuity between such an upbringing and commitment to radical action is often pointed out. Neville Alexander "became a radical socialist because I was a radical and very sincere Christian." "Marxist ideals were for me," Hani

*xxii*

has said, "a natural development of my Christian upbringing." The three great influences in the life of Itumeleng Mosala are Jesus, Marx, and Steve Biko, the leading thinker of black consciousness. Slovo describes Jesus as a liberation leader whose religion is not an opiate. Men and women such as these appreciate the religious disposition of the mass of people and the role that religion and the church can play in the new South Africa. Hani, in particular, emphasizes the concrete services that the church can perform, especially in rural areas.

Exiles observing hopeful trends within South Africa during recent decades were impressed by the influence of black theology, also referred to as liberation or contextual theology. This influence is implicit in the tidy summary given by Cheryl Carolus of the sources of her values: "the church, the democratic struggle, the ANC and the Party." Many young people who were disenchanted with the church were not opposed to "a God who is related to their lived experience," according to Chikane, formerly secretary of the Institute of Contextual Theology. Non-Christian radicals could easily make common cause with Christians like Chikane who followed "a God who calls the people out of bondage into freedom." Enriching such an appeal are African traditional values — the communal humanism of *ubuntu* — emphasized by Stanley Mogoba and Ruth Mompati.

What of Afrikaners? Their church has justified apartheid on biblical grounds and has been characterized as the National Party at prayer. The largest by far of the three Dutch Reformed Churches has slowly moved away from the ideology of apartheid and toward nonracialism and unification with its "daughter churches." (Two — the African and the Coloured — were themelves recently unified.) In October 1994, when unification had not yet been effected, an emotional high point was reached in the evolution of the largest DRC: in a standing ovation, an apology was extended to Beyers Naudé and two of his early mentors.

To say that what has happened in South Africa is a miracle is misleading: it implies that hopes for national unity and democracy are not solidly based. But they are. Power tends to make responsible, as the leaders of revolutionary struggle in South Africa have demonstrated. But power also tends to corrupt, and awareness of this danger appears in the pages that follow. One woman, asked what fundamental values she is prepared to die for, answers: "freedom of speech, freedom of association and freedom of belief — first generation rights." Another: the church "must insist that the government is honest and ensure that the cries of the poor are heard." And another: "Never again in this country should we give unchecked powers to the security forces." Still another: democracy is "an important antidote against tyranny, a dangerous possibility that lies deep within the human spirit." If at any time in the future "injustice were meted out by blacks against whites," Frank Chikane pledges that he would again "defend the underdog. Indeed if I were not prepared to return to prison in so doing, the gospel I preach would be without integrity." The imponderables in South Africa's future are worrisome, and its problems may become overwhelming; but the values of many of its new leaders give hope that they will be overcome. Underlying this hope is an extraordinary spirit of goodwill that animates not only black but, increasingly, white South Africans.

—Thomas G. Karis
March 1995

# ACKNOWLEDGEMENTS

Acknowledgements begin with the very busy people who gave time for these interviews. I hope that the huge privilege that was mine and the richness of discussion which I shared with some of the greatest South Africans of our time, is in some small way reflected in the pages that follow. In some instances I have drawn on media and other interviews to augment the extensive interviews which I conducted. Footnotes have, however, been kept to an absolute minimum. In each case those interviewed were given the final draft of the interview, in order to ensure that they were correctly represented.

A range of people have facilitated this study, locating information, arranging and assisting with interviews, helping with the recording and writing process. These include Peter Grassow, Pat Lawrence, Ebrahim Moosa, Gerrie Lubbe, Farieda Omar, Nan Oosthuizen, Barney Pityana, Sheila Sisulu, Anil Sooklal, Mark Stephenson and Deborah Williams. My colleagues in the Department of Religious Studies at the University of Cape Town have provided useful comment on a range of emphases included in the book. Wendy Arendse transcribed the interviews. Jane Parry is responsible for the final editing process. Mothobi Mutloatse, editor of Skotaville Publishers agreed to publish the book. John Pobee provided funding through the Theological Education Programme of the World Council of Churches. The Centre for Scientific Development also provided assistance through the Religion and Social Change Unit at UCT. The Mayibuye Centre at the University of the Western Cape made extensive archieval photographic material available. Photographs were also provided by *Dimension*, *South*, the *Sowetan*, the *Star*, Rashid Lombard at the Cape Town Press Centre, Beyers and Ilse Naudé and the South African Chapter of the World Conference on Religion and Peace. Diana Russell granted permission for the use of her photographs, lodged in the Mayibuye Centre. Each photograph is individually acknowledged. To each of these people and organisations I am extremely grateful.

Having completed a writing project, I feel the need and the desire to acknowledge my personal indebtedness to my immediate family, Eileen, Heidi and Tanya. Their long-suffering and direct involvement at a number of levels in this project I appreciate and readily acknowledge.

# INTRODUCTION

*I am being driven forward*
*Into an unknown land*
*The pass grows steeper,*
*The air grows colder and sharper.*

*A wind from my unknown goal*
*Stirs the strings*
*Of expectation*

*Still the question:*
*Shall I ever get there?*
*There where life resounds,*
*A clear pure note*
*In the silence.*[1]

**Dag Hammerskjold.**

This book is about people driven towards freedom. It is about the unquenchable, universal will to be free that resides deep within the human soul. "Human beings," suggests Paul Tillich, "cannot renounce being human. They must think; they must elevate being into consciousness; they must transcend the given... When this has happened, there is no way back."[2]

The spirit that energises people so driven, blows widely. It refuses to be confined to any narrow ideological constraints. Too dynamic and diffuse to be a simple process within which an undiluted Charterist, Black Consciousness or Africanist word becomes flesh, the spirit of liberation is best left undefined and unnamed. Seeking to affirm this ambiguity, no attempt is made to synthesise the insights of the interviews that follow, to identify the differences between them, or to articulate the many common values that bind those interviewed into a broad and heterogeneous democratic tradition.

---

1.  Dag Hammarskjold, *Markings* (London: Faber and Faber, 1964), p.31.
2.  Paul Tillich, *The Socialist Decision* (New York: Harper and Row, 1977), p.44.

## Image-Bearers

These are people who have helped mould and influence the struggle for a new South Africa, while both explicitly and implicitly responding to and being shaped by a series of ideas whose time has dawned. Some are important players and image-bearers in the emerging new age. Others will be remembered for past contributions. There are, of course, additional people who have contributed to the new age, who remain unidentified and unsung. Having suffered, fought and bled, their obscurity and anonymity remains. To the extent that their values and aspirations remain hidden and ignored, however, to that extent will the new age fail to be realised.

Heroes, martyrs and saints (but also heretics and scoundrels!) all reject the superficially calm and regular course of things. They dare to question the dominant notions of 'common sense', while being moulded and chastened in the crucible of seeking to stretch, push, beat and lure the existing order in a new direction. Hegel suggests that they draw "from a concealed fount . . . from that inner Spirit, still hidden beneath the surface, which, impinging on the outer world as on a shell, bursts it in pieces".[3] They portray the collective consciousness of those who longed for a new age, transcending past and present contexts, enabling the new to rise out of the ashes of the past.

## Drinking From Our Own Wells

St Bernard of Clairvaux, an eleventh century monk, mundanely observed: "Everyone has to drink from his (her) own wells." Gustavo Gutierrez uses this axiom to describe the spiritual journey of Latin American Christians as he asks: "From what well can the poor of Latin America drink?"[4]

The subterranean streams that have fed the different wells from which the South African democratic struggle has drunk, drawing on a complexity of traditions, cultures and religions, have sustained a social revolution that has endured for centuries. As people reached into the depth of their wells, they have in different ways contributed to a vision that must be kept alive for future generations. To do so is to affirm what the Xhosa people call the *izithethe*, the memory of people who have laid the foundations of ages both present and yet to come.

---

3. Hegel, p.30.
4. Gustavo Gutierrez, *We Drink From Our Own Wells* (Maryknoll: Orbis Books, 1985).

To do so is not an exercise in hagiography. The banned Pan Africanist Congress leader, Robert Sobukwe, was dying of cancer in Groote Schuur Hospital in Cape Town, when I visited him shortly after the murder of Steve Biko in 1977. I spoke of the contribution which he, Steve and others had made to the struggle. He spoke of the vicissitudes of time, of the limitations of individuals and the combination of strengths and weaknesses that constitute the human condition. "That's why," he observed, "we must cling to the message and not the person — and this is a message of faith, of hope and of glory. Don't forget also glory." The people interviewed for this book are bearers of a message of hope.

Hope in the face of despair can perhaps only emerge in the intensity of struggle. It is an expectation of the kind that resounds in the words of Martin Luther King, on the eve of his assassination:

> I've been to the mountaintop. . . I've looked over and I've seen the promised land. I may not get there with you. But I want you to know tonight, that we, as a people will get to the promised land. And so I'm happy tonight. I'm not worried about anything. I'm not fearing any man. Mine eyes have seen the glory of the coming of the Lord.[5]

In an intriguing interview conducted with Chris Hani shortly before his assassination, he observed:

> I am an atheist. But I see religion as a philosophy, like other secular or materialist philosophies, engaged in the important task of grappling with and seeking to unveil the mysteries of the universe. Perhaps I understand religion better than I did when I was most at home within it.

Arguing that morality has its roots in diverse sources and traditions, Nadine Gordimer suggests that "religious people who are inclined to promote a specific religion or ethical system ought to give more attention to this commonality". The common ground between the persons whose stories are told in this book is expressed in the words of Govan Mbeki: "Life is about freedom. Where there is freedom there is life. Where freedom is denied, rebellion and revolution are inevitable."

---

5.  David J Garrow, *Bearing the Cross: Martin Luther King and the Southern Christian Leadership Conference* (New York: Vintage books, 1988), p.621.

# Religion and Culture

Talk to people about religion and their value systems come tumbling out. To the extent that religion is about the quest to be fully human, this is to be expected. What is interesting is the way in which people who are atheists or not particularly religious, often talk about life in a near-religious manner. Joe Slovo's words acquire a poetic ring: "To be human is to reach beyond ourselves to what we ought to become. . . There is, I believe, a certain drive to this kind of fulfilment which is part of the human soul — a notion which I employ in a non-religious sense. Maybe I need to say I am agnostic rather than an atheist!" Equally important is the extent to which the believers interviewed, in turn, affirm the inherent moral and spiritual insight of non-believers. This is nowhere more clearly stated than in Archbishop Tutu's interview. Speaking of God's self-revelation in different places, persons and traditions, he rebukes Christians for taking themselves too seriously. "For me Jesus Christ is the revelation of God, but I am opposed to proselytism. . . For goodness sake, God was able to look after God long before we were around. It is not for us to decide who God is and where this God is to be found."

Many of the people interviewed for this book have been jailed, banned and driven into exile for their political actions. All of them had been actively engaged in the anti-apartheid struggle long before it became popular to be so. This suggests that context and shared experience might be more important in the shaping of human values, than the religions or philosophies to which people adhere. Living together goes a long way towards the creation of a common vision. Believers who are prepared to explore the frontiers of life, often have more in common with unbelievers who challenge the preconceived notions of existence than they do with fellow-believers who regard the sphere of disbelief as dangerous territory to be avoided at all costs. Certainly the divide between belief and unbelief is less clear than is often suggested.

The interviews that follow focus on the religious and cultural identity symbolised in the lives of those whom the majority of South Africans regard as leaders with values worth emulating. The study is an attempt, through biography and story, to give expression to a *popular religion* which is rarely identical to institutionalised religion. Each story that follows is an exercise in biography as theology, which is grounded in people — expressed in social behaviour rather than doctrinal beliefs, made known in lived experience rather than abstract ideals.

The book is an attempt to engage in a different kind of contextual theology. Preoccupied with the spiritual forces of the universe and correct theological belief, the history-making influence of people (created, says the Psalmist, to be just a little inferior to God) is often neglected in theology.

Differently understood, the book is an act of moral discernment. The enlightenment philosopher, Immanuel Kant suggested that when it comes to religious belief, "two things occupy the human mind, with ever new and increasing wonder and awe". These are "the starry heavens above and the moral law within".[6] An attempt is made in what follows to uncover the moral law and social values that have driven people who represent the democratic struggle for a different kind of society. Many of those interviewed relate these values to historic events, individual experiences and often to nature. A consequence is an emerging common memory, a set of goals and a communal vision of a just dispensation.

All cultures are not the same and may not ultimately be judged to be of the same social value. What is of lasting value will however, only emerge in an encounter between different cultures. This can only happen where each person's values and cultural affirmations receive equal recognition. Bound into a common ethical vision, without the identity of any of the constituent parts being lost in the greater whole, a new national soul needs to emerge if a new nation is to be born. Drawing on the African tradition, Sheena Duncan speaks of the need to rediscover the fullness of humanity — the idea of *ubuntu*.

> It involves the need to belong to one another and to care for one another. We need an attitude to life that breeds compassion. Many of us are at the same time concerned to be ourselves and to realise our potential as individual people in life, sometimes feeling that involvement in the lives of others prevents us from attaining that goal. What is needed is the will and the skill to be ourselves in community with others.

In a revealing study on social ethics, Paul Lehmann traces the roots of the English word 'ethics' to its Greek root, meaning dwelling or shelter. Ethical norms, he suggests, have something to do with behaving in accordance with agreed custom.[7] Certainly the early

---

6. Immanuel Kant, *Critique of Practical Reason* (Indianapolis: Bobbs-Merrill, 1956), p.166.
7. Paul Lehmann, *Ethics in a Christian Context* (New York: Harper and Row, 1963), pp. 23–24.

Greeks regarded good custom as providing security for humanity in much the same way that the shelter provides security for animals. Accepting the need for custom to change to meet the new challenges of each age, Lehmann argues that new ethical values and behaviour need constantly to be forged and reforged on the anvil of social change.

A new South African culture is still in the making. The memory of many events will ultimately generate the central images of this culture. Words uttered, songs sung, literature, music and art will all need to be drawn on to complete the mosaic that constitutes an inclusive identity, capable of sustaining a nation that is in the process of being cobbled together. Cultures, religions and secular world views will need to 'find one another' on the basis of mutual acceptance, trust and enrichment. A vast corporate memory will need to emerge to bind the nation to itself. The symbols, memories and events that have hitherto been part of an alternative (and subversive) culture, which comes partly to expression in what follows, will need to become part of the national identity.

Martin Prozesky's observation is important. Cultural pluralism involves "the right of every woman, man and child on this planet to be as fully fulfilled a creator of the spiritual means of production as all others".[8] This democratic right to share in the creation of the religious and cultural identity of society is a somewhat utopian view of religion and culture. It is also an important one, if only because there is usually someone else who defines these things for ordinary people!

This book suggests that African traditionalists, agnostics, atheists, Buddhists, Christians, Hindus, Jews, Muslims and others have more in common than the twice born zealots and thoughtless perpetuators of these traditions are often prepared to allow. The failure to recognise the common ground between traditions (without denying the differences that exist) often results in an elitist and parochial understanding of what it means to be human. This ultimately undermines the spirituality that religious people claim to pursue. It is worth recalling Hannah Arendt's critique of exclusivist religion and ideology which "shields . . . (us) from the impact of reality . . . ruining

---

8. Martin Prozesky, "Religious Liberty in A Secular State: Some Challenges for South Africa." A paper read at the Unesco/WCC consultation on, The Role of Religion and Religious Institutions in Dismantling Apartheid. Geneva, November 1991.

the mind's capacity for judgment and for learning."[9] It undermines humanity.

'Every person has a price,' suggests the cynic. Struggle is at the same time an ennobling experience. Should those who have stood firm one day capitulate, they will have betrayed a dream far greater than themselves. Should this happen, it should neither destroy our dream nor our quest for the kind of society of which those interviewed for this book once caught a glimpse, and gave us a foretaste.

It is this conviction, rather than a starry-eyed optimism, that underlies the title of this book: *The Spirit of Hope*. The stories told here challenge the world-weary notion that human beings have lost the capacity to do anything right. Frank Chikane's words are important in this regard: "If at any time in the future a situation were to emerge where injustice were meted out by blacks against whites, I should be obliged again to defend the underdog. Indeed if I were not prepared to return to prison in so doing, the gospel I preach would be without integrity."

Hope (in the biblical sense) is grounded in the conviction that history is incomplete and that the world is unfinished. It insists that the future is open-ended — and that what we do can make a difference.[10] The people of this book are people of hope — all of whom were interviewed in 1992 and early 1993. They believe that what one thinks and does is important. If this conviction is lost, hope withers. If hope is lost, the possibility of a new future slips from our grasp.

---

9. Hannah Arendt, "Lying in Politics," in *Crisis of the Republic* (New York: Harcourt, Brace, Johanovich, 1972), p.40.

10. See, Cornel West, *Beyond Eurocentrism and Multiculturalism*. Volume 1, *Prophetic Thought in Postmodern Times* (Monroe, Maine: Common Courage Press, 1993), p.6.

*Conversations on
Politics, Religion
and Values*

PHOTO ACKNOWLEDGEMENT: *South*

# NEVILLE ALEXANDER

*No need for the God Hypothesis*

Neville Alexander is a person of discipline and near uncompromising principle. He regrets not having met Steve Biko, who had come to Cape Town specifically to speak with him about establishing a united front of organisations in exile. "He stood two metres away from my backdoor and I refused to meet him, as much as I would have liked to have done so." Biko in fact waited for three hours while Fikile Bam, a Robben Island friend, tried to facilitate the meeting, placing himself, Biko and Alexander at enormous risk.

Compelled to leave Cape Town without having accomplished his mission, Biko was arrested while driving back to King William's Town with Peter Jones. Detained, interrogated and tortured, he died in custody — killed, as many before him, by a security system committed to eliminating all dissent.

> It was in many ways a natural thing for us to talk. Biko's Black Consciousness Movement was an organisation of militants, wrestling with many of the key issues of the time. On the international front it was grappling with the implications of black power, anti-Vietnam politics and student protests in Europe. On the national level it was the only legal black organisation confronting the ravages of apartheid, the Soweto student revolt and at the same time seeking to co-ordinate underground activity on a national level. . . We, a 'no-name brand of insurrectionists' in the Cape, were planning a revolution.

Alexander's group had sent word to Biko in King William's Town requesting that he deal with the divisions in the Black Consciousness Movement and certain organisational issues before their meeting could take place. Although there was some confusion whether Biko received the message, Alexander thought he was trying to force the meeting. "He seemed to think that his physical presence and the risk of having driven to Cape Town would force me to acquiesce. Our group had, however, decided that I should not meet Biko at that time, and I have always taken such disciplined decisions as binding. When I look back I realise that this is perhaps the folly of being too principled. . . I was so hard, I was so principled. I would have loved to have met Steve. I know from subsequent discussion with other people that we were, in many ways, kindred spirits. I am really sorry that the meeting never happened, but that is how it is. I acted in a principled manner, knowing that principled behaviour and self-sacrifice were the key to our survival in a time of terrifying repression. I had not been mandated to see him and could not get a mandate in time." Alexander thinks for a while before continuing: "I have always been a disciplined person, ever since I was a child. At times perhaps too much so."

## Discipline and Religion

Born in Cradock on 22 October 1936, he was the first of six children born to Dimbiti Bisho Alexander, a primary-school teacher, and David James Alexander, a carpenter. From his mother he learned religion and from his father discipline.

It was in the rural Eastern Cape that I also learned, and to a significant extent absorbed, the ingrained racism which characterises South Africa. I was strongly anti-white, having learned from an early age that whites are oppressors. "Keep whites at a distance, always maintaining your dignity and independence," my father told me. On the other hand, I soon learned to work closely with Xhosa-speaking people. Despite the racism which from time to time emerged between the Xhosa-speaking and coloured rural people, there was a very close relationship between us in the community of which I was a part. My mother in particular taught me to respect everyone, especially Xhosa-speaking people, calling them Oom (Uncle), Aunty and so on. Having learned to speak Xhosa as a child I lost a great deal of it in later years. When I went to the Island I again learned some of the language.

A gentle woman, his mother was the daughter of a slave who was captured in Ethiopia and released by a British patrol in Algoa Bay in the 1880s. His grandmother grew up on the Bethelsdorp Mission, marrying one of the missionaries, a Rev Scheepers, who was a member of the African Peoples' Organisation. "Her piety was passed on to my mother who, in turn, implanted a sense of biblical values in me which I still uphold. The Dominican nuns of the Holy Rosary Convent, a school that I attended after completing standard two in Steytlerville, completed my Christian upbringing." Here, under the strict discipline of German-speaking nuns, many of the norms, habits and practices of his life began to take shape. "Somehow I did not see the nuns as white. They were different from any whites I had ever met. They were almost saintly in the service they rendered us. They were dedicated people, becoming formative role models in my life." Speaking with great affection, he remembers particularly Sister Veronata. "She instilled in me a fondness of German, she was so methodical and inspiring. . . I met her again a year or two back. 'Oh, you were the boy who could recite *Barabara Frietchie* (a poem on the American Civil War) so well!' Her entire life was dedicated to her pupils."

> The nuns taught me to enjoy reading, to discover what a beautiful thing it is to express oneself in writing and to appreciate poetry. They taught me German, how to think logically and how to live a disciplined life. They introduced me to logic, philosophy and theology. I read Albertus Magnus and Thomas Aquinas and from an early age engaged in complex metaphysical debates; learning how to question, pry and investigate all propositions and proposals.

5

They also introduced me to the lives of the saints. St Martin De Porres of Peru and Teresa the Little Flower of Spain (St Teresa of Lisieux) became lasting influences on my life. St Martin offered his life to be sold to raise money for the poor and St Teresa dedicated herself to ensure that in her 'little way', she would serve the ordinary people — the poor and the exploited. I came to believe that to be a Christian was to work to ensure that the poor would inherit the earth. This was the religious ethos that I imbibed from a very young age. The prophetic teaching on justice was implanted in me and I understood Jesus to be a friend of the poor. I was taught that religion had to do with loving one's neighbour. Today I am an atheist, but I still believe that is what religion is all about. Its great positive contribution to society is to teach people to love and respect one another.

Neville Alexander's father was a dominant influence in his life. "He was a disciplinarian. The discipline and rhythm of life with which I still live must in many ways be attributed to him. He taught me to be strong, to organise my life and to work hard." Having lost a leg through serving in the armed forces during the war, he later lost his other leg. "I remember the only occasion on which he was able to visit me in prison. 'You're in this now,' he said, 'be obedient but do not lose your dignity.' The discipline which my father had taught me as a child in some ways taught me to be a model prisoner!" Alexander has an abiding appreciation for his father who, having been educated only to standard three, was only semi-literate. He could read only with difficulty, but became a master carpenter, deciphering a building plan with great skill. "My father's life taught me a great deal about the lower-class coloured people who hit their heads against the wall in trying to cope with life," he observes. "My father's natural and acquired skills and his self-discipline were intermingled with a hedonistic will to enjoy life. He revelled in such pleasures as dancing, celebrating, drinking and so on. Then, as the pressures of life mounted up, his frustration increased and he indulged more and more in drink. It was his way of seeking relief and coping with what life threw at him." Reflecting on this experience, Alexander observes:

> Life treated him badly, he was physically disabled — a major blow for an active and creative person. Apartheid was systematically being imposed on coloured people, reducing them to the social, economic and political status that African people were already experiencing. It was simply too much for him and his frustration increased.

> In this situation I began to understand a lot about coloured

militancy and progressivism — the dialectic of it. Lower middle-class people aspired not to be white, but to the standards which white people enjoyed. Deprived by apartheid of the possibility of attaining these standards, some capitulated and internalised their oppression. Others became increasingly militant.

When I think about this process, I realise why people like myself developed the values and sense of determination that we have. Although obviously driven by different ideological considerations and social aspirations, we are facing the same social frustrations that people like my father faced. In brief, we are driven to create a social system within which there is maximum social and economic egalitarianism; ensuring that the marginalisation and exclusion of the poor never happens again.

In many ways Alexander is a blend of the values that drove his mother and father. Her religion taught him to care for the underdog. His father's drive and discipline, together with his defeated hopes, gave him a sense of determination. "My mother was gentle and kind. My father was passionate and at times quite obstinate. I like to think I am a balance of the two!" He smiles: "I have the capacity for balance. I also have the capacity for passion and drive. Put this together with the values and skills I was taught by the Dominican sisters and it is clear that I am to a significant extent a product of my early Cradock experiences."

When Alexander left school he wanted, like many educated coloured and African students, to become a medical doctor. "My problem was that the nuns had taught me German instead of Mathematics! That closed the door of any medical faculty to me. So I decided to become a priest instead. The nuns had taught me to go to mass every morning, and I thought I could become some kind of modern day Martin De Porres." His parents, both being Methodists, would have nothing of it and decided he should be confirmed in the Methodist Church. "I refused and became nothing!" In this situation he left for the University of Cape Town (UCT) where he registered for a BA, majoring in History and German. "I did so as a deeply religious person, quite convinced that anything like socialism or communism, in so far as I knew anything about it, was the anti-Christ. At this level, I was the victim of the worst kind of religious bigotry. My encounter with the secular environment of the university would, however, shortly terminate my religious belief. I had fallen among rationalist thieves! It would also enable me to give expression to my deepest ethical values in a new 'religionless' manner."

# Cape Town

Neville Alexander's move to Cape Town was the beginning of a radically new phase of his existence. He began to discover a whole range of new intellectual and political ingredients in life:

> At first I fought like hell against these new ideas, but within six months I was a religious doubter or an agnostic. I was also becoming a socialist. . .
>
> In retrospect it all makes sense to me. I became a radical socialist because I was a radical and very sincere Christian. Rationally I could no longer explain the existence nor the moral necessity for God. At the same time I believed more firmly than ever before in the fundamental ethical values of the Christian faith. I today still believe that there is a sibling relationship between the Judeo-Christian ethic and socialism in the sense that both draw on the same aboriginal ethic, although Judaism and Christianity of course both predate Marxism. Antecedents aside, both give expression to an ethic of 'love thy neighbour'. This is a relationship which religious and secular socialists need to explore and build on.

Quick to point out that it took time for him to accept the inherent link between the two, Alexander insists that his own early exposure to a socially aware Christianity has always enabled him to understand the importance of religion among the masses. "At no time in my life have I been a militant atheist."

Asked to speak about the journey that took him out of the Church, Alexander insists: "It was through debate and agonising questions. I have never taken kindly to people who try to impose their views on me." He tells how his journey beyond religion began when he came into contact with atheists in the Teachers' League of South Africa, an affiliate of the Non-European Unity Movement (NEUM). "They posed questions and lived moral lives without the religious metaphysics that I thought was an inherent part of moral living." His visits home during university holidays at the same time kept him in touch with the religion of his youth. "These were rigorous and often tense visits. I had grown up at the feet of Rev James Calata in Cradock. The ANC and the activities of the Anglican Church were, under Calata's ministry, more or less one and the same thing. In participating in a procession you were never too sure whether you were joining the Church or the ANC. When I returned home I was again drawn into this milieu. As time went by Rev Calata, other ANC people in Cradock and I got into long and, at times, uncomfortable debates. We were beginning to differ ideologically, but at no time did it occur to us that we could not work together. There was enough common ground to convince all of us that we were essentially on the same side. Calata had a way of including people rather than excluding them." (Calata was General Secretary of the ANC from 1936–49.)

Alexander became more deeply involved in the various structures of NEUM:

> It was here that my anti-whitism was knocked out of me. I met some incredible white people and came to realise that while in South African racism and economic exploitation were intertwined, this was not a synthesis which could not be undone. I was forced to grapple seriously with the works of Marx and Trotsky, with class analysis and the basis of socialist economics. The emphasis was placed on theory, intellectualism and eurocentricism, and I was being forced to read widely. If you did not know Hegel, Marx, Shakespeare, the poets and English literature you were simply left out of things. My present political ideology and interest were at the same time beginning to take shape; while the Christian ethic which I had imbibed as a child in Cradock was transformed into a socialist project. It was in many ways the most natural and obvious development that could happen. I had always been taught to think of other people first. That is why it was so easy for me to become a socialist.

UCT was another decisive factor in Alexander's life. It reinforced the intellectualism of the Unity Movement. "My education there was narrow, even myopic and certainly within the liberal paradigm. For all practical purposes Africa did not exist as far as my curriculum was concerned, neither did the world of the Communist Bloc, except to be dismissed. My encounter with the latter took place outside the classroom and my knowledge of African history and thought had ironically to wait until I was in prison. Such education as I did receive was nevertheless sound. It equipped me well for my years in Germany which lay ahead. My German professors were in their own slightly arrogant manner amazed at the learning which I had acquired before meeting them!"

## Germany

Having completed his MA in German Literature at UCT, he won an Alexander Humboldt Stiftung scholarship to Tübingen University where he remained from October 1958 to July 1961. "I was a committed Marxist by then, although not a rigorous or uncompromising Marxist. I was also not a militant atheist; in fact I have always objected to the approach of those who try to mobilise people by attacking their religion. I, at the same time, had firm views about values, ethics and religion." Having been told by his Unity Movement friends to be open to the various intellectual and political ideas which he encountered, he sought to do just that. "Germany was a hot bed of anti-French, pro-Algerian protests and I became friends with a number of Algerian students. In many ways they were like us. I also made friends with several Cuban students." He joined the Socialist Democratic Students' Union which was involved in the organisation of European student revolts in the 1960s. He met Trotsky's wife in Paris shortly before she died and became influenced by Trotskian thought, which made him very critical of the South African Communist Party (SACP) and more particularly of Stalinist ideas that prevailed among many communists. He recognised the successes of the Communist Revolution and believed it to be correct to defend the Soviet Union against the propaganda of the West. He, at the same time, had no illusions about what was going on in the Soviet Union.

> The SACP and many young people in South Africa refused to face up to the reality of what was happening in Eastern bloc countries. I did not know the depth of the brutalisation, but suspected that things were happening in the name of socialism that would one day return to haunt us. . . I spent more and more of my time involved in the Algerian movement, almost having myself thrown out of Germany for my activities. I was quite a character!

Alexander also became involved in the German Metal Workers' Union, which was seeking to organise Italian contract workers in an attempt to prevent them from undercutting wages. He was asked to write on Trade Unionism in Africa, which required him to research the topic widely. When he eventually returned to South Africa he was equipped to address many of the problems which were beginning to emerge among black workers. He had also experienced the reality of Sharpeville from outside of the country. Alexander remembers the deep sense of anger and foreboding fear which gripped him as he contemplated the implications of the massacre. "I was in a pub that night, drank heavily, got into an argument and ended up in a fight, attacking my opponents with a small pocket knife. Frustration can be self-defeating. It is also at the root of constructive counter-action." Within this context he began to consider seriously the feasibility of guerilla warfare and the possibility of initiating revolutionary movements in South Africa.

## Returning Home

Returning home in 1961, with an exposure denied to most black South Africans, he was immediately seen by many as a natural and well-equipped leader. "I wasn't afraid to lead, but I never saw myself as a political leader and never have up to this day. I am simply someone who wants to make a contribution to the cultural fabric of the people. I am interested in politics only to the extent that politics can contribute to this process. Politics is not *the* thing for me, it is not my all-embracing concern. It is only part of a bigger concern; it is a means to the realisation of a vision. My major concern and vision is not power. It is freedom."

Alexander recognised, however, that power is a major step en route to freedom and he immediately submitted his ideas to NEUM, suggesting that they prepare themselves for guerilla warfare. The youth responded warmly, while the older people were sceptical of both his plans and his agenda. He was suspended from the movement and together with Kenneth and Tilly Abrahams and some others he formed the Yu Chi Chan Club (YCCC), which committed itself to research guerilla warfare. They subsequently formed the National Liberation Front (NLF) to bring together people committed to the violent overthrow of the state, irrespective of their political ideology.

Emphasising the importance of a military arm in political struggle waged in a non-democratic situation, Alexander makes a point of referring to the fact that some of the most influential SWAPO leaders were members of the Front and the Club. "As such," he says, "the club played a major role in getting SWAPO leaders to opt for a guerilla war — although this would probably be denied by many high-ranking SWAPO government ministers today."

> Had APDUSA, (the African People's Democratic Union for Southern Africa; an off-shoot of NEUM), for example, become the mother body that SWAPO became for militant elements in Namibia, we could have had a very different situation in South Africa today. Umkhonto we Sizwe would probably still be the dominant military force among the liberation movements, but we may well have had an additional political current being promoted by armed struggle rooted among the people, especially in rural areas.

> But because APDUSA refused to provide the necessary support, we were compelled to forge an organisation from scratch and that was a mistake. We now know that we should rather have entered

*11*

the ANC or even the PAC. But we were too prejudiced against these groups for that to happen.

People both in NEUM and elsewhere thought that those promoting guerilla activities were just a group of silly young intellectuals who did not really know what they were doing. "And to some extent they were right," says Alexander.

> We were very inexperienced, very green. We had no mature or older people to caution us against certain excesses. We had no military tradition, no conspiracy tradition, no knowledge of secret work. We learned from scratch; literally from encyclopedias. We were an accident waiting to happen!

> Some of us were arrested and went to prison. Some of our people went into exile, one or two were killed and our structures were destroyed. When I was released from prison I met up with a few old friends, but essentially we had to find a new political home. That's when I made contact with the Black Consciousness Movement.

"But that is going ahead of things," he notes. "Before Black Consciousness Movement came Robben Island." Neville Alexander is a systematic person. He thinks historically and tells his story with chronological and logical precision.

## Robben Island

"For me the Island was a disaster in so far as I was obliged to stay there for ten years (1964–74). It was brutalising. Some of the prisoners were almost impossible to live with. The guards were in many instances uncouth, near-illiterate victims of a terrible system. On several occasions we complained to higher-ranking officials that every time they decided to change the prison personnel, we had to educate them all over again. Those negative things I try to forget. It was also an ennobling and enriching experience. It was empowering and most of us came out of it much better people. We were strengthened by the experience." Alexander speaks of the importance of personal relations forged between prisoners.

> There were people of such incredibly high calibre on the Island; people like Nelson (Mandela) and Walter (Sisulu). They set a fine example. . . It was quite remarkable that despite initial suspicions, periodic friction and occasional serious rows, people of such different political persuasions could actually get on so well —

12

even when confined to such small, unpleasant quarters. I learned here to disagree with people, while continuing to respect them. The experience was an example of true democracy and political pluralism. Robben Island was the seed bed in which we learned that we actually need one another. It is this realisation that must form the basis of a new nation.

Speaking of the education programme that was developed in prison, Alexander recalls: "We had some of the sharpest and keenest brains in the country together in a small place." Apart from obtaining an Honours degree in History while in prison, he read both widely and deeply. Hegel, Goethe, Schiller and Shakespeare, as well as the classical English novelists, were among the texts he read and re-read. "We taught one another what we knew, discovering each other's resourcefulness. We also learned how people with little or no formal education could not only themselves participate in education pro- grammes but actually teach others a range of different insights and skills." Building on this experience, Alexander has engaged in research on the restructuring of the South African educational system. "The 'University of Robben Island' was one of the best universities in the country . . . it also showed me that you don't need professors."

Alexander's self-discipline and personal integrity emerged perhaps nowhere more clearly than in his refusal to attend church services while in prison. "I refused to attend not because of any objection to religion *per se*, but because I had personal objections to what I thought was opportunism. Too many prisoners simply attended the services as an outing. It gave them something to do. I would never have been prepared to do this. Maybe I am simply too puritanical, but I refused to pretend that I was worshipping God when I knew very well that I was not. When I look back on the position that I adopted I realise that I was probably being too harsh in my judgement of those who used the church as an excuse to get out of their cells. At the same time I expect of others only what I demand of myself — personal integrity."

Alexander is someone in whom other people are ready to confide. "I think it has to do with an ability to listen. I have no aspirations to be this kind of confidant and no pretensions about having any particular counselling skills. In fact I often find the willingness of people to confide in me a little irksome." He suggests that the ability to listen has to do with energy; simply taking the time and expending the energy carefully to follow the often complex and contradictory line of reasoning of someone. "Robben Island helped me to try to unravel and understand the complexity of my own personality and life. This has, in turn, given me the capacity to involve myself in the labyrinthine lives of others. I suppose I have the mental discipline to do so."

He recalls too the inter-personal relations. "To get to grips with oneself and to take other people seriously, necessarily involves relationships. Robben Island was a kind of hot house where things happened with intensity. Some deep personal relations were forged there, and some serious and deeply-based differences emerged. In that kind of situation it was necessary to learn to say: 'I am sorry' or to say, 'I was wrong' without feeling humiliated. That is something one has to learn, it does not come naturally. It has to do with the Napoleonic thing: 'You can only command if you can obey'. Truth, honesty and integrity must be the measure of all debate and all relationships — against these we must judge ourselves in the same way that we expect others to be measured by them."

Speaking of the sensitivity which emerges between people who learn this kind of trust and honesty, Alexander relates his insights to physical human relationships. "It is a natural thing for people to want to be close to one another." He speaks of the taboos with which some people came into prison concerning not only homosexuality but any form of physical contact with a person of the same sex. "It was, however, completely natural that the kind of emotional and political intimacy which emerged among us on Robben Island would manifest itself in a person putting his hand on someone else's hand or around his shoulder." Seeing this to be the extension of the relationship which often exists between a father and a son or two close brothers, he suggests that under the pressure of their prison experience the prisoners often discovered things about themselves which they had not hitherto known. "Close human relations require the texture that comes from physical contact, without this necessarily acquiring homosexual overtones when it happens between people of the same sex." Relating this to gender relations, Alexander argues that conversely, males are often unable to relate to women without craving physical contact which is overtly sexual. Recognising that attitudes on gender, sexism and human relations are strongly influenced by experience he observes: "I was very lucky when I came out of prison because I met a few very confident, very knowledgeable and very progressive women, mostly classified 'white' (which is why they were confident etc), who were anti-sexist and real feminists in the positive sense of that term. In two or three years they got the last vestiges of sexism out of my life forever."

14

I could go on and on. The process of sorting out our relations with others, whether of the same or a different sex, is part of learning how to relate to people generally; it has to do with putting aside our prejudices and presuppositions, while learning to be neither opinionated and aggressive nor submissive and capitulating. It has to do with meeting one another as equal members of the human species; it has something to do with learning what it means to love one's neighbour.

## Black Consciousness

Critical of certain aspects of black consciousness, Alexander insists that "the ideology and practices of black consciousness were among the most creative phenomena of the 1970s". It was quite natural that he should have sought to make contact with the proponents of this philosophy on being released from prison.

He still regards his essay "Black Consciousness: A Reactionary Tendency?" which he wrote while under house arrest in 1974, as the basis of his critique of black consciousness.[1] Recognising that the Black Consciousness Movement was less dependent on US influences than he realised at the time, he says that today he would "emphasise much more the indigenous — especially Africanist and, paradoxically, Unity Movement — influences on the evolution of the ideology and the political practices of the Black Consciousness Movement." This having been said, it is important to note Alexander's criticism of black consciousness in America. He states: "Any cultural product that enhances humanity by weakening the perpetuation of the system which enables men to exploit others, is beautiful. Anything, whether black, blue or red, which does the opposite or tends to do so, is ugly." He regards black consciousness as being an important political tactic. His concern is, however, that to the extent that it comes under the control of the wrong people it can degenerate into simply another exercise in reform. "If the present crop of leaders is bought off by the powerful and all-pervasive oligarchy to become satellite 'capitalists' or apologists for these, the Black Consciousness Movement will become another conformist attempt: it will become a consumerist

---

1. For a reprint of "Black Consciousness: A Reactionary Tendency?" and reassessment of this argument see, Neville Alexander, "Black Consciousness: A Reactionary Tendency?" in N. Barney Pityana, Mamphela Ramphele, Malusi Mpumlwana and Lindy Wilson, *Bounds of Possibility: The Legacy of Steve Biko and Black Consciousness* (Cape Town: David Philip, 1991) pp. 238–252. "The original is reproduced warts and all, including incidentally the male chauvinist language which I continued to use unproblematically at the time." — Alexander.

movement providing the ideological basis of firms catering for Afro-styles. It will give the appearance of militant opposition while in reality constituting a necessary and even a vital aspect of the Establishment."

Relating this problem to the South African situation he argues: "The Black Consciousness Movement correctly stresses the unity of the oppressed people of South Africa." He obviously recognises that the oppressed are for various historical reasons identifiable in the majority of cases by their colour. His concern is, however, that oppression be not only associated with the plethora of apartheid signs and institutions — a concern which is, of course, clearly shared by the proponents of black consciousness. His argument is that a critique of apartheid must necessarily go beyond colour. It must penetrate the socio-economic roots of the apartheid system. "It is not the 'white' man," he writes, "but the system that oppresses us." He at the same time shares the Black Consciousness Movement's rejection of white liberals, while suggesting it would be a mistake to believe that all liberals are white. Pointing to the close links that have emerged between liberals and the Black Consciousness Movement in South Africa, he believes that all such links should be severed if the Black Consciousness Movement is to become an independent movement and refuge for the oppressed. "In the long run," he suggests, "liberalism is a greater danger to the struggle of the oppressed than fascism."

Again, as if to ensure that no simple answers be allowed, he insists that the Black Consciousness Movement correctly upholds the dignity and inalienable rights of black people. It is quite wrong, however, when it promotes these rights on the basis of these people being black. "Blacks," he stresses, "have these rights because they are people, a link in a great chain of humanity. The oppressed have an historic mission not because they are black but precisely because they are oppressed and have, therefore, a vital interest in the restructuring of a society that is rotten to the core."

Commenting on recent developments in South African politics, both the 'compromise' options being considered for a post-apartheid society as well as the suspicion and violence that exist between various ethnic groups, he observes that his critique of black consciousness "has stood the test of time".

Firmly committed to the principled unity of the oppressed people, his plea back in 1974, addressed as it was to the 'militant youth' within the Black Consciousness Movement, was for a critical reassessment of the central ideas of the movement in relation to the total history of struggle in South Africa, to ensure that it enter into meaningful debate with the rest of the tradition of struggle. This unity was high on the agenda of the abortive meeting between Alexander and Biko. So was the need for debate.

## After House Arrest

During his years as a banned person under house arrest, Alexander worked in a supermarket and as a book-keeper in a doctor's surgery. He also wrote a book entitled, *One Azania, One Nation: The National Question in South Africa*, published under the pseudonym, 'No Sizwe' in 1979. When his banning was lifted he researched Namibian history, again as a fellow of the Alexander von Humboldt Foundation. He later lectured part-time at UCT and became the Cape Town Director of the South African Committee for Higher Education (SACHED). In 1983, sensing a shift in political developments, he helped launch the Cape Action League (CAL) and was instrumental in the formation of the National Forum. In 1986 he became Executive Secretary of the Health, Education and Welfare Society of South Africa (HEWSSA), a trust designed to mediate funding for various community-based organisations. He helped establish the National Language Project and published *Language Policy and National Unity in South Africa/Azania* in 1989. In April 1990 Alexander was elected head of a new political formation, the Workers Organisation for Socialist Action (WOSA), committed to promoting working-class interests. In 1991 he was appointed Director of the Project for the Study of Alternative Education in South Africa in the Faculty of Education at UCT.

## No Need for the God Hypothesis

"My task and that of WOSA," says Alexander, "is to be the voice of the urban and rural poor." Concerned that the middle-class leadership that has emerged in the political structures of the oppressed will compromise to the point where the vast majority of the people will continue to be marginalised, his commitment is to ensure that the poor are afforded the opportunity to participate in the creation of their own future. He argues that while capitalism is presently being celebrated in global and local politics, the contradictions of capitalism will once again explode. The task of WOSA and similar organisations is to ensure that when this happens there is a sufficiently strong infrastructure for that moment to be seized.

Obviously we know that at certain critical times in history numbers count. We are realistic about our influence at present and have few utopian ideas as to what South Africa is likely to look like in the short- to medium-term future. We are at the same time ready to network with similarly minded groups in other political formations, recognising, as we do, that such groups exist in the ANC, the SACP, PAC, religious groups and elsewhere. We can do so, however, only on the basis of socialist principles which promote the interests of the working-class, the unemployed, the marginalised and the poor.

Despite the goodwill and noble intentions of others, it is this constituency alone that has the capacity to confront the present system because they alone have nothing to lose — except their chains. The material poverty of the poor puts them in a position where they have little or nothing with which to compromise. It is this that makes them the dynamic force for change that they are.

Alexander recognises that in a certain sense his life has done a full circle, while in another it has never changed — his priority is, as it was as a pupil at Holy Rosary Convent, the well-being of the poor. "The programme of WOSA," suggests Alexander, "is almost biblical in its simplicity because we genuinely say that the most urgent need in our country today is the need to feed the hungry, clothe the naked, house the homeless and care for the sick. These are the things that really matter in life, it is part of the injunction to love one's neighbour." What has changed since his school days is that today Alexander insists he is an atheist.

My commitment, if you like, is to ensure that the kingdom of heaven occurs on earth. I am not even agnostic about the rest — I am not even prepared to say that if there is a heaven that will be great. There is no logical proof of the existence of God.

Yes, it is important to intellectually explore the frontiers of the quest to understand reality. As a literary person I certainly understand the power of the metaphor. I also recognise that the materialist paradigm is itself a metaphor. I further know that there is a dialectical relationship between body and mind, between matter and spirit. It is in fact wrong to ask which is primary because in saying that the mind is a function of matter, there is a sense in which we are saying that matter is a function of the mind. There is no way to get beyond a certain point of reasoning.

Almost as if annoyed with his own intellectualism at this point, Alexander quickly insists that the majority of people have a need for religion to give life some kind of meaning and a mental construct by which to survive. "There are very few people, usually intellectuals, who can actually sublimate that need in other ways." Himself an intellectual, he observes: "I find myself agreeing with Pierre Laplace (the French astronomer and mathematician) who, when he was asked whether in contemplating the universe he was not compelled to allow for the existence of God, observed: 'Monsieur, I do not have the need for that hypothesis.' " Alexander's interest lies elsewhere. It is with the creation of a genuinely moral, decent and caring society, which allows for the fullest participation and sharing by all sectors of society. He speaks of the need for materialists and believers to find one another in social and ethical concerns rather than by engaging in endless doctrinal disputes. "There is a need," he insists, "to find the kind of meeting place that Palmiro Togliatti (the Italian communist of a half a century ago) was seeking for when he spoke of the need for an 'historic compromise' between the Christian Democratic Party and the Communist Party in post-Mussolini Italy. Socialists of different kinds need to find one another in order to keep the hope of the poor alive." Recognising that there is a working-class majority in most Church denominations, he insists that the identification of the institutional Church with capitalism is an unnecessary one. "It is also," he reminds us, "a distortion of the message of the historical Jesus."

PHOTO ACKNOWLEDGEMENT: Mayibuye Centre, UWC

# RAY ALEXANDER

*Ultimately a Trade Unionist*

Ray Alexander was born on 31 December 1913 to
Simka (Simon) and Dobe Alexandrowich, in
Varklian, a small town in Latvia. Later she moved to
Riga, where her closest friend, Leah, was arrested
for political activities. Concerned that young Rachel
might meet a similar fate, her mother immediately
made arrangements for her to immigrate to South
Africa on board the German East Africa liner, *Ubena*.

Her elder sister, already living in Cape Town, met her at the docks on 6 November 1929. "I was bitterly unhappy when I arrived," she recalls. "It was the day before the twelfth anniversary of the Russian revolution; an event that seemed to be passing by unnoticed. I asked myself how I would possibly survive in such a country. My consolation was that on board ship I had met some members of the German Young Communist League and representatives of the Internationale Rote Hilfe, an international organisation committed to assisting political prisoners. They had told me that if I was unhappy in South Africa they would collect the money for me to return home. I had already resolved to take them up on the offer when, a few days later, I was buying fruit and vegetables from a roadside hawker in Canterbury Street and I saw hundreds of workers streaming out of the factories. I began speaking with them and discovered that while some industries had trade unions others did not. Many of the workers did not belong to trade unions, others belonged to what were called yellow unions — lifeless appendages of industry — rather than the red unions which actively promoted the cause of the workers. I realised that I was walking on virgin soil. There and then, at the young age of 15 years old, I decided to remain in South Africa and help build a labour movement. I've been at it ever since."

A person with vast and varied experiences, it is difficult to get Ray Alexander to define herself. We speak of her Latvian origins (which she traces back to the 1500s) her Jewish roots, her involvement in socialist movements, her membership of the South African Communist Party and her engagement in worker organisations. "I am a socialist, a communist, a member of the ANC, a fighter for justice, a woman, a mother, a wife," she observes. "Yet I prefer to see myself simply as a human being. From the time I arrived in South Africa, trade unions and my involvement in workers' movements have been the locus of my political schooling. This is where my political identity and social character have been formed."         .

## Atheist and Socialist

The young Rachel Ester Alexandrowich was raised in a political home. Her parents were engaged in underground activities during the 1905 and 1917 revolutions. She recalls the oppression of Jewish people in ghettos and the discrimination they experienced in Tsarist Russia, where they were prevented from entering universities, and from learning professions and trades. "My early experiences of anti-Semitism prepared me well for my later struggles against apartheid. I cannot understand how Jews can fail to see the link."

Alexander speaks at length of the formative influence of her father on her life. "Fluent in Yiddish, Russian and German, he had an education which was much wider than was customary for Jews living in Latvia at the time. He taught Hebrew and gave instruction in the Talmud to the children in our neighbourhood. A leader in the Progressive Movement, he was well versed in the writings of socialism. There always seemed to be people at our home, listening to him speak. He loved nothing more than to teach, nothing gave him greater pleasure than to dispense knowledge and learn from other people. I recall the stimulating conversations he initiated in our home, and the many books which he brought home for us to read: Victor Hugo, Tolstoy, Dostoevsky and a whole range of Yiddish writers whose names I have now forgotten. I can still see the copy of *The Letters of Rosa Luxenburg to Sonia Liebknecht* which he gave me to read. I read this correspondence which was between Rosa (while she was in prison) and her friend Sonia Liebknecht, the wife of Karl Liebknecht. Together with Rosa he formed the extreme left-wing Spartacist movement which was responsible for the Berlin uprising in 1919. Both of them were killed after being arrested for their part in the uprising. I read at night and in the morning rose early to discuss what I had read with my father. 'I wish I had lived in those early days of the revolution,' I told him. I still recall his response: 'There are many more interesting times to come. You must learn to have patience, your time will come.' Several years ago I found a copy of The Letters in a second-hand bookshop in Leipzig. I treasure that book today because it is for me a symbol of an important phase of my life with my father. He was more than a father to me. He was a mentor and the best friend I had as a child."

Alexander's father died when she was twelve years of age. "I was devastated. He had taught me that God was just, that God cared for his people — especially for children and the weak. I now questioned the justice of God. 'How could God do such a thing to me?' I asked. 'Why should he destroy the wonderful relationship that my father and I enjoyed?' I conjured up the most hideous images of maggots eating his body. This was a turning point in my life. From being a deeply religious person, I became a non-believer. I hated God. I was an impetuous child, determined to have answers to my questions, with a wild greed for knowledge."

"As time passed my anger subsided, but I remained a non-believer. I

23

simply drifted into atheism. In later years I worked happily with Bishop Lavis and other religious people, while coming to have a deep respect for the religious conviction which inspired many of the workers whom I organised in the trade unions."

With her father's death, Alexander 'discovered' her mother. "This was the beginning of a different kind of relationship with her. Up until this time she was simply 'there', although in an important way. She cared for the family and kept a spotless home — you could eat off the floor — while showing a keen interest in working-class concerns. Having spent five years as a young person in Leeds in England, she had learnt to speak English and encouraged her children to do the same. "We were, however, not very close until my father's death. Then, on the day of his death I went to her and said, 'You are now both my mother and my father'. It was the beginning of a new-found relationship. I moved into my mother's bedroom, sleeping in my father's bed."

Her mother, in turn, became very protective. "She was deeply concerned that I was reading Marx, which was prohibited at the time. Although scarcely literate, she nevertheless showed a keen interest in my reading, and listened attentively when I read articles and stories of interest to her. When I boarded the ship for Cape Town I realised just how close my mother and I had become."

Another early influence in Alexander's life came from Leibe Yoffe, her father's best friend. He was headmaster of the school she attended in Varklian and took responsibility for her education. He was the founder of the *Arbeiter Heim*, a workers' organisation committed to the promotion of socialism and care of workers. He exposed her to further socialist ideas, supplying her with books, pamphlets and other reading material. "I won the school prize for reading the most books during the year; I read 80 books, most were on politics and history." A promising student, although only 14 years old, she was invited to participate in a debate organised by the Zionist Organisation on the Balfour Declaration, supporting the establishment of a Jewish state in Palestine. "I immediately went to the local Zionist Organisation, for reading material. This seemed to me the logical thing to do. As I read I became convinced that anti-Semitism could not be overcome by Jews fleeing to Israel. They needed to learn to live with other people, to become part of a broader human struggle against exploitation, rather than to endeavour to withdraw from this greater struggle. I was also outraged to think that they would be

24

prepared to occupy Palestinian land. I realised that the talk of the Jews being a people without a land and Palestine being a land without people was nonsense. I decided to tell the Zionist Organisation that I was opposed to the Balfour Declaration and that I felt obliged to say this in the debate. Their response was to try and prevent me from attending the debate. Leibe Yoffe objected. So I attended, but did not speak.

If the death of her father was the beginning of her break with religion, it was this event that marks the beginning of her alienation from the Zionist Organisation. "The Zionists," she explains, "affirmed Jewish identity in an exclusive kind of way. The socialist Jews, people like Leibe Yoffe, were fighting for a new world, a world where not only Jews but everyone would be free. This they saw not as an idle dream but as a historical necessity, with the Russian revolution as the beginning of the process. The debate on the Balfour Declaration enabled me to make this distinction in my own thinking. From then on, while still self-consciously a Jew, I began to think beyond the narrow confines of an exclusive Jewish culture and identity. In brief I realised I was a socialist."

"I wanted to become a doctor. As a child I was overwhelmed by the extent of human suffering, and thought the most practical thing I could do was to care for people." Having to pass Latin to study medicine, Alexander attended classes given by a Catholic priest at a local seminary. Unfortunately, the course was never completed because of Anti-Semitic threats from some German students at the seminary who object to the Jewish students.

"I was faced with an impasse: On the one hand I was fighting anti-Semitism, on the other I soon came under attack from the Zionists. The school I was attending decided to celebrate the opening of the Hebrew University in Jerusalem. I said I was happy to celebrate the opening of a place of learning wherever it was to be found — in Jerusalem or Timbuktu — but reiterated my opposition to the occupation of Palestine. Needless to say the Zionist Organisation was not happy. I was, however, fast moving away from observing Jewish festivals, holidays, dietary rules or customs."

The outcome of all this was the decision to study further in Riga, the capital of Latvia, located about a hundred and sixty miles away from Varklian. Whilst attending a technical school there, Alexander also attended classes at the Volks Universitäte, a left-wing community institution, and took classes in dialectical materialism from a Russian woman working in the Russian trade office. It was at this point that Leah was arrested and Ray was sent to South Africa.

Reflecting on her early years in Latvia, Alexander sees a number of influences that came together, providing her with certain formative values that have shaped her engagement in life. "My early religious teachings persuaded me of the need to be sensitive to the fate of the least powerful. The Torah, which my father read to me, taught me that as a Jew I was obliged to love and respect the stranger, remembering that the Jews were themselves strangers in Egypt. This Jewish memory which reminds Jews of their ties to the oppressed, together with the anti-Semitism which I experienced in Latvia, gave me an early bias in favour of everyone who was exploited and oppressed. So when I started reading Marxist and other forms of revolutionary literature, I took to it like mother's milk."

> My fight against apartheid was in a sense an extension of my fight against anti-Semitism; my fight against the Zionist occupation of Palestine a consequence of my commitment to oppressed and exploited people whoever they may be; and my fight for the rights of women a logical consequence of my fight against all other forms of exploitation. My opposition to capitalism was, in turn, a direct consequence of my fundamental belief in the equality of all people. This convinced me that a system which exploits the poor to satisfy the whims and the wants of the rich is unjust and wrong. The struggle for justice is an integrated struggle. You cannot fight for the rights of some and not for the rights of others. Once you start the struggle, there is no curtailing it. That's just the way it is.

I left Latvia with all the ingredients that made for moral indignation — eager to become involved in the struggle of the exploited people of the world. I was sent to South Africa because my mother's two sisters were living in Upington, my sister and brother were living in Cape Town and my mother had this drang (desire) to live in an English-speaking country as a result of her years in Leeds. I could not, however, have landed in a better place. It was a place ready-made to receive me. The saddest day of my life was when Jack (Simons) and I went into exile in 1965. Among the happiest was the day we returned home, to be part of the struggle among the people who had received me as an orphan 61 years earlier."

## Trade Unions

Within days of her arrival in South Africa, Ray Alexander attended a discussion group of the Communist Party of South Africa (CPSA), where she met John Gomas, James la Guma, Joe Pick, E. J. Brown and other leading CPSA members. They suggested that she become Secretary of the Party. "I laughed," she recalls, "telling them that I was only 15 years of age and wanted to work in the Young Communist League. They invited me to attend a meeting of the Party. There I met Comrade James Schuba, Secretary of the Cape Town Stevedoring Workers' Union and a key member of the near-defunct Industrial and Commercial Workers' Union (ICU). My life's work was about to begin. My pent-up energy was about to be released, and the moral values that had been taking shape since my childhood were about to be directed into the trade union movement."

Employed in a dress shop, Alexander worked in Schuba's office during the weekends, accompanying him on his visits to dock and harbour workers. Within three years of her arrival in South Africa she was elected Secretary of the Commercial Employees' Union in Cape Town. When she lost her job at the dress shop in 1935, she became full-time organiser of the Non-European Railway and Harbour Workers' Union, as well as organising workers in a number of other industries. Deeply involved in the Party, for a while she served as Secretary of the Western Cape district committee of the CPSA. She later devoted her energy to full-time trade union work and in 1941 she became General Secretary of the Food and Canning Workers' Union. Six months later the workers at H. Jones and Co in Paarl went out on strike. Although many of the workers were not unionised, Alexander eventually managed to get almost 100% support for union demands, forcing management to settle after a three week work stoppage. What was important was that the new union had won its first victory. Workers discovered the power of organisation and collective bargaining. Alexander's work was, in turn, extended to cover a large area. She continued working in the leadership of trade unions until she was served with a banning order preventing this work in October 1953, after which time she continued her activities underground. In 1957 she was elected Life General Secretary of the Food and Canning Workers' Union and in 1986 Honorary President of the Food and Allied Workers' Union. In exile she continued her trade union work by serving on the Executive Committee of the South African Congress of Trade Unions (SACTU). Since her return to South Africa in 1990 she has again given her support to trade unions.

## Non-Racism

Ray Alexander's link with the trade union movement has always been in association with the SACP. Shortly after her arrival in Cape Town in 1929, she joined the CPSA which had been formed eight years previously. Her early work in this organisation (banned under the Suppression of Communism Act in 1950, and reformed as the SACP in 1953) makes her a veteran member.

She speaks of the contribution of the SACP:

> The communists have not been without fault in the South African struggle — no-one has achieved that distinction. We have, however, consistently been involved on the side of workers who have been exploited at every level of society. We have also seen the unemployed, the marginalised and the weak as the focus of our special concern. Our long history in this regard speaks for itself.
>
> Communists have promoted non-racism in a sustained and relentless manner. Some of our members were, of course, influenced by the all pervading racism of South African society, in giving expression to the slogan, 'Workers of the world unite for a white South Africa'. It has also been argued by some people that the promotion of a Native Republic is further evidence of racism in the Party. I would argue differently.
>
> The idea of a Native Republic was a specific strategy aimed at the mobilisation of Africans. James La Guma spoke at the time of white workers being "saturated with imperialist ideology". Certainly the 1922 strike showed beyond doubt that white workers were ready to side with management in return for certain racially-based job privileges, turning their backs on black workers. In this context I was firmly on the side of those favouring a Native Republic. It was a policy grounded in democracy, aimed at wresting power from a white minority government and the capitalists. The establishment of an independent Native Republic, run by black workers, was to be a first step towards the establishment of a racially socialist state.
>
> However this particular event is interpreted, what cannot be denied is that the Party soon returned to its non-racist vision, committing itself to a social programme favouring the disadvantaged — workers, women, the unemployed and blacks. That distinction no-one can take away from us. It is a heritage that we have bequeathed to the democratic struggle that others joined later.

Today, Alexander is uncompromising in her support for democracy and non-racism. "It constitutes all that I believe in as a human being. We must learn to live together, we must learn to live democratically and we must learn to accept the consequences of democracy. I am a socialist, but fully realise that the time has not yet come when the majority will vote for socialism. I am content to accept that decision, while seeking every opportunity to promote my ideals. I learned to compromise in negotiations with industry. Sometimes you are obliged to settle for less than you want, in order to be around to fight another day." Firmly opposed to racially-based politics, she made herself available as a candidate for one of the three native representatives' seats in Parliament. "Some regarded this as 'joining the system'. Having discussed it with comrades in the Party and the ANC, we saw it as a strategy to promote something far more than Parliament symbolised. The government obviously saw it the same way, because I was issued with a banning order on the steps of Parliament, preventing me from taking my seat in the House on the very day I was due to do so in April 1954. I've been banned from doing so many different things, I can't recall them all!" she observes. "A short while later I was issued a further banning order preventing me from using the parliamentary library, and after that they found various other things to ban me from doing."

## Women's Rights

A year prior to her attempt to enter Parliament Alexander had been banned from a different activity. On 1 April 1953 she had met with Francis Baard, Florence Matomela, Helen Joseph, Gus Coe and others to discuss the formation of a women's organisation. The Federation of South African Women was formed and Alexander opened the first meeting on 17 April 1954. She was elected Secretary of the organisation, but banned almost immediately, preventing her from participating further in the organisation.

Alexander believes in the equality of all people and this has informed her concern for the rights of women throughout her life. "It is a concern, however," she insists, "that I have never been prepared to promote outside of the broader political struggle. For this reason I refused to join the National Council of Women when approached to do so many years ago. I saw it as a bourgeois organisation, supported by the wives of wealthy businessman and company directors. The women's struggle is for me an inherent part of the broader political struggle in which I am involved. It is not something apart from or adjacent to it. I become deeply concerned when it is promoted apart from the struggle, on the assumption that women somehow constitute a homogeneous group who have a common set of interests that transcend race and class. The lives of women, like those of men, are influenced and moulded by race, class and other factors. To suggest that these factors can be ignored in promoting the rights of women is tantamount to suggesting that the divide between rich and poor women, or black and white women can be glossed over or even accepted. I believe in equality between women and men, I believe in economic and racial equality between all people. The one cannot be separated from the other."

Conceding that the trade union movement has been as male dominated as most other organisations, Alexander also insists that the time has come for the affirmation of women's rights: "Women realise that liberation which excludes women's rights is not liberation at all. An increasing number of men are, in turn, beginning to realise this as well. New beginnings are always important times in history. We must grasp this 'new time' in South Africa to advance the cause of liberation at every level, and that includes the liberation of women. If we miss this moment, the struggle could be set back at every level for several generations."

## Into Exile and Back

Ray Alexander and her husband Jack Simons were married in 1941, sharing a political commitment that united them in a common struggle. They went into exile together and returned to South Africa together.

When Jack Simons' banning order came in 1965 it was severe. It included a ban on writing. "Although we at first thought he could continue to write despite this restriction, the frequent visits by the security police made it impossible," Alexander explains. "We had just moved to a house in Onrust when, one morning, a security policeman presented Jack with a new banning order. It included a clause prohibiting any communication between the two of us. I exploded, insisting that the policeman immediately take me to the magistrate in Hermanus. He did so and I demanded that the clause be removed from the order. After some altercation it was dropped." Things were eventually so restrictive that Ray Alexander and Jack Simons left for Zambia. From there they went to Manchester University where Simons received a fellowship and Alexander studied Labour Relations, Russian and German. In 1969 they completed their important book, *Class and Colour in South Africa: 1850–1950*. Exactly ten years earlier they had also co-authored a book, entitled *Job Reservation and the Trade Unions*.

And what of her hopes and fears for the future? She fears the white right-wing. "I do not dismiss their threat to resort to arms. I remind myself, however, that they are a small minority and cannot ultimately win. What they can do is cause a great deal of suffering in the short to medium term. This apart, I am reasonably confident that we are about to take a significant step in the direction of the kind of society for which I have spent my life struggling. We are about to have a democratically elected government, although some compromises are likely to take place in the process. Clearly we are not about to move into a socialist situation. That is something for which we need to continue to struggle. Despite the set-backs which socialists around the world are forced to accept, I continue to believe that the contradictions of capitalism are such that an alternative kind of economy will eventually emerge."

Does she have any significant regrets when she looks back on her life? "I've had my disappointments, but essentially no," she says. "Each phase of my life has had its own meaning, preparing the ground for the phase to follow. There is also a certain continuity running through it all."

Suggesting that the values that have governed her life are those of the Jewish and biblical tradition, I enquire whether religion plays any part in her life today. Her answer: "No, religion has not been part of my life for a very long time. I am simply motivated by a moral vision which I like to think is part of the universal quest to be human." Does she think religion could serve this universal end? "It all depends on the kind of religion you are talking about," she responds. She is, of course, absolutely correct.

PHOTO ACKNOWLEDGEMENT: The *Star*

# FRANZ AUERBACH

*A Jewish Humanist*

Born in Germany, Franz Auerbach came to South
Africa with his parents in 1937. His father was an
unemployed electrical engineer at the time and his
mother, the head of a dental clinic in Wuppertal, had
been dismissed from her post shortly after Hitler
came to power.

Unable to afford the cost of the three years of further study which were required for her qualifications to be recognised in South Africa, she found a job as a machinist in a clothing factory. His father rode a bicycle through the streets of the Johannesburg immigrant areas — places like Doornfontein and Hillbrow, selling polony to other refugees. Although still at school, the young Franz helped augment the family income by teaching English to other immigrants whose English was worse than his! Needing to find a full-time job, he left school at the end of standard eight and joined a commercial company as an accounts clerk, while studying further part-time. He passed his matric by attending night classes at the Technical College and earned a BA degree by correspondence. He later acquired three further degrees, including a Ph D from the University of Natal.

> I can trace one branch of my family back to Frankfort-on-Main in 1397. My family were Jews and I was reared in the Jewish religion, which had been a formative influence on my life. I was also influenced by the racial persecution of Jews in Nazi Germany and a subsequent knowledge of the holocaust, as well as through associating myself with Jewish institutions and organisations in South Africa. These include the South African Yad Vashem Foundation and the South African Jewish Board of Deputies.

> But that is only part of me. I have lived in South Africa since 1937, and feel committed to this country particularly since it accepted my parents and me as immigrants. To be committed to South Africa means, of course, to be involved in its problems. I feel strongly, especially because of the experiences of my youth, that all South Africans are my fellow citizens. For me, racial classification was always secondary to citizenship. I am at the same time aware that my 'white' racial classification has meant that I have shared the privileges of that status as they apply in South Africa.

> Having spent most of my life in education, I am deeply committed to the teaching profession. Even though I taught in African night schools for over twenty years, my work was mostly in central Johannesburg. However, during the past few years I have been working in Soweto. . . When Soweto shudders, my heart feels the tremor.

> I nevertheless neither deny, nor am I ashamed of, my roots, while wanting to stress that I do not have a single loyalty or group identity. There are many strands within me and together they make up the single human being who, I hope, has a harmonious personality perhaps best defined as a human male named Franz Auerbach, born in 1923. I mention the year of my birth because like everyone else I am also a child of my time, with experiences and

perceptions somewhat different from those of earlier and later generations.

Because of my spiritual background and my commitment to the human race, I like to define my life as the voyage of a Jewish humanist.

Recognising an inherent link between the human suffering of Jewish people and black South Africans under the apartheid regime, he observes, "I have never been able to understand how Jews who have suffered from racial discrimination and religious persecution for centuries can be indifferent to racial discrimination in South Africa or anywhere else."

## South African Jews

It is important to understand the history of South African Jews and the special circumstances that brought them to South Africa. Auerbach speaks of the circumstances that brought his family to South Africa:

My parents actually decided to leave Germany in March 1934, a little more than a year after Hitler came to power, intending to settle in what was then known as Palestine. This was not possible. Immigration was confined to those who were able to make a cash deposit of £1 000, or who were farmers. Not having the money nor being farmers, my family went to a place in Luxembourg where academics were trained to become farmers in order to meet the requirement for entry into Palestine. By November 1936 we had still not received clearance to enter the country, so when my parents heard of a ship, the *Stuttgart*, that had been chartered to take people to South Africa, they opted for settling there instead. When the 537 passengers arrived in Cape Town there was an anti-Semitic demonstration on the quayside — the result of a protest movement against Jewish immigration led by the Greyshirt Movement and actively supported by some staff and students at Stellenbosch University. Prominent among them was Dr H. F. Verwoerd, Professor of Psychology at that university at the time."

Auerbach speaks of the three major phases of Jewish immigration to South Africa, stressing that it is important to recognise that two of these are directly related to periods of anti-Semitic persecution in Europe. The first Jews to settle in South Africa did so prior to the discovery of minerals, with the first Jewish synagogue in Cape Town dating back to 1841. The second strand of Jewish migration was in the latter part of the nineteenth century. Auerbach thoughtfully recalls the process: "This was caused by the emergence of anti-Jewish pogroms in various parts of the Russian Empire. . . Many of the

*35*

Jewish people who fled the area went to the United States, while a significant number of them came to South Africa where new goldfields drew immigrants from many lands. Most of the Jewish immigrants came with few material resources, and had to work hard to make an adequate living. They maintained their Jewish identity by joining or founding congregations and charitable institutions; many of which still exist. Jews from Lithuania were particularly prominent among the immigrants, and those who had made good invited members of their families to join them. This went on until well into the 1920's." The third strand of Jewish immigration is that of which Auerbach's own family was a part. They came in the wake of the rise of Nazism in Germany. By this time, however, South Africa was restricting the immigration of people from Russia and its neighbouring territories — only Jews in that part of the world wanted to immigrate to South Africa. Because the restrictions did not apply to other parts of Central Europe, Jews from those areas were still able to enter the country as freely as any other white immigrants. Auerbach recalls: "When, however, over 2 000 Jews entered the country in 1936, the Hertzog government required that a £100 deposit be paid by each immigrating family, whereas prior to this, all that was required was a guarantee of £100. In effect, this limited immigration in a significant manner, and in order to avoid the pending change in requirements the German Jewish Aid Organisation chartered the *Stuttgart* that brought us to South Africa. Within less than a year of our arrival the Alien Act of 1937 was passed which, *inter alia*, established an Immigrants' Selection Board, making Jewish immigration extremely difficult."

Auerbach refers to three social realities which need to be taken into account in seeking to discern the moral ethos of South African Jews.

> The first is the extent of poverty which characterised the arrival of Jewish immigrants. The majority of them were required to eke out a living in whatever way possible. Some worked as labourers, some as pedlars, others opened shops on the margins of the cities and in the rural areas. Some immigrants could recall having had a better socio-economic status in Europe prior to the persecution that drove them out. With this came a commitment to hard work, the education of their children and a determination to ensure that second and third generation Jews in South Africa would have a better deal in life. It paid off. Jews were able to become medical doctors, lawyers, teachers and to enter other professions. Although South African Jewish immigrants were traditionally prominent among the supporters of liberal and even radical causes, in

the process of climbing the social ladder of life, they tended to become increasingly supportive of the white status quo. Perhaps this was inevitable. It is a well-known sociological fact that with material wealth comes a certain degree of economic and political conservatism.

The second factor is the anti-Semitism, in its various forms, which was part of the social milieu with which Jewish immigrants had to contend. People sometimes remember that President Paul Kruger had a friend called Sammy Marks. The implication, they seem to think, is that Jews were respected and well-treated in the Afrikaner community. The reality is that blacks, Jews and Roman Catholics never had the vote in the old Transvaal Republic. I have already referred to the anti-Semitism of the 1930s; and the pro-Nazi stance of some politicians who would eventually occupy the highest offices in successive National Party governments is well known. Aware of their minority status and remembering the persecution that drove them out of their homes once before, the Jewish community was politically sensitive, ready to interact with the existing political establishment and willing to become quite submissive in return for a space in which to live. The irony is that some Jews in this country have since even been prepared to support and promote the political policies of the National Party that has not only a history of anti-Semitism, but has systematically exploited and persecuted people on the grounds of race and ethnic identity. This is the kind of policy that accounted for the Holocaust.

Thirdly, the religious factor that has shaped the moral behaviour of Jews in South Africa. Jewish orthodoxy looks inward. While not all Jews who came to South Africa were strictly speaking 'orthodox' as opposed to 'reformed', their sense of vulnerability in a hostile social environment caused many of them to look towards other Jews, to protect their Jewishness, to practise Jewish rituals and generally to take care of their own community. Within the South African community, which separates groups and encourages people to affirm their own separate identities, this kind of Jewish exclusivism intensified. Given the fact that all Jews in this country are white, it has meant that this exclusivity has in practice been a white exclusivity. A consequence of this has been that even when Jews have ventured out of their own religious and social communities, they have felt more comfortable among whites than blacks. For a number of conservative Jews (some of whom almost blindly supported the Israeli position concerning the occupied Palestinian territories) this isolation was exacerbated by the fact that many coloured people are Muslim and show an understandable sympathy for Arabs on the receiving end of Israeli policy.

Many Jews in South Africa, for a variety of reasons, have isolated themselves from the broader South African context. They have certainly not opposed the apartheid structures in the way in which their history and theology would suggest they should.

## An Ethical Incentive

Auerbach, however, sees an ethical incentive within Judaism that needs to be elevated and promoted in the quest for a democratic South Africa. He relates his own religious experience as a Jew and his understanding of this incentive. He feels that Jewish ethics, if conscientiously applied, has a profound contribution to make to the development of the just and equal society which is now hopefully taking shape in South Africa.

Auerbach had his Barmitzvah in Luxembourg and has been part of the Johannesburg Jewish community since he arrived in South Africa. "I have always had a strong awareness of being a Jew. I have, however, never been ultra-orthodox and I do not claim to be a strictly observant Jew, in the sense of keeping a kosher home or observing all religious aspects of the Sabbath. Yet in the 43 years of our marriage, every Friday we have had wine and bread, which is the traditional *Kiddush* in the Jewish family. As a family we observe the Passover, the New Year and the Day of the Atonement. I have also been on the Council of the congregation where I have worshipped for the past 25 years. Religion means a great deal to me, but I have always held that the ethical values of my religion are far more important than the minutia of legal and ritual observances, although I do not discount these as being unimportant."

Auerbach has a strong sense of Jewish history and speaks of the importance of the Jewish understanding of what it means to be truly human. "Jewish scripture sets for us a high goal as human beings. It holds out the possibility of human improvement — and quite frankly, I sometimes feel we place too much emphasis on the sinfulness of humankind." He developed this theme in the Eighth Desmond Tutu Peace Lecture, which he delivered at the WCRP Annual Conference in November 1992.[1] Expressing concern that it is sometimes taught that human beings are naturally aggressive, and that little can be done

---

1. Franz Auerbach, *Peace Education — Failure of Our Century* (World Conference on Religion and Peace, 1992). Extracts of this lecture have been synthesised into Dr Auerbach's verbal responses to questions in the interview conducted in November 1992.

to curb human nature, he drew on the words of the Norwegian John Galtung:

> We do not think there is either evidence or theory to corroborate the assumption that man is inherently bound or programmed to engage in aggression or dominance. . . There are undoubtedly combinations of structural and ecological conditions that prompt human beings into direct and structural violence, but these conditions are modifiable . . . they are changeable. . . On the one hand there is the conservative distrust of man as not only unmodifiable but also as fundamentally evil or at least weak, bound to engage in violence. The best one can do is to contain him geographically or hierarchically. On the other hand there is the radical confidence in man as modifiable, at least to a large extent conditioned by structural changes.

Auerbach quoted Psalm 8:

> What is man that you remember him
> And the son of man that you think of him?
> Yet you have made him a little lower than the angels
> And have crowned him with honour and glory.

"That is not the description of a creature seen as inherently aggressive, evil or even weak," he continued. "Nor does Judaism believe that human beings are born sinful. In spite of our weaknesses, we are assured each year during the Day of the Atonement that God's judgement will be tempered by forgiveness and benevolence through prayer, repentance and the practice of justice through charitable deeds . . . I believe that humanity can make greater progress towards peace and harmony."

Acknowledging the centrality of sin in Jewish thought, he insists that the other side of the theological equation, which speaks of humanity being able to rise above weakness and aggression, is all too often neglected. He argues that this pessimistic trend in Judaism is historical rather than theological. He sees it as a consequence of twenty centuries of being a persecuted minority group in most countries. "Jews have a profound pathological sensitivity to anti-Semitism which is quite understandable. My concern is that we should not internalise this sense of persecution to the point of withdrawing from mainstream society, or simply declaring that this is the way the world is and that we must, therefore, ourselves respond aggressively towards everyone else."

Auerbach recalls a recent visit to Europe. "I punished myself by taking a trip to Auschwitz, discovering that it is a devastating thing to do so alone, without anyone with whom to share your emotions. In addition to all else, it reinforced in me a concern that I have had all my life. It has to do with the question of how Jews, who have experienced the racial discrimination and genocide of the holocaust, whether vicariously or directly, can remain indifferent to racial discrimination in South Africa or anywhere else." Making this kind of link between Nazism and apartheid has earned Auerbach a measure of opprobrium over the years because many Jews regard the holocaust as a unique event, feeling it is almost blasphemous to compare it to any other event. "There is a sense in which it is unique, since the planned total destruction of a people had never before been carried out with such diabolic scientific planning. But one must not lose sight of the fact that Jews were persecuted by the Nazis not because of their religious beliefs but because of their race or ethnicity — and discrimination and persecution on the grounds of race clearly has other parallels, especially in South Africa. The great contribution which Jews can make, by drawing on their memory of the holocaust, is to ensure that this kind of discrimination, which was the root cause of the holocaust, will never happen again — whoever the victims of this discrimination may be." Emphasising that it is his duty, as a Jew, to make this point he continues:

> The predominant theological and ethical feature of the holocaust is that the Nazis regarded the Jews and some other human beings as being of less worth, or less human, than themselves. This can and indeed has happened elsewhere in the world, and is what apartheid is all about. Once you have started the process of declaring some people to be of more worth than others, it is almost inevitable that you will eventually conclude that some are less than human. Such people become expendable. When they cannot be controlled you simply wipe them out. In South Africa blacks have not been wiped out but they have been marginalised, deprived of their citizenship and a systematic attempt has been made to force them to be content with less than what is due to any human being. Many have been killed in the process. There is no great and impregnable divide between Nazism and apartheid. For Jews to refuse to see that, is for Jews to fail to make the contribution which they can and ought to make to the elimination of racial discrimination in the world.

Auerbach speaks too of the Israeli-Palestinian problem. "There is a strong perception in the Jewish community world-wide, promoted of course by successive Israeli governments, that no Jew should criticise

Israel unless he or she is prepared to live there and accept the consequences of being a Jew in what is essentially an Arab region of the world. I do not accept this. I believe that Jews everywhere have an obligation to work for justice and peace in the Middle East and elsewhere in the world. To vigorously share in the debate on the Israeli presence in occupied territories can only help to sensitize Jews and others inside and outside of Israel to the situation. In this way the difficulties involved can be discussed and, hopefully, an equitable solution found. As in South Africa, where people have lived in conflict and confrontation for so many years, it is very difficult to create a situation of mutual trust between Israelis and Palestinians. South African perceptions of the Middle East confrontation are often confused. For example, because Jews in South Africa are white and most Muslims are black, the Israeli-Palestinian and Israeli-Arab problems are often interpreted as racial conflicts. The truth of the matter is that most Jews in the Israeli army tend to look a bit like the coloured people of this country. This aside, Israel is a harsh occupying force in territories that she will ultimately need to vacate. I am committed as a Jew to see this happen and there are increasing numbers of Jews in and outside Israel who are saying more or less the same thing. The world-wide movement for democracy and self-determination is slowly beginning to make its influence felt in Israel as it is in South Africa."

> If I had a pessimistic understanding of human nature I would be a despondent person. I fundamentally believe, however, that by God's grace and with serious moral resolve we can rise above our conflicts and create a better world. I think the Jewish faith has something to teach us in this regard. We must reclaim our status as people called of God to be makers and creators of a world within which we, and indeed the whole of creation, can live in harmony.

Auerbach refers to a comment made by Mr Yitzchak Navon (then President of the State of Israel) who was wanting to underline the common humanity of the people of the Middle East, during his first state visit to Egypt in 1980. He told a story from the Talmud, in which a wise man answered the question as to why the Holy One had created millions of fish, trees and animals but only one human being. "It was," said the wise man, "so that no one human being could say to another 'My father is more important than yours'." Stressing that we have all, whether rich or poor, Jew or non-Jew, white or black, come from one and the same person, Navon continued:

Another wise man said that there was another reason God had created only one man. It is here that we can see the grandeur of the Holy One, Blessed be He, for when a human king makes coins out of the same mould all coins are identical. But God created all human beings from the same mould — from the first man — and there is no human being identical to another. . . As far as origin is concerned we are all equal; there is no one who is more distinguished or better than anyone else. At the same time we are all different; it is our right to be different. The whole cosmos testifies to this. The whole of nature is evidence of this difference, of this variety. Together with this there is harmony. We must recognise our differences, respect them and respect our equality. If we go in this direction, we may progress one step forward.

With an abiding commitment to, and belief in, the importance of education, Auerbach quotes Julius Nyerere (in *Education for Self-Reliance*) who wrote that societies educate the youth to "transmit from one generation to the next the accumulated wisdom and knowledge of society and to ensure their active participation in its maintenance and development". As an educationalist Auerbach believes that what we teach and the way we teach it can improve harmony in society and contribute towards peace in the world.

## Education for Peace

Taking Peace Education as the theme of his Desmond Tutu Peace Lecture, Auerbach insisted that no society can afford to allow some of its citizens to live without hope for a better tomorrow. To do so would create the conditions in which frustrations would express themselves in widespread crime, in mindless hatred and in social destruction. Locating his observations within the context of Abraham Maslow's hierarchy of human needs, he noted that the most basic need is for physical well-being, for food and shelter. The second is for security. Until the need for regular food and shelter is met and people feel that they live in relative safety, they are unlikely to devote much time or energy to the fulfilling of other needs. Maslow's third level of need is the one for love and affection. The fourth is the need for self-esteem, the need to be accepted as a person. The highest need is for self-actualisation, "the need to feel that we are expressing our personalities in our lives, and making a worthwhile contribution to the world". Against this assessment of human needs, Auerbach emphasised the need for the total well-being of people to be addressed before any

42

serious attempt can be made to teach and enable people to aspire after such values and ethical ideals that can make for a better and more humane society.

We have known for a hundred years that hungry children cannot learn properly. Therefore most civilised countries have school feeding schemes to ensure that no pupils attend classes on empty stomachs. It is simply another example of the fact that until basic needs for food have been fulfilled, the satisfaction of a higher need, viz. learning, cannot get the attention it requires. In this connection it is a disgrace and a sign of our neglect of basic public needs that we have had no school feeding scheme as part of our education programmes for the past forty years. Some private agencies have, however, jumped into the breach and are doing splendid work to ensure that the children they feed can benefit from teaching. It is time for the state to do its duty in this regard without delay.

Auerbach speaks about the need to promote certain educational truths that could make for a more peaceful world. The first, he suggests, is the imparting of the firm knowledge of certain basic facts. Most children, he points out, learn some basic facts at school and know them for life. These include such basic truths as: Pigs can't fly, three plus two makes five, and the sun rises every day, even when it is hidden from our view by clouds. His concern is that there are, however, people who believe all sorts of other things which they should also have learnt to reject as simply not true. Such beliefs include the myth that ethnic origin predetermines human character and that natural disasters are caused, for example, by the wickedness of individuals who cast spells on their innocent neighbours. "All children everywhere should learn some basic facts about physical inheritance and social learning, about the causes of disasters and diseases, and also about some of the limits of human knowledge at the present time. If they did, many of the prejudices that cause severe conflicts locally and globally would not survive. It is here that I believe our teaching has failed."

Secondly, he argues that there ought to be contact between people from different backgrounds. "There is ample evidence from many quarters that children are not born prejudiced, that little children play together quite happily with children who look different. Prejudice is generally acquired, it is learnt."

Thirdly, Auerbach stresses the importance of teaching attitudes and values, recognising that "what is caught is more important than what is taught". Noting the extent to which racial superiority and the lack of tolerance is inculcated in people as a result of upbringing and imposed or taught attitudes, his point is that the opposite can also be cultivated in our children.

Fourthly, his concern is that we should teach mutual respect for one another. In this regard he finds fault with the emphasis placed on individual achievement and competition in the classroom, suggesting that more emphasis should be placed on co-operative and shared learning techniques. He similarly suggests that the flaunting of expensive clothes and possessions before our children undermines the values of mutual sharing and caring for one another. Auerbach believes that if we can impart these basic lessons to our children early in their lives we may move one step further forward on the path to peace and harmony in South Africa. We will have taught our children that it is not in fierce competition or in the aggressive promotion of ourselves through individual achievement but in co-operation and mutual respect that we will build a better society. "This fact," he reminds us, "is wonderfully expressed in the tradition of African humanism: Umuntu ngumuntu ngabanye — a person is a person through other persons."

## Being Jewish Today

For Auerbach, what does it mean to be a Jew in today's world?

It means being part of a group of people world-wide that has all kinds of sensitivities and fears, which it has acquired historically, and yet it has also an ancient history with a tradition of peace and justice. You need to be aware of both the positives and the negatives of this community if you are to play a meaningful role within it or to enable it to share positively in the creation of the larger community.

It means being part of a minority community that has often protected its identity by isolating itself from the larger community. There are signs, however, of the Jewish community being prepared to grow towards the broader human community. Jews will always be Jews but will hopefully be prepared to share in and shape the future in a more creative manner.

Concerned that in the midst of our difficulties and in the struggle for a better world we do not lose hope, Auerbach suggests that one of the joys of teaching young people is their sense of idealism, hope and impatience. This is something that makes older people in every generation grumble about the unrealistic expectations of the youth. Yet we have a special obligation to keep such dreams alive. As he speaks I recall the final paragraph of his Peace lecture. It includes the words of hope written in the diary of a fifteen-year-old German Jewish girl, as Europe burned, in July 1944.

> It's really a wonder that I haven't dropped all my ideals because they seem so absurd and impossible to carry out. Yet I keep them, because in spite of everything I still believe that people are really good at heart. I simply can't build up my hopes on a foundation consisting of confusion, misery and death. I see the world gradually being turned into a wilderness, I hear the ever-approaching thunder, which will destroy us too; I can feel the suffering of millions and yet, if I look into the heavens, I think that this cruelty too will end, and that peace and tranquility will return again.

The words are those of Anne Frank. She did not live to see the return of peace ten months later.

PHOTO ACKNOWLEDGEMENT: *South*

# CHERYL CAROLUS

*Struggle Not Politics*

Cheryl Carolus is forthright and relaxed, not easily
phased. I ask her to respond to a sexist comment
made in a feature article on her in the *Beeld*, an
Afrikaans daily: "Sy is mooi, sy is jonk, sy is sexy, sy
is knap en sy is 'n kommunis. Haar ster is aan die
styg in the ANC en die SAKP." (She is attractive,
young, sexy, intelligent and a communist. Her star is
rising in the ANC and the SACP.) She laughs.

Ignoring the choice of labels, she observes: "I am an ordinary human being, struggling to be human in a dehumanising world, where it takes everything you've got to be a whole person."

The first formal meeting between members of the African National Congress and the South African government at Groote Schuur (the official residence of the State President) shortly after the unbanning of the ANC and other organisations in February 1990 included Cheryl Carolus. Her participation in that meeting attracted widespread interest. Speaking at the National Congress of the ANC in July 1991, Mandela referred to her as a possible future leader of the ANC and likely successor to the present Minister of Health. Also a disciplined member of the South African Communist Party and an active proponent of socialism, she has attracted attention from the public media.

Carolus is committed to open debate, and insists that she is not a politician — politics being no more than a means towards the creation of an open, democratic and just society within which, she says, "we can all learn to be human and enable one another to attain our full potential as people".

What is it that would save her from politics; even her own politics? She is quite emphatic: "I am involved in politics precisely because I am not a politician. I am damned if I am going to allow any politician or the political process itself to determine my future. I am deeply committed to the creation of a space within which people can shape and direct their own lives in relation to the needs of all others. In this sense I prefer to regard myself as not primarily engaged in politics, but rather in struggle. I don't really care whether I am personally elected to office or not." Quick to switch into Afrikaans to emphasise a point she observes: "In die opsig sal ek enige regering se nagmerrie wees." (In this sense I shall be any government's nightmare.) "I am jesting," she continues, "although what I say is laden with truth. The day that I cease to speak-up when my conscience tells me to do so, is the time to quit politics."

## The Formation of a Conscience

Born into a working-class family in 1957, Cheryl Carolus imbibed what she calls "ordinary, conservative, family values". She respects the values of her parents, who worked hard, lived frugally and affirmed honesty and basic Christian values.[1] She speaks with deep feeling about her father, who worked most of his life as an 'assistant' in the printing industry. "He worked long hours, overtime at every opportunity and during weekends, while my mother managed to care for the family on a very limited income." Dismissed from his job on several occasions because he intervened on behalf of workers who were unjustly treated by management, he is today a pensioner suffering from tuberculosis, caused by inadequate working conditions. Carolus is equally moved when speaking of her mother, who underwent nineteen operations before being cured of epilepsy. "My mother worked as a nursing aid to augment the family income, often carrying the entire financial burden while my father was unemployed." She continues:

> Some people say that if you are poor it is your own fault. It is because you are lazy or irresponsible. I soon learned that this is not the case. I discovered that if you are born into a working-class family, capitalist structures are such that it is very unlikely that you will ever be able to be other than a worker. Unless they are on the right side of apartheid, which was specifically designed to improve the lot of whites, very few workers are ever able to significantly improve their position in life. I learned early in life that while workers produce the wealth of industry, they are rarely able to control or benefit from that wealth.

Recognising that her political views have a great deal to do with the social context within which she was raised, she notes: "It is almost inevitable that I should hold socialist views. I've seen and lived with the underside of capitalism all my life and I am determined to ensure that no one has to live with its effects in the future. What I stand for today is grounded in my lived experience." Always thoughtful in speaking of her family home, she insists that it was there that she learned to respect all manner of people, irrespective of their social standing, intellectual status or level of deprivation. "My parents taught me never to call anyone 'kaffir' or 'baas' (master), because no person is ultimately of less or more value than another. My parents were poor but proud — something for which I am deeply grateful. I

---

1. My own interview with Cheryl Carolus has been augmented with material from two other interviews, one by Elsa Krüger and the other by Hennie Serfontein, published in the *Beeld* and *Vrye Weekblad*.

have often seen how poverty has dehumanised and belittled people."

Enrolling for a BA degree at the University of the Western Cape in 1976, she soon became involved in the Black Consciousness Movement through her involvement in the South African Students' Organisation (SASO). "My lived experience convinced me that black people are oppressed and that white people are the oppressors." Black consciousness was an important phase of her life. It taught her, she says, "to trust in my own resources, to speak my mind and to celebrate who I was". As such, she regards black consciousness as an essential transitionary ideology for many of the activists of the 1970s. "It was a phase that ended for me," she says, "in the wake of the Soweto uprisings of 1976. To have clung to that phase of my life would have led to stagnation, even racism... I was by then, of course, reading Marx and beginning to see oppression well beyond the confines of race." She remembers how diligently she read Das Kapital, without seriously understanding most of what she read. "It was nevertheless important to read it, and let everyone else know you had done so!" She also realises that this was a time when she slowly began to establish a theoretical and intellectual framework in which she began to understand her own lived experience and that of her parents in a new way.

"Theology also became part of the process," she says. "Raised an Anglican and encountering Black Theology while at university, I began to realise that the essential ethical categories of Christianity were actually supportive of what I was fighting for. I soon discovered that not all that the Church stood for was, in fact, what the New Testament taught. It was a time when the soft legitimation of the apartheid status quo by the 'non-racial' Churches was beginning to be challenged by an increasing number of activists and theologians in the Church. This enabled me to accept that it was not necessary for me to choose between what I believed and what the dominant voices within the Church were telling me I was supposed to believe. In a strange way, my estrangement from the Church drew me closer to it. I felt OK about fighting the Church. At the same time, I discovered that there is something within religion. Today faith is still an important ingredient of my life — although not in a conventional Church sense."

By the end of the 1980s Carolus was deeply involved in the political struggles of the Western Cape. "Die *Kaapse politiek* (Cape politics), with all its limitations, has taught me a great deal. The different organisations in the Western Cape exposed me to a variety of often conflicting ideologies, and sometimes these were manifest within the ANC structures. But this is all right. There is nothing wrong with political diversity, provided it is openly debated and honestly integrated into a positive struggle towards the bigger goals that unite us."

She was a founding member of the United Democratic Front in 1983. Having been detained on several occasions, she was in hiding between 1985 and 1990, pursuing her political work underground, and emerging only to address important meetings and share in the leadership of key campaigns. Carolus is quite clear in her own mind as to where she comes from: "In brief, my political roots lie in the home in which I was raised. The values I hold were taught to me in the church, the democratic struggle, the ANC and the Party. There has been a great deal of continuity in my life. I see no serious contradiction between the different phases of my existence."

## An Idealist

Carolus is concerned that the anger of pre-February 1990 politics has given way to a measure of disillusionment and a loss of expectation, and is determined to rediscover the resourcefulness of humanity.

People often say that I am an idealist. Well, I suppose I am. . . . What separates us from other animals is, *inter alia*, our ability to rise above our location and status in life. It is to reach beyond where we are born, to transcend the limits of what is often called the 'possible' and to create something new. Kill that in the human psyche and you have killed the human spirit.

This is what I regard as the spiritual dimension of humankind. It has to do with the will and the ability to be free. Freedom necessarily involves the freedom from hunger and other material needs. It is about the freedom to vote, to an education, to work and so on. But it involves more than that. Freedom also has to do with freedom to dream and to pursue one's dreams, while always remembering that one's own dreams have ultimately got to be worked out in relation to the dreams of others. This is what the pursuit of the common good is all about. . . For me, freedom and justice are therefore two sides of a single coin.

My concern is that society has over-emphasised the negative side of humankind. We are told that we are all sinners and need therefore to settle for the existing models of what is possible, lest in our desire for something more we end up killing one another. We are predisposed to believing that we are devoid of all decency, that we are incapable of living together.

Politics is the art of the possible, but it is time to dream a new dream of what is possible. In the process we will disagree, threaten and fight with one another. That, I suppose, is part of the process. . . It is at the same time important to remember that we belong together and will, like it or not, be obliged to live together. This is why we must share our dreams in struggling together to make them a reality. If that means I am an idealist, guilty of some heinous utopian dream, so be it.

The purpose of politics is, for Carolus, the creation of structures within which the process of dreaming and social reconstruction can take place. "We need a government," she reminds us, "precisely because society is made up of people with different values, different ethical ideals, different social, religious and cultural norms. We need to co-exist." This diversity has previously been suppressed in South Africa, with people being forced into separate chambers of parliament, homelands and cultural ghettos. Her plea is for a new dispensation within which people are no longer dictated to and told who to be and how to behave. "What we need," she argues, "is open structures of government and civil society that enable everyone to participate in the national debate in the pursuit of a more inclusive, more flexible and more dynamic society." The writing of a constitution, a bill of rights and the institution of government is important for her, precisely because it provides a framework within which this open debate can take place. "I bring you back to my earlier comments," she continues, "I prefer to talk of struggle rather than politics. Politics, in its highest form, is surely about an inclusive, national struggle for individual and communal humanity."

## Socialism

"The failure of Eastern European socialism does not disqualify the quest for socialism in South Africa." About this Carolus is adamant. "In South Africa it is capitalism that has failed, bringing the economy to the brink of collapse. It has impoverished the overwhelming majority of people." Emphasising that her primary concern is the welfare of the poor, she stresses the need to rise above theoretical debate about free-enterprise and socialist ideologies, in the pursuit of an economy that serves the actual needs of the exploited.

> The supporters of capitalism like to tell us that we have had a distortion of capitalism in South Africa, and that we must now adopt a free-enterprise system that is without these distortions. These same people are not, however, prepared to apply the same principle to Eastern Europe. They refuse to allow that the socialism practised there could in some way have been a distortion of true socialism. . . My concern is that we learn from the failures of Eastern Europe and South Africa, and that we be honest enough to adapt, change and fine-tune our economic visions to meet present realities.

> It is important to realise that apartheid has been used to promote the capitalist system, in that black people were deliberately exploited as cheap labour to augment the wealth of whites. To merely scrap apartheid laws now that the deed has been done is not sufficient. While across-the-board nationalisation would be inappropriate in South Africa, it is the task of a democratically elected government to intervene in the economy, devising responsible ways of ensuring that all sections of society share in the wealth of the nation. *Laissez faire* capitalism will not do that, it will take a strong socialist ingredient in the economy to correct the historic imbalances which face the nation.

Adamant that it is quite immoral for a few people to live off the wealth created by others, she insists that people who create the wealth must both have access to it and some form of control over it. "Eastern European socialism was based on the simplistic notion that the state represents the interests of the people; that the state is the Party and that the Party is the people. That is, of course, total nonsense. I am fundamentally convinced that the only means of ensuring that a government, any government, serves the good of the people is to ensure that it is answerable to the people. This means it must rule with the sure and certain knowledge that it can be removed from power by the people whenever it fails to serve their needs."

Carolus finds it quite incredible that anyone who regards him or herself as a Christian can be other than a socialist. She sees capitalism as a violation of the teaching of Jesus, who cared for the poor and promoted the interests of the marginalised and the needy. She becomes quite spirited in making her point:

> Socialism is the logical outworking of the New Testament ethic. I challenge anyone to show me otherwise. Indeed, to the extent that I understand other religious beliefs, I would argue that it is the necessary consequence of Islam, Judaism, Hinduism and most other faiths. . . To the extent that religion includes the need for its adherents to care for one another, showing particular concern for those less fortunate than themselves, religious people ought to show a special inclination towards socialism.

Accepting that all socialists have been severely shaken by the collapse of Eastern Europe, Carolus is quick to point out that the internal contradictions of capitalism will yet take their toll on the West. "Perhaps it is only then that the real economic debate will begin."

## Ecology

"For me," says Carolus, "freedom is a broad and inclusive concept, related to the total quality of life, which includes the air we breathe, the water we drink and the environment of which we are a part. In the same way that we need to get beyond a culture that allows any one nation, group of people, or any individual to exploit and dominate another, so we need to learn that we can no longer exploit and dominate nature, without this having the gravest consequences for the entire universe."

Her election to the National Working Committee of the ANC put paid to her plans to do a BSc degree in Agriculture or Forestry. Keen to ensure that any future government adopts a responsible environmental policy, she wants ecology to be seen as more than a preoccupation of a few middle- or upper-class people with the time and resources to devote to nature conservation. "It must become a serious issue for the working-class majority in South Africa. The poor who live in the squatter camps surrounding our cities and the dispossessed who live in the resettlement camps of the homelands, instinctively understand the dangers of filthy air, inadequate sewerage and polluted water for the simple reason that it is their children who are dying from such hazards. Part of the democratic process of sharing in the creation of a better South Africa involves taking responsibility for the natural environment within which we live."

Carolus' ecological concern includes a sense of holistic mysticism. She sees a continuity between the natural order and the quest for a realisation of one's full humanity:

> We are all part of the same creation. To destroy part of that creation is ultimately to destroy the entire creation. To disregard the sacred dimension of life wherever it is manifest — whether in trees, rivers, the fish of the sea or in humanity itself — is to promote a sense of indifference, aggression and greed that the world can no longer afford. To promote a reverence for life in its diverse forms and manifestations, on the other hand, promotes a sense of respect for the 'other', whatever form that 'other' may take. This can only contribute to a kinder and better society. It is time for South Africa to become green!

She is convinced that ecological awareness and a new appreciation of the natural order are vital if we are to survive. "We need to promote a new sense of urgency to deal with ecological concerns. Hopefully the bitterness of our political divisions will soon be behind us, in fact we simply *must* place these behind us, so that we can face some of the bigger challenges that are threatening this sub-continent. These include drought, soil erosion, the destruction of the environment by urbanisation and industrialisation. The preservation of the life cycle - of which humankind forms but one small part — is the challenge facing us."

## Religion

Carolus speaks with concern about the social disintegration of the nation, which she calls "the erosion of the moral fabric of society". This disintegration reveals itself differently in different parts of the nation. "In the more affluent sections of society it is manifest in marital and family violence, unfettered greed and indifference to the suffering of the majority. In the townships there is a growing disregard for the life of others. There is gangsterism and disrespect for any form of authority. People are afraid of their own children . . . Obviously we can talk about the cause of all this, and apartheid will need to be located high among the essential causes of this predicament. The question is, however, what we are going to do to remedy the prevailing situation." She continues:

> The last thing we need is religion, in the sense of the Church or any other religious institution preaching at those guilty of such

behaviour. What we do need is a sense of values which can restore a measure of communal concern and respect for life. We need further to enable our people to gain a vision of a new and more complete understanding of life. Precisely how this is to be done is difficult to say, but it has something to do with a discovery or rediscovery of what it means to be human.

If religion is concerned about this, and I would argue that it ought to be, then religion has a role to play. For this to happen, religious institutions will, however, be obliged to change the perception which many people have of them in the townships and elsewhere. . . For me religion has to do with exploring the potential of the human spirit which is God-given. This means that there is a resourcefulness that is inherent to humanity, which needs to be rediscovered, unleashed and nurtured. Religion has an enormous contribution to make in enabling disenchanted, alienated people to rediscover what it means to be human. We are rapidly forgetting that in our society.

Carolus is again speaking of the struggle to be human. "For me religion is an important component of human spirituality. It involves a wrestling with the question of life. It is an exercise in redefining yourself for yourself, both as a human being and as part of the greater created order. It involves discovering the greatness of humanity, knowing that you can make a difference, while realising how small you are in relation to the total order of things. When you understand that balance, I think you are beginning to take your rightful place in society. My theology tells me that to the extent that we are less than what we ought to be, falling below what God intended us to be, we are less than human. To this extent we are inadequate. When on the other hand we try to pretend we are greater than what we are, trying to usurp the place of God, we are arrogant, and again we are sinners. But that stuff I must leave to the theologians!"

Is she a religious person? "I prefer to see myself as a spiritual person, raised within the Christian tradition. As such, I employ Christian ideas and symbols in pursuit of answers concerning my identity, location and role in society. At the same time, however, I recognise that others are in pursuit of the answers to such questions via other religions, secular traditions and disciplines such as art, poetry, literature and so on."

Does she attend church? "Sometimes, although quite frankly I find the average church service simply too restricting. It tends to contain and limit my quest for wholeness, rather than liberating me from myself and freeing me to be a better person. In brief, I do not think that the Church is exercising the liberating and enabling function which it ought to exercise in society."

Is there a God in her life? If so, who is God? "Yes, I believe there to be a dimension to life which I call God. I believe, however, that it is demeaning to think of God as a person. God is Creator, a creative spirit. Any attempt to define God in our own image is extremely arrogant. It is a restricting exercise, which undermines the greatness and otherness of God. Again I am into theology, but let me stay with it for a moment. We need to find a metaphor which expresses both the otherness and the proximity or immanence of God. God is an unfathomable presence, which we cannot define. God is, however, also human. God is present in all human beings and human endeavours. But God is also in the trees, rivers and the air we breathe." Carolus argues that institutional religion all too often limits rather than expands the sense of the divine. In prescriptively telling us who God is, religions destroy the spiritual quest of people. "We need *more* metaphors for God, multiple metaphors, that give expression to the mystery, exhaustiveness and greatness of the divine dimension of life."

What about male metaphors for the divine? "My problem with metaphors such as the 'fatherhood of God' is that they tend to be used exclusively. God is more than a father-like figure. God is equally more than a mother-like figure. We need, therefore, to learn to celebrate both the male and female dimensions of God. Some feminists argue that to say God is a male is the same as saying the male is God. Well, maybe. I simply want to argue that God is greater than both male and female. I experience God as a disturbing presence, which requires me to be more than I am at any given point of my existence."

## Secular and Religious

Says Carolus: "I am both secular and religious in a spiritual, rather than an institutional sense. There is a strong correlation between what I do and what I believe. I try to reflect both critically and imaginatively on what I do. I also believe that the major cause for which I am fighting, is a secular, political manifestation of my innermost spiritual and ethical beliefs."

Stressing that we are living through a major epoch of transition, the significance of which will only be fully understood in centuries to come, she is adamant that it is time to rediscover values and goals that are worth striving for. "Socialists have been forced to rethink what some thought were the answers to life's problems in the wake of the collapse of the Soviet Union and Eastern Europe. My concern is that people who are not socialists are, by and large, not doing so. . . People who live on the edge of their respective religions and philosophies of life, or hold, only with difficulty, to such established doctrines and philosophies, tend to wrestle with what may have been hitherto unquestioned presuppositions. This makes for renewal. The tragedy is that others, content and all too often arrogant in their beliefs, are not prepared to do the same."

I ask a final question. What are the fundamental values for which she would go to the wall, for which she is prepared to die? She thinks for a long while.

> I suppose those values which are sometimes referred to as 'liberal values' — although I think it is a bit of a nerve for society to label them such. They are fundamental *human* values, grounded in a range of religious and secular traditions. I am referring to the freedom of speech, freedom of association and freedom of belief — first generation rights. I say this because without these all talk of social and economic rights will come to naught. Workers will have food to eat and roofs over their heads one day, not primarily because a Bill of Rights states that they should, but because they have the right to get out there, organise politically, and fight for those rights. Take these rights away and we will be back to square one in this country. At the same time, try and isolate these rights from second and third generation rights, from socio-economic, ecological and developmental rights and you have undermined the very essence of the right to the freedom of speech, association and belief. They become an empty abstraction that makes sense only to the rich who already have shelter, food and the necessary material ingredients of life.

The struggle to be human is what stands out in the interview. "There is a deep longing inside us," she tells me, "for a place in the sun. I am zealously fighting for that right for all people — for all God's children. We cannot rest content until that has been found. That 'place in the sun' includes material things, make no mistake about that. Human beings, however, need more than that. We need bread to stay alive, but we do not live by bread alone. We are in a restless quest for human fulfilment, for the need to live meaningful and useful lives. We are looking for inner, as well as outer, peace. If religion is about that, then please write me up as religious. Religion certainly need not be the opium of the people."

PHOTO ACKNOWLEDGEMENT: Mayibuye Centre, UWC

# FRANK CHIKANE

*Spirituality and Struggle*

"I was young, black, unknown and expendable. I was in prison and wondered whether I would come out of it alive. My theology, spirituality and present understanding of life are grounded in that experience," observes Frank Chikane, General Secretary of the South African Council of Churches (SACC).

By all standards Chikane has always been a deeply religious person, with prayer, worship and devotion having been a part of his life for as long he can remember. He has been a loyal member of the Apostolic Faith Mission, immersed in the Pentecostal holiness tradition from the time of his childhood. He nevertheless observes, "I became most religious at the most intense political moment of my life. It was in prison that I discovered the importance of faith in a manner that made the religion I had previously known pale into insignificance." Although arrested and detained on four separate occasions between 1977 and 1982, it was the six weeks of torture and interrogation which began with his arrest in the early hours of June 6 1977 that have influenced his attitude to life.

> I thought of Nelson Mandela and others who had been sentenced to life imprisonment. Many had been killed in prison. I was beaten to the point of confusion. I lost control over my body and lapsed into unconsciousness. When I awoke, I was alone, powerless and abused. "Why don't you simply commit suicide and end your misery?" an interrogator asked.

> I realised that there was not much more they could do to me. That was a liberating moment. I told my interrogators that I was not going to answer any more questions. They had done their job. I was not going to give them any information. They were free to kill me but decided to leave me alone.

Chikane speaks with the fervour of an evangelical preacher as he tells how he discovered the meaning of seemingly conservative and traditional religious teachings which he had hitherto simply ignored. "I thought of Paul's words in the New Testament which refer to his completing the suffering of Christ. 'Could I conceivably regard myself as sharing in the suffering of Christ?' I asked myself. The very thought was almost blasphemous to me." It was in that context, says Chikane, that his present Christological thinking was born. "The Church tells us that Christ came into the world in order to die to save us from our sins. The truth of the matter, as I see it," he observes, "is that Christ *simply had no choice but to die* given the extent of evil in the world. He would not have been allowed to live. His fight against evil cost him his life, and the ongoing fight against evil exacts the same price today."

"As followers of Christ we are required to engage in the work of Christ, accepting the inevitable consequence — which is to suffer in one way or another. To work for the kind of society for which Jesus worked, requires us to confront institutions, structures and empires which contradict the values which he taught. . . It would be most foolish to imagine that in so doing we can escape suffering. Understood theologically, this suffering is an extension of the work and suffering of Christ — we are completing his suffering in the world."

In a more relaxed manner, Chikane speaks of the significance of biblical teaching for contemporary living. "Once I understood what Paul meant when he spoke of completing the suffering of Christ, I also understood what he meant when he said, 'I live, yet not I. It is Christ who lives within me.' Paul was speaking of the vision and power of the Spirit of Christ that was also his vision and power."

Chikane believes religion and politics are inherently linked. "The pendulum of Christianity swings between devotion to God and devotion to those who suffer. It has to do with the love of God and the love of neighbour. It concerns spiritual empowerment and political engagement. To be a Christian is to be engaged in struggle," says Chikane. "I once told a policeman this and he responded: 'Die Bybel het jou a terrorist gemaak!' (The Bible has turned you into a terrorist!) Struggle is the necessary and logical outcome of all that I believe. It is a direct consequence of my devotion to God. It is the enactment of my theology. Without it, all that I believe and teach would be without integrity."

## Journeying from Below

Chikane smiles when he recalls that during the interview for his job as General Secretary of the SACC he was asked whether he thought he could maintain the devotional life of the Council.

> My entire life has been a deeply devotional struggle both against faith and for faith. This, in a sense, is what the Pentecostal tradition is all about. It is a quest to understand and make spiritual sense of one's life experience. I cannot imagine life without devotion. It is the bedrock of my entire life and it must necessarily be the foundation of the engagement of the Churches in society. At the same time, if that devotion does not lead to practical engagement in the struggle for a decent society then it is no more than escapism and ultimately an exercise in rejecting the Christ who calls us to fight against evil in the world. . . Few people have perhaps been converted to religion solely as a result of the ethical behaviour of its adherents. The moral indifference of religious people has, on the other hand, sent many would-be adherents

scurrying off in the other direction. I know sufficient people who, in justified anger, declare themselves atheists when faced with those who speak of a God who cares, while their lives contradict the moral values of religious belief.

Chikane is one of the few Church leaders in South Africa to have come to his present position as a direct result of his involvement in the grassroots struggle against apartheid. His story is vividly told in his autobiography, *No Life of My Own*. "If you are black in South Africa and of my generation," he writes, "you cannot be sure of your actual place of birth because, often, what you are told is likely not to be true."[1] If it were said that he was born in Bushbuckridge in the Eastern Transvaal in his grandparents' home, where his mother was staying at the time of his birth, the apartheid Influx Control laws would have prevented him from living and working in Soweto. "So. I was born in Johannesburg!"

A good student, he obtained a first class matriculation, before attending the University of the North in Pietersburg, created exclusively for Africans in the wake of the 1959 University Extension Act. In his final year of study towards a BSc degree, the university prevented him from completing his exams after his participation in what became known as the 'Frelimo Rally', organised to celebrate the liberation of Mozambique in 1974. His attempt to complete his degree through the University of South Africa, was also foiled by his being repeatedly sent to prison. After serving as a probationer minister in his Church he was ordained in 1980 and the following year was suspended from the ministry for twelve months, because of his involvement in politics. Chikane was imprisoned a short while later and his wife and children were evicted from the manse. Protests from his wife about the callous action by the Church, were met with the following response from a delegation of pastors: "When your husband did what he did he must have been aware of the consequences." Then, at the end of the twelve months, Chikane was instructed to return his ordination certificate to the Church. His status as a minister was completely withdrawn. It was not until 1990 that this decision was reversed and Chikane was reinstated in the ministry, with an apology from his Church. In May 1993 he was elected President of the newly united Apostolic Faith Mission in South Africa, which brought together the African and coloured

---

1. Frank Chikane, *No Life of My Own* (London: Catholic Institute for International Relations, 1988), p.26.

sections of that Church. Asked to explain his stubborn loyalty to a Church that rejected not only him and his family, but also the essential tenets of the convictions for which he has been prepared to die, he says: "To have done that would have been to deny an essential part of what drives me in life."

> My Church's handling of my case was clumsy. It dealt with the problem in a less politically astute and sophisticated manner than that which the mainline Churches would have used. I am at the same time convinced that the other Churches would also, in their own way, have got rid of me. . . My commitment is not to see the emergence of a more slick or even competent, liberal way of dealing with things. It is to a Church honest enough to face the full implications of the gospel.
>
> Some who shared my convictions in this regard suggested that I form a separate Church committed to the gospel values which I affirmed. I was not convinced that a new structure was enough. My fear was that sooner or later this new structure would be no less inclined, under different circumstances, to fall prey to the temptation of escaping the challenge of the gospel.
>
> So, I decided to stay. I refused to resign and I committed myself to continue to work for the things that I believed to be of God. My task is to fight evil, to challenge those who capitulate before the demands of those who do evil and to be obedient to God in whatever situation I find myself.
>
> There is a sense in which my struggle with my Church is for me a parable of the larger South African struggle. I refuse to run away from evil, I dare not ignore its challenge and ultimately I must serve God in all that I do, accepting the consequences that may follow from that.

Denied the opportunity to function as an ordained pastor in his Church, Chikane joined the Institute of Contextual Theology (ICT), and was appointed General Secretary in 1983. He was instrumental in the writing of the *Kairos Document* — the most significant statement of belief to have emerged from (essentially black) Christians committed to radical political change in South Africa. Having delivered the opening address at the launch of the United Democratic Front in Cape Town in 1983, he was elected to the executive of the UDF and was involved in a range of civic organisations. In February 1985 he was again arrested. This time he was charged with treason. Released from prison on bail in May of that year, he was served with a restriction order that made it an offence to be involved in politics, confined him to the Johannesburg area and placed him under house arrest from dusk to dawn. His house was attacked with fire bombs and plans were made for his assassination. Acquitted of treason in December, he went into hiding when the State of Emergency was declared the following year. He left the country illegally but, six months later, decided to return home to share in the struggle. "Theologically speaking," he says, "this decision was a practical expression of all that I believed. Not to have returned home would have been a denial of my faith." Before his departure for home he wrote a letter to his friends and supporters — "those who cared".

> The decision has been made and I am on my way into that beleaguered country, South Africa. . . My action looks senseless, futile, suicidal, inconsiderate, stupid, and one can continue end-lessly with these descriptive words which characterise my state of affairs. In short I can't defend this position.

> But why have I moved against the tide of reason? The cries of my people at home, the call of those who are in distress, who live between life and death on a daily basis; those who are in the heat of things, who have no other option but to face the guns of the apartheid security forces; the call of those who have left their families and have been in hiding or underground for the last nine months since the State of Emergency — and these are in their thousands; the call of women, men and children in Soweto who believe that my presence, in terms of my ministry, will make a difference. This is the call that sends me home.

> . . . I have begun to see the story of the Passion in a new light. This experience has opened my eyes to a new and deeper reality about the gospel of the Cross. . . No-one wants to go to the Cross, or the way of the Cross, but it has dawned on me in a new way that it does not look as if we can achieve our liberation in South Africa without going through the Cross.

"I was ready to die or to face whatever other fate awaited me. I again went into hiding, working underground and eventually I re-emerged," Chikane recalls. "Those were wild and chaotic days. I was not arrested. But others were and many died. Our history is a history of many silent, anonymous martyrs."

Chikane's election as General Secretary of the SACC in July 1987 was not without its controversy. Many within the Church regarded him as too political. They regarded his controversial background as render-ing him unable to facilitate the reconciling role expected of the SACC and his membership of a small black Church (that rejected him!) as an inadequate base from which to address the mainline Churches. When the selection committee presented his name as their choice for the position of General Secretary, a leading cleric observed: "I would feel a bit better about this if he belonged to a proper Church. Can't he be persuaded to transfer his membership to one of our Churches?"

"I realised," says Chikane, "that when I was appointed to the SACC I was moving into a bureaucratic position and that the onus was on me to prove that I could assist the Church in doing the work of God. Foremost in my mind was the need to prove that I was not the kind of activist who simply wanted to demolish and destroy. I had learned the importance of democratic consultation through my involvement in grassroots politics, and made good use of this in dealing with the Church leaders."

Working hard at uniting the Churches around the actions of the SACC, Chikane continued to confront a range of political and social justice issues. Political assassinations were numerous and two attempts were made on his life. On a trip to Namibia he became ill and was forced to return to South Africa. Then, while travelling in the United States, he collapsed and was hospitalised. Medical diagnosis and subsequent investigation showed that his baggage had been sprayed with a poisonous substance which was absorbed through his skin.

## The Church Missed the Moment

Looking back over his years as General Secretary of the SACC, Chikane provides a double assessment of the Church. "In 1988," he argues, "the Church missed the opportunity to provide effective moral and spiritual leadership for the nation." The occasion was the Convocation of Churches which met in Johannesburg. A decision had been made to launch the 'Telling the Truth Campaign' and a strong statement was adopted by the meeting. Although several of the Church leaders were unhappy with the statement, the majority accepted it. After the Convocation few Church leaders promoted the programme of action. "The problem," says Chikane, "was that the Christian activists wanted the Church leaders themselves to take to the streets. When they refused to do so, some activists became disenchanted and abandoned the campaign. Those who continued to work actively in the Church, often expressed contempt for the Church leaders. In abandoning the campaign, they let the Church off the hook." Chikane notes that the Church is infinitely poorer for activists having turned their backs on the institution. "It is likely to remain that way for some time to come," he says.

Chikane at the same time sees another side to this story. "The Church leaders, despite having failed to do all that was asked of them, did provide a space in both Church and society, within which activists could work. The Church leaders did not openly repudiate the position of the Convocation, nor did they oppose Christian activists — in fact they usually defended their actions." Emphasising the importance of the institutional Churches, he observes: "Too many people have given up on the Church as an agent of political change. This makes the task of those of us who remain in the Church more difficult. Politically concerned people must remain within the structures of the Church and force these structures to face up to the practical implications of the gospel."

Chikane speaks of a God who continually calls us into struggle. Accepting that God is part of the struggle for justice, is God more than that? Who is this God, of whom he talks? His reply is measured: "That is not a question that I often ask myself. I did not grow up with that question and the vast majority of people in South Africa, do not ask that question — simply because they operate with the assumption that there *is* a God. The question for them is not whether there is a God but rather *where* is this God at work? *What* is this God doing? *How* is the will of this God to be accomplished? The essential theological discussion among most of our people is not a cerebral enquiry about the existence or nature of God. It is a question of the extent of God's concern for their lot in life."

We speak about atheism and the many young black people who have become disenchanted with the Church. Do these people operate with the God assumption of which Chikane talks? "Many do not consciously do so, but a significant number continue to show an interest in liberation theology for example. They are opposed to the Church, not to a God who is related to their lived experience. In that sense they are more theologically sophisticated than many self-declared atheists who, in turning their backs on the Church, assume that they must reject God."

Does he regard it as important or helpful for people to be religious? Chikane recognises that there are many remarkable atheists and agnostics who are deeply engaged in the fight against evil and the struggle for a better world, and he has no desire to persuade them to adopt his religious views. He laughs as he says: "I sometimes think that what I experience as evidence of God's existence is simply differently understood by others. Perhaps this doesn't even matter. It may even be that God does not really care about this. My religious tradition requires me to seek to convert people to Christianity. I am, however, very cautious about doing so because many who claim to be converted Christians are on the side of those who resist justice. The Bible teaches that what we *do* is more important than what we say or think."

## The Least in Life

We discuss the importance of evangelism in the Christian tradition. "The essence of the gospel is for me the call to become engaged in the mission of God, which is to build a society of justice on earth within which those whom the Bible calls 'the least' — the poor, the marginalised and the oppressed — are given their rightful place. Once a person has acquired that vision, he or she experiences an inner compulsion to promote this vision among others. That is what evangelism is all about. In that sense I am an evangelist. Should a person, however, be committed to this process on the basis of a secular philosophy, I am ready to accept that. I am against proselytisation in the sense of converting people for the sake of converting them! If this conversion results in transformed lives and a commitment to a new order of justice that is different."

Developing the notion of 'the least', Chikane speaks of the changing political mission of the Church. "Prior to January 1990 it was our task to promote the broad liberation struggle," he observes. "In so doing we looked to the liberation movements as the authentic voice of the poor and the oppressed." He states his position quite deliberately: "I firmly believe that in so doing the Churches were converted by the liberation movements. In listening to these movements which gave expression to the deepest aspirations of the oppressed people, the Churches heard the cry of the poor and in that cry they discerned the voice of God. Today the focus of the oppressed people is in the process of shifting away from the politics of liberation to the pursuit of political power. I accept the necessity of this. It is not, however, the task of the Church to follow suit. Our mission is a different one. It is to keep alive the concerns of 'the least' which are so often forgotten or overlooked in the encounter between the major players in any negotiation process. This requires us to look to the workers, the unemployed, women, the youth and other marginalised groups. These are 'the least' and it is there that the voice of God is to be discerned."

Arguing that it is always the task of the Church to be the voice of the voiceless and to promote the interests of the poor, which the powerful can afford to rationalise or play down, Chikane insists that this constituency can change from one situation to another. "If, for example, at any time in the future a situation were to emerge where injustice were meted out by blacks against whites, I should be obliged again to defend the underdog. Indeed if I were not prepared to return to prison in so doing, the gospel I preach would be without integrity."

"I have already stated that politics and religion are inherently linked. They must at the same time not be reduced to one another. Politics is about power, which often requires compromises. This is inevitable, and to be encouraged to the extent that it promotes the well-being of society. Theology, on the other hand, while being obliged to promote the best realistic option available at any given time, has an obligation to keep alive a vision that is beyond what a particular political situation may be able to accomplish at any given time. Theology ought to be the cutting-edge of radical politics. The Bible tells us that this vision is one that must favour 'the least'. In our situation it means that the Church's measuring stick of justice is the people of 'the dump' in the Transkei and elsewhere. We are obliged to measure all reforms and the policies of any political party or government in terms of the effect these have on the people in squatter camps, resettlement camps, impoverished rural areas, the unemployed — those at the bottom of the socio-economic pile."

## The God of the Oppressed

"God is never willing to allow us to be content. Just when we think we know who and where God is we are made to question our presuppositions. We learn yet again that God is no longer who we would like that God to be, or located in a place of our choosing." The thoughts behind these words of Chikane, have done much to challenge and shape theological debate in South Africa.

He tells how the first theological shift in his thinking about God came when he was still at school. He began to question in his own mind the claim made by whites that they were extending the mission of God in South Africa.

He tells of the long conversations which he had with schoolmates while at high school. "They would insist that the whites had traded our land and freedom for their Bible." He tells how he began to understand how humility, submissiveness, long-suffering and a refusal to stand-up for one's rights — all virtues that the Church commended to black people — could lead to black subjugation. "This kind of religion is indeed an ideology of oppression. It is the opium of which I heard my classmates speak, drawing as they did on their understanding of Marx. I was confronted with a choice: either I was to reject religion or begin to understand religion differently. I began to read the Bible with all these questions in mind and slowly I came to realise that the God of the Bible is a God who empowers the poor and calls people out of bondage into freedom."

Arriving as a student at the University of the North, Chikane joined the Student Christian Movement (SCM) and later the South African Student Organisation (SASO). Within this context theological debate intensified. He recalls reading a paper on Christianity and Black Consciousness. "Black theology, as far as I was concerned, provided the answer to all my questions; and I still regard the black theology debate as the most important theological debate ever to have taken place in South Africa. We cannot, however, deify or absolutise any system of thought," he insists. "God is a disturbing and destabilising God, constantly requiring us to be shaken out of our self-complacency and theological contentedness."

Chikane speaks of the challenge of feminist and womanist theologies. "It took the rude challenge of women in the late seventies and early eighties for me to discover that black theology was a male-dominated discipline. In that situation women were 'the least' and within the voice of women I again heard the disturbing God requiring me to question the very answers of black theology, which had freed me from the God of the white oppressors. It was painful for me to discover that we who talked about a black liberation theology could ourselves be oppressors. We must continually be vigilant in theology. Oppressive dimensions so easily creep into what we say. We must be constantly open to the 'victims' of our theology, those who can better see the limitations of what we say than we can."

> Liberation theologies are an attempt to give expression to the God who liberates. To suggest that any one of these theologies has the final word on God is absurd. God can never be reduced to the control of a theological system. To protect our theology from internal and/or external criticism is to isolate it from the truth question. To locate theology in the protective care of any particular group of custodians is, in turn, to exclude it from the renewing,

disturbing and challenging presence of the God who refuses to be held captive by the ideologies of even the best meaning people.

## Violence

Deeply concerned about ongoing violence in South African society, Chikane insists that three factors need to be taken into account before we pass any judgement on large sections of people in the black communities who resort to violence.[2] Firstly, he argues that theoretical moral debate on the subject is really only the privilege of a very few people. "Debate on violence," he tells us, "can only take place where there in no war or where war does not directly involve the participants in the debate. It is the privilege of those who do not experience an immediate threat to their lives . . ." Secondly, he regards the space for debate on violence and non-violence as space often created by violence. "Most white people and some privileged blacks dwell in this space, condemning the violence of townships and expressing abhorrence at all forms of violence while they themselves are 'protected' by the violence of the security forces". Thirdly, he suggests, there comes a point where serious moral debate on violence and non-violence is simply not possible for the oppressed masses. "In situations where townships are turned into war zones, with hit-squads and so-called 'third-force' elements being able to attack residents, burn houses and assassinate people, often without the security forces acting against them, self-defence and counter attack are sometimes the only realistic options available to people. When under violent attack you either run or fight back. There is no time or space for moral debate when you are confronted with an AK 47 rifle or a panga wielding assailant."

"This," says Chikane, "is why the violence issue cannot be separated from a political settlement. We have got to create a situation where political violence is eradicated and where the government and security forces acquire a sense of legitimacy in the community, before we can begin to address the other forms of violence in society." Arguing that violence has become an endemic and habitual part of South African society, Chikane realises that the building of an alternative culture within which conflicts, suspicions and fears are addressed in non-violent ways will take time. "We are likely to live with the sins of a violence-generating apartheid society for years and

---

2. See, Frank Chikane, "Where the Debate Ends", in C. Villa-Vicencio (ed.), *Theology and Violence: The South African Debate* (Johannesburg: Skotaville, 1987), pp.301–309.

perhaps generations to come. It is the task of the Church not merely to sit in moral judgement of this situation, but rather to engage itself in the healing process which the nation so badly needs. In addition to promoting conflict-resolving skills and what are often referred to as Education for Democracy programmes, it is the task of the Church and other religious groups to create a new 'soul' for the nation. This has to do with generating new values, a new respect for life and a culture of tolerance based on justice and kindness. Unless this soul emerges from within the culture of the oppressed majority, as well as from that of the oppressing minority in this country, there is little hope that a new nation can be born."

## Grounding Theology

"For theology to be at the service of the oppressed who seek to understand and respond to the challenge of the liberating God, it must be grounded in the struggle for life in which the poor are engaged. It must give expression to the cries, the agony and the hope of those who the Bible tells us are the special concern of God." This comment informs all that Chikane believes the Christian message to be.

As General Secretary of the SACC Chikane travels widely. He has contact with many of the most powerful political players in South Africa today. He is courted by big business and constantly invited to deliver lectures at major universities throughout the world. Now that his status as a minister of the Apostolic Faith Mission has been restored, he has also chosen to serve a small congregation in Naledi, on the far western side of Soweto.

> People call it the Wild West. Impoverished, violent and depressed, it is here that my ongoing struggle to make sense of the Christian faith is grounded. If what I believe and preach does not make sense in this kind of situation and emerge from within the crucible of 'the least' in society, then it is not the kind of theology which will ultimately matter too much in South Africa.

> The situation of the people in Naledi is my measure of the success or otherwise of renewal in South Africa. I am mindful, of course, that there are many people in the rural areas, in the so-called homelands and elsewhere who are even worse off than those who have managed to get a foothold in the Johannesburg area. But then, I must be grounded somewhere.

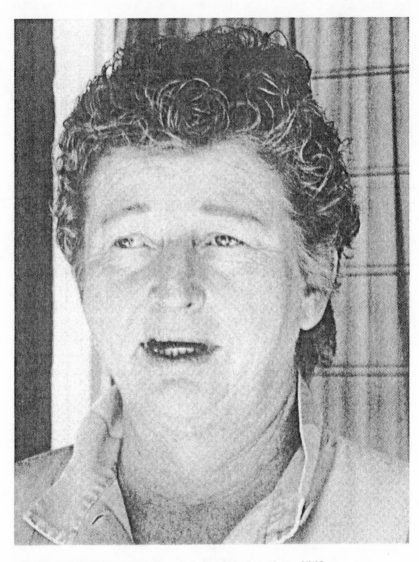

PHOTO ACKNOWLEDGEMENT: Diana Russell and Mayibuye Centre, UWC

# SHEENA DUNCAN

*Surprised by Joy*

Relaxed and quite unaffected by her prominence as a leading figure in activist, Church, women's and political circles, Sheena Duncan is capable of standing up to anyone who may venture to cross her.

Extremely well-informed, she has been described as knowing more about racist South African laws than almost anyone else in the country — something acquired through more than two decades of voluntary work at the Johannesburg Black Sash Advice Office. Is she a feminist? "Some feminists hate men, others do not. I am among those who do not. I prefer to regard myself as being anti-sexist, rather than a feminist."

She speaks of the incredible drive of her mother, Jean Sinclair, one of six women who met in 1955 to establish Black Sash (or the Women's Defence of the Constitution League, as it was known in those days), serving the organisation as President for fourteen years of its existence. "After the initial support which the organisation enjoyed at the time when the government tampered with the Constitution, removing coloured people from the common voters' role, the membership of Black Sash was reduced to a small core of people. It was my mother's tenacity and drive that kept it going." Duncan admits to a certain amount of youthful rebellion against her mother in earlier years, although she eventually succeeded her mother as President of Black Sash in 1975. She suggests it was her father whose influence impinged most strongly on her as a child and young adult.

> He was a Scot who came to South Africa after World War I with a very strongly developed sense of justice which made a formative impact on me as a child. Seeing himself as part of an oppressed group in Scotland, he often spoke of the Highland clearances, in which people were pushed off their land. I don't quite know the details or how he was involved. It was probably his mother who was directly affected, but the memory of the event was an important part of his identity. As a good Scot he further resented what he saw as the domination of his people by England.

One of five children, born in Johannesburg in 1932, the young Sheena completed her schooling at Roedean (a private girls' school in Johannesburg) with the "rather eccentric but remarkable" Ella le Maitre as principal. Intensely religious, le Maitre established friendships with Alan Paton and Trevor Huddleston, and carried her religious and political insights into the school. Sheena was then sent to Scotland to study domestic science at the Edinburgh College of Domestic Science. "That exercise was not exactly a waste of time because it has assisted me over the years to run a household without it becoming a great big thing in my life. I have been able to maintain our home reasonably efficiently, and be involved in all the things that have characterised my life."

Sheena Duncan's life is a full one. A past President of Black Sash (1975–78 and 1982–86), she was Vice-President of the South African Council of Churches from 1987 to 1990 and Senior Vice-President from 1990 to 1993. She is National Co-ordinator of the Black Sash Advice Offices, a member of the National Executive of Black Sash, a member of the National Co-ordinating Committee for the Return of Exiles, a member of the Independent Board of Inquiry into Informal Repression, a Patron of the Society for the Abolition of the Death Penalty in South Africa and Canon of the Cathedral Church of St Mary the Virgin in Johannesburg. The position of Canon has traditionally been assigned to "a learned and discreet priest". The language was, however, changed to "learned and discreet person" and St Mary's had two women Canons before the Anglican communion in South Africa agreed to the ordination of women to the priesthood! Duncan is involved in the End Conscription Campaign, in human rights activities, paralegal work, Church related programmes on justice and peace and in areas of non-violent direct action. Having won international awards for her work through Black Sash, she was made a member of the Order of Simon of Cyrene by the Bishops of the Church of the Province of Southern Africa in 1988, an order created by the South African Anglican bishops to honour outstanding contributions by lay people. She also holds honorary doctorates from the University of the Witwatersrand (1990) and the University of Cape Town (1991).

## A Religious Experience

Raised in the Presbyterian Church from the time of her youth, Duncan remembers the sense of guilt she experienced while in Edinburgh. "I used to lie in bed on winter mornings listening to the church bells ringing, thinking I would not attend church that morning, and then invariably rush out into the snow to get to church on time. I have always had what you might call a religious conscience. Holding to the moral values which were taught to me in the Church and in my childhood home, the practice of religion was however a rather burdensome thing. There was no real integration between what I intellectually knew Christianity to be and my religious practice, neither in terms of my devotional life and worship on the one hand nor my actual moral engagement in life on the other."

The change came quite unexpectedly and sadly. In 1958 Sheena and Neil Duncan's first child died of gastro-enteritis at the age of eighteen months. They approached a friend, David Jenkins, an Anglican priest in Salisbury (Harare, after Zimbabwean independence), where they were living at the time, to make the necessary funeral arrangements. "Returning from that meeting a strange thing happened, a kind of a moment of recollection, and my life seemed to come together. I realised that I could no longer sit around as a spectator, taking no more than an academic interest in politics and in what was going on in society around me. That is where it all began, as a religious experience."

Conscious that this kind of event is capable of many different interpretations, she interprets it in terms of what lay theologian C. S. Lewis described as an experience of a certain kind of joy. Having been raised in the Christian Church, Lewis in time became an atheist. Then, as he put it, "surprised by joy" he rediscovered the essence of a religion that he had hitherto never fully understood. A quotation from his autobiography makes the point:

> And with that plunge back into my own past there arose at once, almost like heartbreak, the memory of Joy itself, the knowledge that I had once had what I had now lacked for years, that I was returning at last from exile and desert lands to my own country; and the distance of the Twilight of the Gods and the distance of my own past Joy, both unattainable, flowed together into a single, unendurable sense of desire and loss, which suddenly became one with the loss of the whole experience, which, as I now stared around that dusty schoolroom like a man recovering from unconsciousness, and already vanished, had eluded me at the very moment when I could first say *It is*. And at once I knew (with fatal knowledge) that to 'have it again' was the supreme and only important object of desire.
>
> . . . To 'get it again' became my constant endeavour; while reading every poem, hearing every piece of music, going for a walk, I stood anxious sentinel at my own mind to watch whether the blessed moment was beginning and to endeavour to retain it if it did. . . But far more often I frightened it away with my greedy impatience to snare it, and, even when it came, instantly destroyed it by introspection, and at all times vulgarised it by my false assumption about its nature.[1]

In time Lewis came to realise that while he could open the door to this joy or keep it shut, it was an experience that came to him unsolicited as he lived life in its fullness and abundance. Duncan's experience of joy thrust her into the midst of life. "It motivated me to rediscover

---

1. C.S. Lewis, *Surprised by Joy* (London: Collins, 1974), pp.62; 137.

and perhaps to discover for the first time what it meant to live a life which integrates spirituality with active living and political engagement. My life was about to begin. And there was much waiting to be learned."

## Black Sash

It was largely in relation to Black Sash that the rest of her life unfolded. In 1955 the government packed the Senate, introducing additional Senate seats in order to obtain the necessary two-thirds majority required to change the Constitution, which had entrenched the right of coloureds in the Cape Province to vote on the common voters' role. Coloured people were outraged, while the white liberal community came out in protest against the activities of the National Party minority government. This resulted in the formation of the Womens' Defence of the Constitution League. Its members started wearing a black sash across their right shoulder, tied at their waists, as a sign of mourning for the Constitution. Dubbed 'Black Sash women' by the Press, the name soon replaced the more cumbersome title originally conceived. "Looking back I now realise that the majority of women who initially joined the Black Sash were less concerned with the rights of coloured people, than with the broader implications of tampering with the Constitution. They feared that if the government was prepared to go to such ends to remove coloured voters from the voters' roll, it might seek to remove the entrenched clause on language as well, which gave English the same status as Afrikaans."

Black Sash membership declined rapidly after the early sixties. The protest against the Separate Representation of Voters Act was a thing of the past and subsequent legislation, designed to curtail all serious resistance against apartheid, was written into the statute books despite protest from the Black Sash and other organisations. By the time the Duncans returned to South Africa in 1963 the initial reaction to the Sharpeville massacre was also over, the ANC and PAC were banned and the Black Sash membership had dwindled from its original 10 000 members to a small group of little more than 1 000 women.

"I immediately joined the Black Sash on my return to the country," Duncan reports. "When my children started going to school I started working in the Advice Office one morning a week. I have been there ever since, although in those days it was very different from what it is

79

today. We would take our knitting or writing material to catch up on our correspondence. Repression was at an all time high, people were scared to ask for advice and the tradition of serving the community, now established in the Black Sash, had not yet emerged. People asked me why I joined the Black Sash. The answer is that there *wasn't* anything else to join."

Black Sash women participated in silent protest stands outside various City Halls around the country and in the vicinity of Parliament, until legislation was introduced preventing stands within a mile of the Johannesburg City Hall and within a certain radius of Parliament. Legal protests were reduced to a minimum and new ways of resistance had to be found. Individual stands were organised. Sash members wrote letters to newspapers and tried to get editors to carry stories giving publicity to Black Sash activities. "My mother told me," Duncan remembers, "that the editor of the *Rand Daily Mail* once told her that it was very foolish to keep the organisation going and that she should rather be working in the United Party!"

When Duncan succeeded her mother as President of Black Sash in 1975, the organisation had recovered from its earlier slump and, particularly after the events surrounding 1976, a lot of younger women started joining. "There was a renewed sense of people saying, 'enough'!" she observes. The hard work which Duncan and others have put into Black Sash since those days has been immense. The prominence of the Black Sash in the mass action campaign, prior to February 1990, bears witness to their work.

Like many organisations, Black Sash has had to adapt to the changing needs of South African politics. Duncan explains the new phase in the Black Sash.

> I think we have already made the transition. Our focus is human rights, education and the process of enabling ordinary people to assert their right to participate in the shaping of their own lives. Before we protested against people being overtly oppressed and excluded from mainstream society. Now that there is a possibility of the legal barriers to participation being removed, we need to equip people to take their rightful place in society.
>
> We are likely to have a Bill of Rights in the future and a Constitution that will hopefully provide a structure for just government, but if ordinary people do not know what their rights are they are not likely to demand them. In similar manner, if people do not have the confidence to use the system, because they are not sure how it works, they are likely to be excluded from it.

Our task is to be vigilant about what is happening to people who are in danger of once again being marginalised by the emerging new system. More than that we need to equip people to themselves be vigilant and demanding of their basic rights. This is why we are taking the Education For Democracy programme so seriously, ensuring that our paralegal work continues. In brief, we are concerned to help people to participate in their own future.

. . . Different members of Black Sash are motivated by different world views and social visions to become engaged in this work. For me personally, there is a direct link between this work and my religious convictions. My concern for the poor and the oppressed is a biblical concern. I further believe that people — all people — are called by God to be the people of God in the sense of needing to realise their full potential as people and to share in the creation of a more just and decent society.

We discuss Black Sash being essentially a white organisation. Is this a problem? Can white women effectively promote the task of enabling black people to realise their own potential and claim their basic rights? I suggest that this goes against the basic lessons we all learned from black consciousness. Duncan recognises these difficulties, warning against any sense of whites doing something for blacks. A strong advocate of a non-racial society she emphasises the need for blacks and whites to work together, seeing Black Sash as a vehicle for mobilising essentially white women to be so engaged. She speaks of 'whiteness' as being a difficulty some Black Sash women are struggling with in pursuit of non-racial engagement.

This is, however, not something that hinders me. Perhaps it has something to do with the political awareness and exposure with which I was raised. I long ago reached a position where I am not conscious whether a person with whom I am meeting is black or white. This is largely due to my involvement in a programme of the Anglican Church, called the Challenge Group, created in response to the World Council of Churches' Programme to Combat Racism. It involved me in working with black people who were excluded from the hierarchical structures of the Church and therefore unable to make their voices heard through the Church synods and other channels of ecclesial authority. It was in that situation that I began intensively, and on a regular basis, to meet with black people who were not merely turning to me for help as they were in the Black Sash Advice Office. Neither did they reject me simply because I was white. We were working *together* on something. After a period of time we discovered one another as people and skin colour was simply no longer an issue for us. This experience taught me the undeniable importance of building non-racialism in South Africa. It is not only a case of needing to do so, it is possible. I discovered that non-racialism can be taught, communicated and culturally evoked in people.

What about her social location in society? Has being neither poor nor oppressed been a barrier in her work? "I suppose the experience of being a woman, has helped me a little here," she replies. "Although I have personally never experienced oppression by men, I certainly think I have an understanding of what it means to be an underdog. I have at the same time been released of an overburdening sense of guilt, and do not ask myself what right I have to possess certain things while others do not, because of my marital status. Our material possessions are not mine, which means I have not had to deal with the daily or annual assessment of my material resources. So there is a sense in which I have been let off the hook on this one. At times this has frustrated me. When, for example, there was a move among some people a few years ago to impose a peace tax on themselves, I did not feel personally affected. Yes, I have been conscious of my privileges, but have tried to ensure that this has not resulted in a sense of paralysing guilt. It has motivated me to commit the resources I have to the tasks that I have taken on, without pretending that I was poor or ever able to know the full impact of poverty."

## The All-Consuming Evils

Duncan identifies three pieces of legislation as the nerve centre of the all-consuming evil of apartheid: the structure of pass laws and influx control, the process of forced removals and Bantu Education. Her track record on amassing detailed information and irrefutable facts on the effects of these systems, and exposing the human suffering of countless people to public scrutiny, is a story documented and well known. Ultimately three and a half million people were forced to move in order to conform to apartheid notions of who should live where. When the process started a group of women, who included Duncan, visited and told the stories of people's suffering and resistance in places like Lime Hill in Natal, Mogopa (in the western Transvaal), Driefontein, Klipgat, and elsewhere. The story she tells of the people of Driefontein whom the government wanted to move to Oshoek, is but one of many. She tells of the minutes of a meeting between Dr Piet Koornhof, the minister responsible for the removals, and the local residents. "You must go because you are squatters," the minister told them. "But we *own* this land," they responded. Back came the reply: "All black people in South Africa are squatters if they are outside their traditional lands." Her story continues:

> The negotiations and meetings went on and on, but the people never faltered. They continued to say that they weren't moving. Then the police arrived at a meeting of the community in the schoolyard, and a policeman called Nienaber shot and killed their leader, Saul Mkhize. That was the turning point in their struggle. Saul had been in the schoolyard, and the policeman was outside a high wire fence, but be claimed he was in danger of his life and that's why he shot Saul dead. The people remained firm and said: "On no account are we going." The women made a plan to dig their own graves, and said: "We will stand beside our graves because we are not moving from here. You can shoot and we will lie in our land forever."[2]

The people of Driefontein eventually won the right to keep their land. Others were less successful. "Nazism was about genocide. Apartheid has destroyed millions of people in South Africa, decreeing that skin colour was sufficient ground to locate and relocate people around the country, provide them with an inferior education and ultimately reduce them to mere vassals. More than that, apartheid has killed millions of people, through starvation, as a result of disease, and in police gun fire. It too is genocide."

## Reparation

The question is, where do we go from here? Her concern is that we do not simply allow economics to replace race as the primary vehicle of repression in South Africa. "Politicians have used race to deprive blacks of their land. It is not merely sufficient to scrap all apartheid laws which have already located the wealth in the hands of whites. A future democratic government will have to make reparations for the past. I fully recognise that rectification is likely to take generations, but we have got to start somewhere."

When she was awarded the degree of Doctor of Laws (Honoris Causa) at the Graduation Ceremony at the University of Cape Town in 1991, she spoke of the need for reparation.

> Occupation and usage of land and property and its distribution are fundamental to economic justice in the future. We simply must not take the present maldistribution with us as we approach the

---

2.  Diana Russell, *Lives of Courage: Women for a New South Africa* (London: Virago Press, 1990), pp.318

first democratic elections ever to be held in South Africa. The repeal of the Land Acts and Group Areas Act will enable some wealthy people who are black to acquire property, but will not make any difference to the dispossessed in the foreseeable future.

We therefore must *not* rush into enacting a Bill of Rights which enshrines the right to private property. A Bill of Rights which seeks to entrench the *status quo* will inevitably be ignored and overthrown, however valuable its other provisions may be.

. . . Has any person the right to own land which he/she does not use at all and to seek constitutional protection to keep those in need of land for shelter or production from making use of it?

Should any person be allowed the constitutional protection of ownership of property, which was unjustly taken away from others, to the exclusion of claims for restoration, restitution or, at the very least, reparation?

Surely the debate must begin with the prior right — that of people to basic protection from rain, wind and heat, the right to privacy and security of tenure, to the use of land for the production of food for family, community and nation? Then we can start to construct a Bill of Rights which will enable these needs to be met in the future.

To take as the point of departure the enshrining of the consequence of past injustice is to perpetuate that injustice and to make it certain that a future, democratically elected, government will be unable to meet the aspirations and demands of the deprived majority. That will lead to the collapse of all order, and bloody revolution.

Conscious that an inevitable clash over property rights looms ahead, she quotes Donald Leyshon, writing in *Leadership* (December 1990): "Vested property interests — like the monarchy, nobility and clerics of revolutionary France — will attempt to thwart the ambitions of the newly enfranchised population as far as possible." Duncan continues: "We cannot protect the rights of existing property owners at the present time in South Africa. Those rights are in direct conflict with the rights of the homeless and landless to shelter and the means of production. We can, however, look for creative ways in which we can address the problems of bringing into being a just social order. This may or may not entail nationalisation of land." Making a distinction between ownership and usage of land, she suggests that ownership, as defined in laws inherited from Europe, is foreign to the people of Africa, who understand land as being something given in trust into the stewardship of the present generation by the ancestors for the benefit of future generations. Duncan links this to the biblical understanding of the use of land: "Your land must not be sold on a permanent basis, because you do not own it; it belongs to God, and you are like foreigners who are allowed to make use of it." (Leviticus 25:23) "We need to note," she continues, "that the people we call squatters rarely move onto land that is being used. The land they occupy is indeed owned but it is not being *used* in any visible way. It is 'empty' just as the history books have taught our children that the land appropriated and used by white settlers and trekkers was 'empty'."

Duncan thinks that the solution may primarily have to do with ensuring a secure form of land tenure for an extended period — say a ninety-nine year cycle. "As such," she suggests, "the land itself remains the property of the state, which can be translated as 'the people' or 'God' according to one's own interpretation or ideologies and beliefs. . . On productive, as opposed to residential, land perhaps the leasehold should be dependent on productive use of the land and should be for a period of 50 years based on the ancient Judaic concept of the 'Jubilee Year' — the year of restoration in which all debts were forgiven."

> Count seven times seven years, a total of forty-nine years. Then, on the tenth day of the seventh month, the day of the Atonement, send a man to blow a trumpet throughout the whole land. In this way you shall set the fiftieth year apart and proclaim freedom to all the inhabitants of the land. . . In this year all property that has been sold shall be restored to the original owner. So, when you sell land to your fellow Israelite or buy land from him do not deal unfairly. The price is to be fixed according to the number of years the land can produce crops before the next year of Restoration. If there are many years the price shall be higher, but if there are only a few years the price shall be lower because what is being sold is the number of crops the land can produce. (Leviticus 25)

Acknowledging that this is old-fashioned and outdated thinking, she suggests it contains an ethical ingredient that is applicable to the South African situation. Her concern is to ensure that the poor will not be further dispossessed in the future by a Bill of Rights which entrenches the injustices of the past.

"In brief, I suppose I am a social democrat," says Duncan. "I am as terrified of this great urge to go hook, line and sinker into a Thatcherist type capitalism as I am of a centralised economy. There are certain ingredients of the communist economic system which must not be dismissed along with what was undoubtedly bad. I recently spoke with a Czechoslovak journalist who told me he had formerly earned only $300 a month, but his child had access to the highest level of education of which she was capable; the family had a roof over its head; and health care was free. He asked whether the demands of the West that the economy of his country be restructured, resulting in unemployment and homelessness, could be ethically defended. The homeless and unemployed in South Africa are asking similar questions. It is the task of all people concerned with the future plight of the poor to ensure that these questions are not ignored when the politicians settle down to plan the future."

## Transcending the Propaganda

"The problem is that most whites are simply unexposed to the lot of black people in this country. They are fed each day on propaganda, told what to believe and brainwashed into believing that the poor have brought their poverty onto themselves." Duncan refers me to William Shirer's *The Rise and Fall of the Third Reich*, in which he talks about the extent to which he found his judgement being affected by reading German newspapers and listening to German radio day after day, even though he was a foreign correspondent with access to the international media. "The tragedy is that this is what is happening in South Africa," she insists. Referring specifically to SABC radio and television as the opium of the people, her concern is also that the average person doesn't want to read investigative journalism even when it does make its way into newspapers such as the *Weekly Mail*. "We prefer to be entertained by the matrimonial affairs of the British royal family, neglecting to take an interest in the tragedy of our country. We do not know what other people are suffering or what their concerns are. While this ignorance prevails we will not be moved to do anything about the situation. . . What this all means, of course, is that the struggle for press freedom is directly related to the New Testament commandment that we love our neighbours. If I do not know my neighbour and am ignorant of his or her plight I cannot possibly love him or her."

## Religion

Sheena Duncan has a tendency to shift her conversation from politics to religion and human values, and I ask her to speak more about her religious worldview. Is it important for her to go to church? "Oh yes, it is important for me to be part of a religious community. I read the Bible regularly. Many years ago I read somewhere about prayer being a state of constant recollection, an exercise in reflection on one's life, one's past deeds and intentions — a kind of ongoing reflection on one's hopes and fears. It is also a recollection or an awareness of the presence of a Supreme Being or the presence of the Holy Spirit. I try to engage in that recollection process on a regular basis. I find it both sobering as well as spiritually and mentally invigorating. I am not by any means a recluse, everyone knows that, but I do need time out. That is a very important part of my life. For me, prayer is both a prayerful attitude towards life as well as actually stopping to reflect."

What is Duncan's notion of God? Who is God? "I find the 'who is' more difficult than the 'what is'," she answers.

> For me God is Creator. My most fundamental understanding of life is that the whole creation is the manifestation or revelation of 'something'. To disregard or disturb the creative order is to live an unfaithful or sinful life — whether in regard to other people or to the environment as a result of using harmful chemicals, fertilizers or anything else. In other words, the 'green thing' is very important for me. If I lived in a situation where I did not have to fight apartheid, I would be involved in environmental concerns. I experience God in the world around me, in people, in nature, in the political struggle for justice. My experience of God is that of being taken by the scruff of the neck, thrown into life and realising that I am in the presence of God.

Acknowledging the difficulty of knowing 'who' this God is and facing the difficulties of speaking about this God, she observes: "I don't think God is a person to whom I speak. God is more of a spirit, a dimension to life. I don't have the right words, but I do not regard God to be a person of some kind." After discussing the need for suitable metaphors as a way referring to, and therefore understanding, God she continues:

> We need to be far more thoughtful and guarded in our use of God-language. To thoughtlessly refer to God as if we know exactly who or what God is, is a dangerous thing. In so doing we disregard the mystery of God, the challenge to experience the richness of God and the need to reach beyond ourselves and our presuppositions of reality to new horizons of life and possibilities of reality — of God if you like.
>
> It is a very difficult thing to talk of God. Sunday school teachers and preachers ought to be far more on their guard in naming God.

They often create serious spiritual problems for people. They ought to enable us to explore various ways of experiencing God, rather than confirming us in our narrow notions of God, which so often make for bigotry and religious intolerance. Feminist and other contextual theologies have begun to teach us to do this, but I do not know many preachers who are prepared to enable their congregations to explore new ways of knowing God. We will probably have to wait for the next generation for this to happen.

What about sexism in God-talk? Does she have difficulties with referring to God as 'Father' or 'He'? Are these problematic concepts for her? "We are back with the problems of *all* religious language," she observes. "No, I personally don't find such notions any more problematic than most other references to God. But I am aware that some women do and pastorally this must be taken seriously. The Church must be sensitive to their needs." She recalls a conversation with Suzanne Petersen, an Anglican priest in Grahamstown:

> I was telling her that I think language is very important and that I found talking about things like 'personholes' rather offensive. I happen to think 'manhole' is okay! This led to an most interesting theological conversation.

> She suggested that if you practise writing prayers without using terms like 'Father' and 'He' you are eventually exposed to a new revelation or understanding of God. To struggle with God-language is a pastoral and deeply spiritual exercise; it is not merely some fad that a few feminists or secularists are into. I find that when priests and others are enabled to understand that, they become far more open to the language issue. The problem is that some of our people are so culturally bound and trapped in traditional language that they genuinely cannot understand the problems that other people have. It is a pity because they are in fact losing out on an enriched experience of the divine.

The Duncans' younger daughter, Carey, lives in Morocco, having married a Muslim. Duncan describes the experience of working with the couple, a Presbyterian minister and an Imam when organising the wedding ceremony. "My own rector wouldn't participate in a service that deliberately excluded any reference to the Holy Trinity. I was disappointed. I also realised how important it is to develop a culture of religious pluralism in this country. How can we speak about religious pluralism, while affirming the truth of a religious experience and the importance of a particular religious culture? That's an important issue which the theologians need to help us with," she concludes.

## Ubuntu

What are her hopes for a democratic South Africa? "It would have to do with the idea of *Ubuntu*," she replies. "Social disintegration is busy destroying the fullness of what it means to be human in traditional African society. Whites need to learn this from blacks, while blacks need to reaffirm the importance of it. The African understanding of humanity has, of course, certain strong similarities with biblical anthropology."

She reviews the usual vision of democracy, non-racism, non-sexism and so on. "There must be certain rights for all and an economy that generates sufficient resources for all. We need not necessarily be prosperous, but there must be sufficient for all of us. My problem is that I am becoming increasingly despondent, wondering whether this can be in my lifetime. The violence, conflict and loss of compassion that are characterising our nation are likely to take a heavy toll for years to come. That is why I speak about *Ubuntu* — the need to rediscover the fullness of humanity. It involves the need to belong to one another and to care for one another. We need an attitude to life that breeds compassion. Many of us are at the same time concerned to be ourselves and to realise our potential as individual people in life, sometimes feeling that involvement in the lives of others prevents us from attaining that goal. What is needed is the will and the skill to be ourselves in community with others."

## Integrated Life

Sheena Duncan is a person as much at home speaking about hard politics and engaging is social analysis as she is talking about things spiritual — prayer, worship and personal devotions. "I need the active as well as the contemplative dimensions of life in order to be a whole person," she observes. "I encounter God in my engagement in the world as well as in solitude and prayer. I try to integrate the two. . . My passion is, of course, the garden. I also read mountains of thrillers. These activities are also part of my quest for an integrated life."

PHOTO ACKNOWLEDGEMENT: South African Chapter, World Conference
on Religion and Peace

# ELA GANDHI

*Part of a Tradition of Struggle*

Granddaughter of Mohandas Gandhi, Ela Gandhi[1]
recalls visiting the Mahatma in India when she was
eight years old. "I remember him not as a dignitary
or famous person, not as a religious leader or the
freedom fighter which he was, but as a grandfather."

---

1. Ela Gandhi has recently reverted to her maiden name, hitherto having used her
   married name, Ela Ramgobin.

"Having spent three months in his home I realise, in retrospect, how privileged I was to have lived so close to him. I don't recall him having sought to impart any great religious or ethical truths to me, he was simply a grandfather who spent time with me and loved me. After I returned to South Africa, I corresponded with him, but I never kept any of his letters. A foolish thing, indeed! Then, after his death, my parents kept the memory of him alive in our family. For me he came to symbolise a kind of spiritual and ethical centre or lodestone that brought together the religious and political struggle in a manner that has been an example that I have tried to emulate throughout my life. His life and example have taught me that politics is about more than power. It is about giving outward expression to certain basic ethical and spiritual or inward ideals. He is on record as observing, 'affection is as basic as bread'. These are good words that we would do well to remember as we strive to build a new society."

Gandhi identifies three aspects of the family tradition in which she was raised: a history of political struggle, the Hindu religion and the memory of Mahatma Gandhi.

I simply grew up believing that it was right, proper and the natural thing to engage in the struggle for the basic rights of people who were denied such rights. Being part of the broader black community in South Africa, we were ourselves denied such rights. So, in a sense my family had struggle thrust upon it. I was raised as part of a tradition of struggle and came to believe that it was better to fight than to lose the essence of what it means to be human. This commitment involved me not only in national and regional politics; macro politics, if you like, but also in community or civic concerns. I was raised to believe that it was simply the decent thing to become engaged in campaigns to ensure that people had access to clean drinking water, that they had houses to live in and that children had access to education. For me it was a simple consequence of being a human being.

Looking back, however, I realise that subconsciously the influence of Hindu thought, as taught to me essentially by my father, was a formative part of my value system. He taught me from the Bhagavad-Gita and the Ramayana, telling me that at the heart of Hinduism was a struggle between good and evil. From an early age I learned of the *dharmic* and *adharmic* forces, which are the forces of righteous and unrighteous rule. I was taught that the *Ramrajya* (the kingdom of righteous rule) was a goal for which I was to strive in society. This, I was taught, was a way of being close to God. Therefore I saw the struggle against oppression and apartheid in South Africa as a natural consequence of my Hindu belief.

Then, of course, there was Gandhiji. He personified the very link between Hinduism and social engagement of which I am speaking.

## The Lessons of Life

"On this tradition I built my life," says Gandhi. "There were lessons ahead to be learned, but as I journeyed along the different roads that life provided for me I came to realise that the basic foundation of my life was sound, enduring and yet sufficiently flexible to enable me to adjust to the changing needs of society."

Her father, Manilal Gandhi, remained in South Africa after her grandfather left the country in 1914, but he visited India to marry after Mohandas Gandhi had chosen a bride for his son and arranged the marriage. Ela's parents settled in Natal and eventually her father shared in the running of the Phoenix Settlement in Inanda and the production of the newspaper, *Indian Opinion*, both of which the Mahatma had established. Always politically active, while in India together with the Mahatma, her father was involved in the Salt March in the 1940s. He was arrested and spent a year in prison for his opposition to British rule. After returning to South Africa, he was imprisoned on several occasions for his political resistance to apartheid. Her mother was also involved in political protests, although language difficulties prevented her from taking a leadership role. Her father's final imprisonment, after being actively involved in the 1952 Defiance Campaign, had the most adverse effect on him and the family. He was eventually released from prison a sick man, and he died of a stroke four years later.

Growing up with her family on the Phoenix Settlement, Gandhi recalls a growing sense of frustration as she encountered the effects of apartheid as a child, travelling to school on over-crowded, segregated trains and observing white children playing in parks and on beaches that were barred to blacks. She also speaks of her more immediate environment at the Ashram on the Phoenix Settlement, where people of different races lived together. "This was an experience that convinced me that a non-racist society was possible. I have also, however, come to understand why and how people acquire racist feelings. Driven by the effects of apartheid and living with the consequences of having both his parents under house arrest, our second son became quite hardened in his anti-white stance. This came home quite forcibly to me when we wanted to buy him a pet dog. Still quite young at the time, he insisted that the dog should not be white!"

Gandhi's marriage (which recently ended in divorce) to Mawalal Ramgobin, with whom she grew up in Inanda, thrust her still deeper into the political conflict. She was banned for eight and a half years and her husband for fifteen years. They were both active in the revival of the Natal Indian Congress in the 1970s, after it had been dormant since the imprisonment and banning of its leadership ten years earlier. She shared in the formation of the National Organisation of Women and in the launch of the United Democratic Front Women's Congress in 1987.

Having earned a BA degree, she later returned to do undergraduate studies followed by Honours in Social Work at the University of Natal. She then practised as a social worker from 1975 to 1989. Since then she has been employed as the Information Unit Co-ordinator at the Career Information Centre for the Natal region. She serves on the Natal executive committee of the World Conference on Religion and Peace (WCRP).

"In brief," she observes, "my life's journey has been a process of discovering the implications of the essential beliefs with which I was raised. In my parents' home I was taught the ethical values of the Hindu religion. I was taught to work for the triumph of good over evil and the realisation of a society within which the basic necessities are available to all and equally distributed among all people. I've dedicated my life to fight for this kind of society. I've studied to equip myself to share meaningfully in this struggle. I've finally come to the conclusion that, despite the failure of Eastern Europe, there are certain important values being promoted by the communist ideology, so I have decided to join the South African Communist Party. I intend giving expression to my ethical and religious ideals through this organisation. If not, well, I'll resign and look for another home." She is also an active member of the ANC.

### Rediscovering Hinduism

We discuss Hinduism at some length. Why are adherents of Eastern religions, including Hinduism, regarded as being indifferent to material things, tending to be less politically involved than adherents of such history-affirming religions as Christianity, Islam and Judaism? "You need to understand the Hindu psyche," she tells me. "Hinduism is not an assertive faith. It does not actively proselytise, nor does

94

it seek to promote its own distinctive identity. This means that as a Hindu I do not feel the need to speak about my Hinduness in my opposition to apartheid. I do not see the need to fly the Hindu flag. My religious identity, however, informs who I am. As such it motivates and empowers me to fight for my basic values and beliefs through whatever channel becomes available to me and in the name of whatever organisation enables me to do so. This means I engage politically in a political organisation as a political person, without pretending that I am *only* doing so because I am a Hindu. I further see no reason to believe that someone else will become a better person or a more effective activist if he or she is a Hindu. As a Hindu I am enriched by sharing with people of other faiths."

Indicating that there are people who continue to be involved politically, who are deep within themselves conscious of their Hindu roots, she is at the same time critical of the dominant forms of Hindu religious practice in South Africa. She speaks of the "enormous privatisation of religion" that has come to characterise the dominant middle-class expressions of not only Hinduism but all religions in South Africa. Focusing her discussion on the South African Indian community she ascribes this privatisation to socio-political rather than religious or theological causes. "In many ways it is a class thing. People who are more or less comfortably off tend to cling to what they have, and regard it as sufficient to give a little to charity as a means of convincing themselves that they are honouring the social teachings of their respective religions. Then as time goes by they become more and more preoccupied with a personalistic type of religiosity, while becoming increasingly indifferent to the needs of the poor. Social and economic ideologies which have little to do with their faith, convince them that there is little or nothing that they can personally do to redress poverty and repression. The outcome is a privatised religion which is, in turn, all too often passed on to the underclasses, who willingly adopt it as a means of escaping the harshness of their suffering. Religion becomes a form of opium which both the rich and the poor happily imbibe. Add to this the attraction which the exotic and symbolic side of Hinduism has for an increasing number of westernised people who are fed-up with what society has to offer, or are simply 'drop-outs' from society, and you have the myth of an Eastern religion through which the demands and challenges of society can be avoided." Gandhi insists that this is a deviation from the historic Hindu tradition seen, for example, in the Indian freedom struggle. Her concern is that the social awareness of Hinduism be rediscovered. She speaks again of her grandfather's faith, of Subhas handra Bose (who opposed the Mahatma's passive resistance movement in India), Jawaharlal Nehru, Aurobindo Ghose (the head of a religious community at the time of the freedom struggle), Swami Vivekananda (who headed Ramakrishna Mission) and of Swami Dayananda Saraswathi (founder of the Arya Samaj Movement) whose slogan 'India for the Indians' was heard among many zealous nationalistic Indians. "In different ways they were inspired to take the political situation seriously by virtue of their religious convictions. They certainly did not ascribe to the kind of privatised, apolitical brand of Hinduism to which too many Indians in South Africa ascribe today."

Gandhi further ascribes the privatised nature of contemporary forms of Hinduism in South Africa to the break-up of the Indian community, brought about by the Group Areas Act. She argues that with the breaking down of the social structure of the Indian community and the traditional organisational infrastructure that bound the community together, Indian people felt an obligation to look inward, concern themselves with their own affairs, and neglect the broader community. "Add to this the fear syndrome — the sense of being a small minority in a predominantly African environment in Natal — and the will to withdraw from the harshness of struggle is intensified. The government and Inkatha threaten that, if the ANC were to come to power, there would be a repetition of the situation in 1949 when Africans attacked Indians. The implication is that it is far better for Indians not to be involved in 'liberation politics'; confining themselves to taking care of their individual needs."

> In a word, the religious escapism that one sees among many South African Hindus is socially and politically imposed. It is a result of social, economic and psychological factors rather than the essential teachings of Hinduism. There was a time when Hindus in South Africa were motivated in their involvement in the political struggle by their faith. Hindu Pandits (priests) were deeply involved in the protests against the Indian Registration Act earlier in the century, and when Gandhiji defended the protestors in courts he was asked by the judge whether what they were doing could be justified in terms of their religion. He replied affirmatively, "Yes! It is part of our religion." The tenets of Hinduism have not changed, it is the social milieu within which people practise Hinduism that has changed. What we need is a rediscovery of a socially active Hindu faith.

Aware that religion can never be reduced to social action, Gandhi speaks also of Hindu spirituality as experienced in her own life. "For me it was always part of a broader reflective and meditative dimension of life. I have never shared in the rituals of the temple on a regular basis, but the evening prayers conducted by my father were a formative part of my youth. He would gather the family around him, invite neighbours and whoever else wanted to attend for a short period of reflection and prayer. These would invariably be inter-faith prayers. We would say a Christian prayer, a Muslim prayer, a Zoroastrian prayer, a Hindu prayer and so on. It was a custom which we inherited from Gandhiji. He was totally inclusive in his devotional life, committed to interfaith dialogue and practice." Family devotions being the only rite to which she was exposed on a regular basis, it is still the only routine religious ritual in which she shares. "I now say prayers in the morning, rather than the evening, which means that fewer friends and neighbours are available to join us, but evenings are simply too hectic in my life. This is a pity because the gathering of a slightly bigger community, as was the case in my parents' home, helped sustain the community. Nevertheless, a period of reflection and prayer is a source of great strength to me. I will often augment devotional reading with so-called secular readings. The spirit of the divine is manifest in different ways and we must be open to discern divinity wherever it occurs."

## The Indian Community

Gandhi is a staunch critic of tricameral politics. "There has been an attempt to exploit the sense of fear and uncertainty in the Indian community to which I have already referred, through the creation of a self-seeking, subordinate Indian identity through the Indian House of Delegates in the South African Parliament." She sees this epitomised in the person of Amichand Rajbansi, the former leader of the House of Delegates and one time minister without portfolio in P. W. Botha's cabinet. "He flies the Hindu *jhanda* (flag) over his house and from what I have read he professes his faith in all the Hindu deities, praying to them on a regular basis. He has at the same time been seduced by social status, lucrative rewards and the structures of power created by the State for Indian politicians. His religion is no more than a private, socially irrelevant, idiosyncratic behaviour pattern that leaves him free to live life according to the demands of extravagant living and the politics of influence. He apparently sees little or no contradiction between his involvement in a variety of highly dubious practices and his Hindu piety. It is this kind of outward religiosity that is a denial of the humility and non-assertiveness that I would regard as a central feature of the Hindu faith. The pious Hindu does not need to tell everyone he or she is a Hindu. It is enough to simply apply oneself to promote good over evil."

Concerned about the apparent support for the government within the Indian community, Gandhi sees the government and the Inkatha Freedom Party co-operating to isolate the Indian community from the black majority in the country. "This is done in a number of subtle ways. The Inkatha Freedom Party's Women's Brigade recently protested outside the homes of Pravin Gordhan of the Natal Indian Congress and Mo Sheik, a member of the Regional Executive of the ANC in Natal. On another occasion a group of Inkatha impis (soldiers) forced their way into the Natal Indian Congress conference in Durban to tar and feather Indian leaders. Certainly there is a widespread belief in the Indian community that the participation of Indian people in the liberation struggle will be severely dealt with by Inkatha. In this way an attempt is being made to force Indians to be content to fit into the niche in national politics created for them by the State. They are expected to either affirm their Indian identity in religious and cultural practices which do not engage them in the liberation struggle, or know that they will face the wrath of Inkatha. Certainly, every attempt is being made to exclude Indians from free and unhindered participation in South African liberation politics. Indians are a minority and are encouraged to maintain their minority identity by isolating themselves from the mainstream liberation struggle. For Indians to fall for this is a very un-Hindu thing to do. The strength of Hinduism is its universalism and willingness to respect others and to share in the common struggle for good over evil."

Unrestrained in her rejection of the role of Mangosuthu Buthelezi, whom she has publicly criticised on several occasions, she regards the strategy against the Indian community as largely a Natal problem. "Even Muslims in Natal are driven to adopt a more quietistic approach to social concerns than one normally associates with this religion. Compare the social stance of Natal Muslims with that of Cape Muslims, for example." The role of Buthelezi and Inkatha in the promotion of separatism on the basis of ethnic, cultural and religious identity is a matter of major concern to Gandhi. "The 'Natal factor' is likely to haunt a future South Africa for decades to come. We need the promotion of a broad South Africanism, a common identity, in order to build a better future for all of us."

# Feminism

The inclusive society, for which Ela Gandhi is striving, includes the direct and unrestricted participation of women. Uneasy with the way in which feminism is used in some circles, she says:

> Feminism has become a swear-word for some. I definitely believe in women's rights, but I am not sure that I am a feminist. It depends how one uses the word. The chauvinistic individualism associated with the feminist movement in many First World situations is something that I cannot support.
>
> I like to talk of gender rights, because there are clearly socially imposed gender roles and discriminations which militate against men as much as against women. There are social impositions on all of us that cause all of us to suffer when we refuse to submit to them. People (both male and female) should have the right to give expression to their individual wishes, capacities and desires without undue hindrance in society. This means that if a women has the ability and the desire to be a bricklayer or a surgeon this should obviously be her right, in the same way that a man may choose to care for the children or maintain the home. It also means that if a man chooses to weep in public this should not be frowned upon. Why should it be socially unacceptable for a man to show tender emotions in public? In a similar way it is quite wrong to argue that women do not have the emotional or physical strength to deal with certain jobs. That is total nonsense.
>
> To argue, on the other hand, that liberated women should not be nurses, social workers or home-makers is equally wrong. Women, for probably biological as well as social reasons, are generally speaking, great caretakers of society. Society would be poorer without them. This does not, however, mean that men should not fill these roles or that women in such positions should not be adequately paid or denied the kind of privileges which men receive in many jobs. I believe in an egalitarian society, I am concerned about equal rights, while at the same time being committed to finding the right person for the right job.

Concerned about the extent to which culture and religion work against this kind of open society, imposing gender roles on people, Gandhi believes that religious and civil communities should critically evaluate the gender roles which they promote in society. "The Indian community does not take easily to change. There is a great emphasis on tradition and past practices, with women largely playing roles that are subservient to men. Yet, if you look at ancient Hindu society you realise that from the earliest times women were priests and sages, although Hinduism, like most other religions, has been male dominated. It does not, however, *doctrinally* restrict women. Social custom has nevertheless been such that twenty or thirty years ago most girls stopped attending school after standard six. Thereafter their task was to get married, care for their husbands and start a family. But times are changing. Twenty years ago approximately 5% of the student body at the University of Durban Westville were women, today more than half of the students are female. We are slowly beginning to rediscover the gender liberating dimensions of the Hindu religion. Some of our most respected priests are women. Pandita Nanakchand emerged from within the folds of Hinduism without the kind of discontent that one observes in sections of the Christian community concerning the ordination of women to the priesthood. Yet, we have a long way to go in rediscovering the rightful role of women in the Hindu society."

Gandhi emphasises that liberation (whether from racial or gender oppression) should never be regarded as simply an indiscriminate pursuit of the characteristics of the dominant culture or person concerned.

It would, for example, be quite wrong for women to adopt all the socially imposed behaviour patterns of males in their quest for liberation from their own captivity. Quite frankly I am concerned when women seek to outdo men in their maleness. We have rich resources of our own to contribute to society. We need to plumb the depths of our respective traditions in quest of these reserves, often forgotten and frequently neglected. Hinduism has, for example, a great tradition of motherhood, which has implications well beyond the home and the immediate family. Society would be the richer for sharing in these resources.

What I am saying is that women make a fundamental mistake if they think that by simply buying into the dominant notion of the 'successful' person of western society (which is male dominated) they are truly liberated people. To be liberated is not necessarily to be westernised. We must learn to be discerning in our quest for liberation, adopting what is good and leaving what is bad. Women also need to realise that they have a mission to enable men to liberate themselves from their male hang-ups, in order that they may discover what are sometimes referred to as womanly characteristics which they have suppressed in their own humanity. There are emotions and resources in all of us which society labels 'male' and 'female', that we need to enable all people, both male and female, to claim as their own.

She hopes that the entire human race discovers the richness of the resources which each participant can bring to the quest for a set of values that will enrich humanity as a whole. Among these are tenderness and understanding. We are again talking about Mohandas Gandhi's notion that affection is as basic as bread.

## The Contribution of Hinduism

I ask Gandhi to speak about the particular contribution which she thinks Hinduism can make to a future South Africa. "The most important thing which my faith has taught me," she answers, "is universalism." Discerning this as perhaps the most needed ingredient in a democratic South Africa, she continues: "I think the Hindu religion is the most tolerant of all the major religions of the world. People of other faiths are welcomed into Hindu temples, without the slightest desire that they should become Hindus. Inclusivism, universalism and acceptance of others are values which any good Hindu cherishes. We want people to be good people, whether Jews, Christians, Muslims, atheists or agnostics. The spirit of divinity is liberally and generously present in all places. We must all learn to accept and respect one another. Maybe Hinduism can help us learn this. But then history also tells us that Hindus often fail to live up to these Hindu ideals."

"Hinduism," she continues, "integrates the spiritual into the midst of life. We celebrate many colourful festivals such as the Festival of Lights, *Diwali*, when lamps are lit and placed in the doors and windows of our homes, signifying the triumph of good over evil. However, it is not only on such festivals that a Hindu thinks of God. Everything that he or she does contains a religious dimension and can be accompanied by a religious ceremony. We recognise the presence of the divine in animals and rivers, acknowledging that God is present everywhere — in all places, all people, all religions and all the creatures of the earth. In brief it is an easy and natural thing for a Hindu to acknowledge God in the midst of life. An ability to view all things as sacred can only make for a kinder and gentler South Africa."

PHOTO ACKNOWLEDGEMENT: *South*

# NADINE GORDIMER

## A Vocation to Write

"I have no religious belief, I am an atheist,"
Gordimer observes. "The only time I seriously
enquired into religion was in my mid-thirties, when
I experienced a strange kind of loss or lack in myself
and thought this may be because I had no religion."

"So I started reading authors like Teilhard de Chardin and Simon Weil. I also read books on Buddhism and other religions. For the first time in my life I learned something about Judaism, the religion of my parents. But it didn't happen. I could not take the leap of faith."

To hear Nadine Gordimer speak of her work as a writer, which involves "a search for meaning which goes on all your writing life" is, in a certain sense, to encounter a deeply spiritual person. "I am not a materialist. I don't think a writer can be a materialist. I am always seeing behind things. I search for the spiritual element." I suggest that this is what religion tries to do, and she responds: "You're probably right, except that I have not since my thirties really explored the metaphysical or religious dimension of life. I simply try to unravel things at a more basic level. . . Sometimes I wonder whether for writers the piece of paper and the typewriter or the pen, or for some the word processor, is a not a father confessor. I am sure it is so."

The recipient of numerous honorary doctorates and the winner of almost every major literary prize in the world, Gordimer won the Nobel Prize for Literature in 1991. Making the announcement, the Swedish Academy observed that "through her magnificent epic writing she has, in the words of Alfred Nobel, been of very great benefit to humanity". Shrugging aside such accolades, she insists: "I am just a writer. I write about the mysteries of life in my home place, a place that happens to be imbued in all its details and scenes with one of the most horrible problems in the world: racism."

Gordimer is of course more than 'just a writer'. She sees herself as living out a vocation to write. "It is perhaps as much a vocation as that of a priest," she observes. "I don't quite know what this means. Sometimes it is quite frightening." To this we later return.

## A White African

Gordimer calls herself a white African. In a widely published interview as far back as 1974 she rejected the designation 'liberal'. She said then: "Please don't call me a liberal. Liberal is a dirty word. Liberals are people who make promises they have no power to keep." The interview led to an angry exchange of letters between Alan Paton (leader of the Liberal Party at the time) and herself. Both stood their ground and Paton eventually concluded: "Let us face the fact that we have wounded each other . . . both of us can make better use of our words." The truce came, however, not before Paton had suggested that "Miss Gordimer should return to her ivory tower and avoid these interviews at all cost".

Gordimer can scarcely be accused of living in an ivory tower. She has defended the rebellions of black youths: "Since the Soweto uprisings in 1976 young blacks have taken their destiny into their own hands. This caused South African whites to recognise the need for change." Long before it was fashionable for whites to publicly support the ANC and Umkhonto we Sizwe, Nadine Gordimer did, and testified in the Pretoria Supreme Court (in 1988) in mitigation of sentence for Terror Lekota and 10 others found guilty of terrorism. She told the Court that while she was opposed to violence, she "could see the time had come for a military wing". Two years later (shortly after the unbanning of political organisations) she told a reporter: "It was really quite moving to walk into a building in downtown Johannesburg and pay my subscription to become a card-carrying member of the ANC."

Her words are uncompromising: "To call yourself a white African means you really have to identify first of all with the black struggle. You have to show you are ready and waiting to opt out of class and race. You cannot simply say 'I am against apartheid', you have to live it in your life as far as you can."

Few question Gordimer's commitment to the anti-apartheid struggle, although some of her radical critics have seen her writing as cold and detached — "holding the reader at arm's length" and "lacking revolutionary content". Others see her ability to portray the complexity of the inner feelings and conflicts of her characters as the genius of her work, something that invites the reader to enter into the ambiguity of their lives.

I remind her that she had once observed: "My consciousness is the same tint as my face." Her response is immediate: "Apartheid has placed all of us into conceptual and moral ghettos." She explains that at a time when she was feeling increasingly isolated from the white world, she was simultaneously being drawn into the world of black friends and colleagues. "A crucial point of transition for me was the world of musicians, journalists, poets and artists — the Bohemian life of the 1950s in Sophiatown and elsewhere in Johannesburg." Then she warns: "In an apartheid society whites should never pretend that they have bridged the racial divide for once and for all time."

Has she ever experienced rejection because of her colour? "Only once," she responds. "And that was in a particular context, when the Black Consciousness Movement had strong support and pressure was placed on black writers to leave the writers' organisation of which I was a part. The alternatives were to become a white organisation or to disband. We chose the latter. For a while I continued to maintain an informal working relationship with black writers, but in time this gave way to an increasing sense of isolation. It was Desmond Tutu who enabled me to make sense of all this. I told him that while I understood why this separation had to take place — that black people had to free themselves from their so-called tutelage by whites and to test their own muscle both intellectually and on the streets — I was nevertheless deeply hurt. I felt rejected and abandoned. His words are still with me: 'Nadine', he said, 'you must realise that you feel like this because you have established a relationship with black people. For whites who do not have a real relationship with blacks, there is no hurt involved, there is no-one to feel isolated from. Your very sense of rejection is your affirmation.' In time things of course began to change. The 1980s saw the re-emergence of non-racism."

## First of All a Writer

Gordimer has repeatedly shunned interviewer's descriptions of her as a hero or having paid a major price for her stance against apartheid. "I've done no more than what can be expected of any morally concerned person, what every white person could have done, which is to use his or her talents to expose and fight against apartheid."

> My writing is all that I can contribute. I at the same time write out of an intense inner need to write — and I sometimes don't really think it is a natural thing to write.

> I sometimes think my writing may have to do with me not being religious. I do not, for example, believe in the after-life. So what is there that survives us? Perhaps my writing is a quest for that something which transcends life. It has to do with discerning what is lasting in the ups and downs of life, what gives us an insight into life itself. It is a quest for something that transcends the particular.

> People die but their contribution to life endures in one way or another. Epochs come and go but something of them remains. It may be that this can only be captured indirectly — in the arts: in music, literature, in painting.

> I try to capture what comes to expression in the time and place in

which we live. There is something unfolding in our midst which is about life itself, an insight into the complexity of humanity, that I seek to capture. Heroes are wonderful people, but it is important to understand that they are also human. They make mistakes. They have faults. In order to be politically correct a writer ought not to mention these contradictions in his or her fictional heroes. It is, however, the task of the writer to show a different kind of integrity. This is an integrity to humanity itself. It is out of the complexity and moral ambiguity of humanity that the transcendent dimension of life emerges.

The characters in Gordimer's stories provide what has been called a 'history from the inside' of South African consciousness. At times it is that of colonials, of capitalists, exploiters, landlords, employers, or guilt-ridden observers. Gordimer has also struggled to free herself from her own white consciousness, in giving expression to the different moods of numbed anger, violent reaction and the quiet confidence of black people. In all the characters she creates there comes to expression what she has (in delivering the William James Lecture to the New York University Institute of the Humanities in October 1982) called "the torturous inner qualities of prescience and perceptions".[1] Does this enable her readers to face the inner conflicts and ambiguities of their own lives? "Prejudice and ideological control is a powerful thing. It takes more than my writing to free people from it. I hope only to be a small part of that process."

Gordimer's unquestioned commitment is to the emergence of a new nation within which imposed racially-based consciousness will give way to a culture within which each person will be free to be him or herself. However, insisting that no creative writer can allow him or herself to be controlled by political correctness, she comments: "I have written and made political comment over many years, but when writing fiction there can be no party line, no propaganda for the sake of some good cause, no political manipulation of the text. A writer must create characters warts and all. For this reason I am extremely grateful that I have never been obliged to merge my politics and writing. Political correctness can be the death of imaginative writing." Recognising the privilege of being able to adopt this position, she refers to black writers often having been compelled by circumstances to give up their separate writing space. "How they managed I do not

---

1.  Nadine Gordimer, *The Essential Gesture: Writing, Politics and Places*, edited and introduced by Stephen Clingman (London: Jonathan Cape, 1988).

know. They wrote from underground, from exile, from prison. They were often under pressure from radical black groups who would have liked them to have restricted their vocabulary to the crudest kind of protest writing. I have never been under that kind of pressure."

Her contextual location in South Africa is at the same time clearly reflected in her novels and stories. "It can be no other way," she continues. "I do not choose apartheid or oppression as a subject. I don't go out and look for it. I write about what I know and feel and see, and what I absorb from the life I live, and the life around me. It's the air I breathe and the food I eat, it's the bus I get on and the cinema I go to. My whole life is implicit with it and so it comes naturally into my writing."

> My writing has enabled me to get to see and understand the depths of our political situation. In the 1980s, for example, I wrote a novel called *July's People*, in which I described a country in civil war. Whites had created a situation within which they were being attacked by blacks and fleeing for their lives. Two years ago I thought of that novel and said 'Thank God, it was fantasy!' Today we are again on the brink of civil war. I am not a seer or a prophet. It is frightening to realise that you perceive and understand the political situation at a level of clarity which you probably would not have understood had you not been a writer. Could that be so?

A sentence from her William James Lecture comes to my mind: "I remain a writer not a public speaker," she told her audience. "Nothing I say here will be as true as my fiction."

## Growing Up White

Gordimer was born in the goldmining town of Springs, to Nan Myers and Isidore Gordimer in 1923. Her father, born in Riga (Latvia) came to South Africa when he was thirteen years old with the orthodox Jewish education of a *shtetl* boy. Having left school two years earlier, he learned the trade of watch-making, and survived in his adopted country by travelling to the different gold mines along the Reef fixing watches. Her mother, born in England to an established English-Jewish family, immigrated to South Africa with her parents when she was six years old.

Her father attended synagogue only on high religious days, while Nadine, her mother and sister never attended. Sent to school at the Convent of Our Lady of Mercy in Springs, the nuns made no attempt to convert her. "As a child I simply never thought a great deal about religion." Growing up in the ethos of the mining community, she imbibed the prejudices of the white community. "My parents had that highly political position which is called 'apolitical'. I didn't have any inkling of what this country was really about until adolescence when I began to think for myself and see reality for what it was."

She remembers the sense of immediate happiness that she experienced when at the age of six her mother enrolled her at the local library. "I was like a pig in clover," she recalls. "I was enthralled by the stories I read, becoming an indiscriminate reader from an early age." At the age of thirteen Nadine's first story was published in the children's section of the Johannesburg weekly, the *Sunday Express*. Two years later her adult short story, "Come Again Tomorrow" was published in the journal *Forum*. Her first collection of short stories appeared ten years later, in 1949. Today she has over 200 short stories, 10 novels and several essay collections to her credit.

Noting that it is impossible to trace the precise evolution of one's development, she identifies reading and her childhood writing as the point at which her imagination began to develop. "The ability to imagine something different is the first step in the change process. In a limited way I was beginning to realise that life need not simply be what I knew it to be. I still, however, had a long journey ahead of me. I eventually left my home town, spent a year at university and began to become part of the more cosmopolitan life of Johannesburg. Slowly I saw the world around me in a new light, but still I had no serious commitment to change it. Racism was invisible to me. It took years before I saw South African society for what it was."

> I realised that the segregation of my life as a white person from black people was not an act of God. It was not a cosmological given. It was not inevitable. It was man-made. I discovered the extent to which I had been denied life by the laager into which I was born.
>
> My journey out of that laager has been both an exhilarating and a painful one. I had to learn that life is more than the narrow white perception on which I was raised. Once the illusion that those who differ from us are inferior is shattered, a whole new dimension to life opens up before us. We no longer reduce what it means to be human to our understanding of humanity. New horizons appear. This involves a journey into the unknown; always a fearful thing. But once that journey begins there is no way of turning back. It involves a kind of farewell to innocence.

Describing life as a continuing challenge to encounter what is new and different, Gordimer views her various stories and novels as ultimately one book within which she struggles to understand what comes to expression in each step along the journey. "My challenge, as a writer, is to understand what life is about through each changing set of circumstances. For this to happen it is necessary to reach beyond ourselves, seeking to discover who we are from another perspective, from the point of view of others."

## A Common Culture

Gordimer sees apartheid as having seriously debilitated culture in South Africa. "It has undermined our ability to grow as a people, to adapt to the changing demands of society and to deal with the challenges of living together as people of different backgrounds and cultural identities. Too many whites still regard culture as synony- mous with European culture, seeing indigenous music, dance and oral tradition as a lower form of existence, which needs to be tolerated rather than something of beauty which can enrich and empower our common future."

Concerned that the need for cultural change could be neglected by a future government, if only because it will be overwhelmed by economic and related needs, Gordimer believes that this could undermine the process of change itself. "Unless we are able to develop a culture to carry us into a new age, to empower us and provide new values, we will not be able to face the material challenges that threaten to tear us apart. This involves taking active steps to create a new culture." She immediately insists: "This is not to suggest that we need cultural commissars. Far from it. Even the idea of a Ministry of Culture concerns me, if this means the control or manipulation of culture. But we do need to take active steps to facilitate the promotion of all the different cultural experiences of our people. What happens beyond that encounter of cultures will be determined by the future. It must not be manipulated."

> The challenge facing South Africa is the creation of a multi- cultural society within which people of different cultural, ethnic and religious identities can be a part. We have exiles returning home with different cultural experiences and an African culture that has been excluded from the dominant or official cultural expression of the nation. We need to ensure that the life-giving resources of these cultures are channelled into the new society.

> The danger is that the prevailing culture will continue to domi- nate, because its symbols, values and structures are already in

place. If that happens millions of South Africans will continue to feel culturally excluded from main-stream society. That will have the most dire political implications, undermining the democratic process and denying us the opportunity to deal with the material challenges of reconstruction.

## Feminism

And what of feminism? Gordimer has been criticised by some feminist critics for failing to be a feminist writer. She once observed that she was simply "a writer who happens to be a woman"; elsewhere that "all writers are androgynous beings". Her short stories and novels nevertheless sometimes portray the subordinate place of women in society. On other occasions she provides an insight into the restlessness and revolutionary tendencies of her fictional characters. She raises the very issues about which feminists are concerned. She is careful, however, not to specifically promote the conscientisation of women in her writing in the same way that she resists promoting other agendas in her fiction. Radical black writers and feminist critics find common cause in their criticism of Gordimer's style. In content, however, her writing provides the very insights into human behaviour of which both causes are made. She observes:

> I don't think I am a feminist in the classical sense. This is because I take the political context of the South African situation seriously. Black women in South Africa have more in common at the level of oppression and deprivation with black men than they have with white women. Of course the sense of gender oppression experienced by some white women is real, but cannot be compared with the additional burdens which face black women. It is this vast gap in the experiences of black and white women which makes me a little sceptical about talking too easily of the common agenda of women. We need also to remember that South African white women have assisted in placing a white minority government in power. They've had the vote. They clearly saw themselves as having more in common with white males than with black women. Some white women who claim to be feminists continue to do all they can to curtail black political and economic advancement.

> In brief, there is a lot of sorting out to be done in the feminist movement. My own position is that all discrimination should be tackled together. Because the women's agenda goes beyond those things we can address through the legislative process such as equal pay and civil rights, I fundamentally believe that the

concerns of women should be included in the struggle for an inclusive culture. Culture must be gender inclusive as well as racially inclusive. No person, whatever that person's sex, racial background, ethnic or cultural identity should feel excluded by the broader culture of a future South Africa.

## Religion

I ask Gordimer to speak about the source of her moral values. "I suppose they emerge essentially from the Judeo-Christian tradition within which I stand. In a more general sense they are part of the collective consciousness of humankind, gleaned from earlier generations and centuries of moral insight, wisdom and different ways of dealing with the mysteries of life.

Gordimer speaks of her Jewish roots. "I get rather annoyed when people suggest that my engagement in the anti-apartheid struggle can somehow be traced back to my Jewishness," she observes. "Not all Jews in South Africa are opposed to apartheid, despite the racial discrimination they have suffered as a people. However, of two whites condemned to life imprisonment as prisoners of conscience, Braam Fischer and Dennis Goldberg, one was a Jew. Other South African Jews have endured imprisonment, banning and exile for their commitment to the black liberation struggle. These Jews had not suffered the racial discrimination suffered by blacks. I refuse to accept that one must oneself have been exposed to prejudice and exploitation to be opposed to it. I like to think that all decent people, whatever their religious or ethnic background, have an equal responsibility to fight what is evil. To say otherwise is to concede too much."

"Where does human compassion come from?" she asks. "I don't know," she responds to her own question. "It is certainly not the exclusive possession of any one ethical tradition or religious heritage. Our values emerge from the many different streams of what we call civilisation. There is a blending of sources and traditions in human history from which people in different contexts and parts of the world can and often do draw. I think religious people who are inclined to promote a specific religion or ethical system ought to give more attention to this commonality."

What does the notion of God connote to Nadine Gordimer? "It conjures up in my mind other people's explanation for what they cannot understand. For me the notion of God is the greatest myth of all time. I say this in a positive and appreciative sense. The idea of

God emerges out of a tremendous human desire for fulfilment — for something more than oneself. Religion in the orthodox sense says it the other way around. For me to be religious I would need to believe that it is God that inspires godliness in human kind. Well, I am simply in no position to posit such a claim. God, for me, is a human construct which different religions personify in different ways. I am intrigued, for example, by the link between religions and the change of seasons. Take Easter, for instance. In the Northern hemisphere this is a time of rebirth and resurrection for bulbs, plants and trees. Why not extend this to human beings? A wonderful idea. I can understand why people are religious. There is perhaps a bit of pantheism in all of us who are enchanted by nature." She discusses established religion, suggesting that were she to become religious she would be a Roman Catholic, primarily because of the ritual, symbolism and preserved sense of mystery, which Protestant Churches have surrendered. "I at the same time find certain religious practices quite offensive," she continues. "I think, for example, of Holy Communion. The very thought of eating flesh and drinking blood is repulsive. For me this is a violation of what is appealing in religion. It is so unspiritual."

Drawing on Simon Weil, Gordimer defines prayer as "a special form of intelligent concentration". She speaks of the need for time to withdraw from engagement in life. "We all need time out to think and be alone. Prayer can be a time of quietness and thoughtfulness. In fact I quite envy people who withdraw in order to pray on a regular basis. Fortunately my work as a writer creates this kind of space in a different way. Certainly I cannot afford not to be alone."

### Fears

Asked to speak about the future, she responds: "My major fear is that we will allow ourselves to be side-tracked by civil strife. Those who want to cling to the past will stand in our way and bloodshed is probably unavoidable. We must not, however, allow this to distract us from our goal, which is a just and decent new order in South Africa, a non-racial democracy under majority rule."

PHOTO ACKNOWLEDGEMENT: Rashid Lombard

# CHRIS HANI[†]

*Almost A Priest*

Chris Hani has been uncompromising in his attacks
on government, fervent in his support for socialism
and committed as former Chief of Staff to a place for
MK officers and soldiers in a revamped South
African Defence Force.

[†] Chris Hani was assassinated on Easter Saturday, 10 April 1993 — three months after
this interview was conducted.

Chris Hani has often been the focus of government wrath, primarily because of his standing within the ANC's military wing, Umkhonto we Sizwe (MK), and the South African Communist Party (SACP). As General Secretary of the SACP he has become the scapegoat of the anti-communism which the government, the established media, business and many religious leaders like to fan. Often associated with bombs, raids on police stations and undercover operations such as Operation Vula, he is held responsible for much of the militancy of contemporary politics. "There is a sense in which I am committed to keeping that image alive. The ANC must not lose that image. Should it do so, it will lose the support of many young people. That will be fatal in terms of our goal to build a nation in the future. If I am to be labelled a 'radical' as a result, so be it. History must be my judge."

He joined the ANC's military wing in 1962, but within a year, on the instructions of ANC leadership, he had to go into exile to avoid imprisonment under the Suppression of Communism Act. After receiving military training in the Soviet Union he crossed the border back into South Africa on several occasions to carry out special assignments. "I was always nervous on those occasions; always on my guard." When eventually granted indemnity and able to return home after the February 1990 unbanning of the ANC and other organisations, he chose to visit the village of his birth — Cofimvaba in the Transkei, where he was born on 28 June 1942. As a child he attended the local Roman Catholic primary school there and he became an altar boy. He also became intrigued with the use of Latin in the mass and, "quite frankly," he observes, "fell in love with the language". At the age of 12 he decided he wanted to become a priest, a notion that remained with him for several years, despite the opposition of his father. "One of the first things I did on returning to my village was to visit the church where my life's journey began. Baptised in the Catholic Mission when I was ten days old, it was there that at a young age I began to try to make sense of the sufferings of my people."

It was a nostalgic and sobering visit for Hani:

> My parents still live there. They must now be well into their seventies, but as you know many old people do not know when they were born. Many of the people I knew as a youth were there to welcome me. The older folk were proud to receive a child home. . . I also met some of my school friends and realised how little had changed. Women were still walking five kms to fetch

water, carrying it on their heads back to their meagre homes. People were still walking 15 kms to the nearest store to buy soap or sugar. A few people had radio, no-one had television and the problems of illiteracy were as sharp as they were when I was a child. I was revisiting my life of 40–50 years earlier. It was a strange and fearful experience.

I visited the church, met the priest, talked with the nuns and remembered how I used to enjoy getting up early on Sunday mornings so as not to be late to perform my duties as an altar boy. They listened to my stories from the past and attended the ceremony later that day to welcome me home. There was no concern that I am a communist and I found myself as much at home among the religious community of Cofimvaba as I had before I left that place in the early fifties.

The church stood out in my visit as a symbol of perseverance. There is a certain continuity there, linking generations and uniting people. I realised that in rural areas in particular, but presumably elsewhere too, such institutions have an enormous role to play in the reconstruction of the country. We need to begin to restore the role of the Church to what it once was in society — rendering service to the people, becoming an active part of civil society. It has an educational role, it can help combat illiteracy, it can enable people to rediscover moral and social values without which no nation can survive.

Acknowledging an abiding fascination with peasant peoples and villages, Hani mentions the Russian novelist and poet, Maxim Gorki, who had a similar fascination and love for the underclasses. "Gorki's writings have a certain religious aura to them. They portray the cultural and spiritual adhesion, the religious centre, that binds a peasant people together in exploitation, sustaining them from one generation to the next. Gorki understood the hardness of peasant life, rebelling against the conditions that condemned large sections of the population to a life of squalor and human degradation, while condemning the intelligentsia who had lost their sense of the heroic. He realised that intellectuals, and let me say many politicians, are distant from peasant reality, even when seeking to be most supportive of the poor. There is a lesson to be learned here. We would do well to get closer to the peasant classes and to listen to them before proposing our grand development schemes. We need to learn that the often strong-willed and visionary peasant communities have much to teach us. They, at the same time, must have their basic needs met and be given access to the resources of life to participate in and enrich mainstream society. I ended my visit to Cofimvaba with a new sense

117

of urgency to address the very problems and answer the very questions that caused me to first leave that place so many years ago."

## From Religion to Communism

Hani wanted to become a priest and became a communist instead. What is the link? Hani again speaks of his village: "I grew up in a poor family among poor people. Many of the males were away, working on the mines, some in Cape Town and others on the sugar plantations in Natal. Most of us grew up under the supervision of our mothers, combining school work with working in the fields and tending the livestock. I was a thoughtful boy and often asked questions about the suffering of our people, finding a measure of childhood relief in the message of the Church which told us that there would be a better world in the hereafter. I, at the same time, admired the selflessness of the priests who worked among us. They lived alone, frugal and puritan in their life style, visiting the sick and ministering to the poor. I learned to admire the discipline of the Mission, I was inspired and challenged by the examples of the priests. To be a priest seemed to me a natural development." After passing what was then called Junior Certificate, Hani attended Lovedale College and eventually Fort Hare University College. In 1957 he joined the ANC Youth League, seeing this as a natural extension of his concern for social justice.

> My father was a construction worker in Cape Town at the time, Chairperson of the Langa Vigilantes Association and a member of the ANC. He was later banished from Cape Town, and found asylum in Lesotho. During this time I was driven by a religious concern for the suffering poor, while realising that it was not sufficient to wait for the next world for relief from that suffering. The ANC helped me give expression to this commitment and I found plenty of biblical justification for the new 'this world' orientation of my faith. My political involvement was a natural outworking of my religious convictions. Then, at Fort Hare, I came under the influence of people like Govan Mbeki and Raymond Mhlaba, and I joined a socialist study group. I read the *Communist Manifesto* and thought it all sounded a bit like a biblical vision of a caring society, although clearly I was beginning to ask more and more penetrating questions about religion. When I joined an underground cell of the Communist Party in 1960 I was still very much a Christian, attending church and participating in the various programmes of the Church. The Party and the Church were for me complementary institutions. I saw positively no contradiction between them.

Things later began to change. "As time passed, I began to view the Church as indifferent to the socio-economic improvement of black people, even though I was sure that the Bible demanded the opposite. The Party and the ANC were at the same time emphasising the need for the suffering of the poor to be redressed, and by 1962 my enthusiasm for religion was on the decline. The dichotomy between the promises of a good life after death and insufficient concern for the suffering of the present age began to take its toll on my thinking. During that same year I joined Umkhonto we Sizwe inside the country and my involvement in the Church simply no longer seemed very important to me." Emphasising that he has, perhaps because of his early exposure to the Mission in his home village, never felt a need to crusade against religion, he continues:

> The most fundamental concerns that initially attracted me to the Church — namely, the suffering of people and the example of the priests in Cofimvaba, were now coming to expression in the ANC and the Party. The essential values which I learned in the Church about the equality of all people, the need to love one's neighbour and the obligation to respect elderly people were for me the very values that apartheid was undermining. In brief, I came to the conclusion that the political organisations to which I belonged were doing far more than the Church to eradicate these evils.
>
> In this ethical context I, in turn, began to question the existence of God. 'If there is a God', I asked, 'what is this God doing about the suffering of people?' But that was, and to a certain extent still is, for me a personal or private concern. I know others who gain strength in their commitment to the very things to which I am committed as a result of their faith. I have also come to gain a new sense of appreciation for the place of belief in political struggle as a result of recent developments in liberation theology and the various related contextual theologies which are presently doing the rounds.

## The Source of Values

Hani speaks of the need to promote moral values and protect the moral fabric of society. "The most fundamental values of our society are being eroded as a result of generations of exploitation and conflict. We are facing a moral crisis that threatens to destroy the social concern and compassion necessary to build a new nation — respect for the elderly, kindness towards the needy and caring for those unable to care for themselves."

Asked about the origins of his own moral concern, he identifies three sources. First, he sees religion as a major formative influence on his early life, stressing that he continues to believe that religious institutions have a particular responsibility to promote such values as are essential for the well-being of society. Political struggles around the world show that religious institutions and leaders have a significant role to play in transitionary periods. "South Africa is no exception. Religious institutions need to become far more self-confident and aggressive in promoting morality; not in some heavy Puritanical manner, but at the level of enabling people to rediscover the fundamental values which make for long-term happiness and peace."

He secondly identifies the ideals of the ANC alliance of political forces as a conveyor of values that sets it aside from many other political groupings in South Africa. Identifying a profound ethical centre to ANC political history, he argues: "I am not for one moment suggesting that our followers are inherently more moral than the followers of other groups; I am merely suggesting that there is an ideal to our struggle which, when taken seriously, makes a significant contribution to the ethical identity of society. The traditional commitment of the ANC and SACP to non-racism, justice, democracy, and more recently to non-sexism, constitutes a centre of values that challenges all of us to live better lives. These ideals have inwardly shaped and directed my life as comprehensively as conventional religious values have influenced others." He similarly identifies the Marxist ideal of a classless society as a moral incentive that has continually inspired his quest for moral values in life. "In a very real sense Marxist ideals were for me a natural development of my Christian upbringing. In some ways Marxism is a secular expression of a biblical social vision."

Hani thirdly points to classical literature as having shaped his moral perceptions. His early encounter with Latin resulted in an abiding interest in the language, as well as a later interest in Latin and Greek literature. He continued to enjoy reading Greek literature in translation and Latin literature in the original for years after graduating with a BA in English and Latin from Fort Hare University (with the degree being conferred by Rhodes University).

> I simply do not have the chance to continue to do so to the extent that I once did, but still do so where and when possible. I covet the time when I will be able to again read Tacitus' *History of Rome*. I am intrigued by the stories of struggle between the Patricians and

Plebians, while at times being moved beyond words by the writings of Sophocles and Euripides. I am fascinated by Homer's *Iliad*. I have read and reread Homer's account of the wanderings of Odysseus and his ultimate regaining of his kingdom in the *Odyssey*. The Greek approach to religion is fascinating. Despite their metaphysical separation of the sacred and the secular, they anthropomorphised their gods in an attempt to make them both intellectually and morally accessible to ordinary people. Their gods bear all the blemishes of human nature, exposing and revealing the good and bad of human struggle. . . I was enthralled by the beauty of the poetry and still today enjoy tracing the link between English poetry in Chaucer, Dryden and others on the one hand and the Greeks on the other. Many of the prayers of the Church reflect similar links. . . We all have our own religious, literary and/or cultural vehicle through which to seek moral insight. For me classical culture was a major location within which I discovered beauty and encountered essential human values. By projection I shared in the ancient Greek struggle between good and evil, discovering its significance for the present situation in which we live.

"The Greek tragedies," he continues, "can be seen as an ancient form of contextual theology, an attempt to relate the common ethical ideals of society to the contemporary issues of the day. The classical tales were a serious quest for human values. Religion is a quest for spiritual fulfilment and moral perfection. Political struggle is about the creation of a better world in which to live. They are for me all facets of a multi-faceted quest for human completion. Intellectuals have a special obligation to make the insights of former ages available for the present struggle. They can assist us not to make the same mistakes and also to forge models of human existence based on the wisdom of the past."

## The Armed Struggle

"Shortly after I was found guilty under the Suppression of Communism Act in 1963, having been granted bail pending an appeal, Comrade Govan Mbeki visited me in Cape Town, giving instructions that I leave the country to undergo military training. It marked the beginning of a new phase of my life." By 1967 Hani had risen to the position of Commissar of the Luthuli Detachment of Umkhonto we Sizwe, leading his detachment in three battles alongside the army of the Zimbabwe African People's Union (Zapu). The strategy on the part of the ANC was to consolidate its position in Zimbabwe in an attempt to establish a base from which to penetrate into South Africa. Then as the level of the Rhodesian security force activity intensified, Hani crossed with a section of his detachment into Botswana. He was charged by the Botswanan authorities with the illegal possession of arms and sentenced to 18 months imprisonment. On his release he went to Zambia. In 1974 he was instructed to infiltrate back into South Africa. "I crossed the Botswanan border alone at about 18:00 hours and walked through the night, making my way to Zeerust which I only reached (after having to take several detours) at 15:00 the next day." Hani went to the station to purchase a ticket to Johannesburg. "I spoke to the guy in the ticket office in broken Afrikaans, thinking he would be more helpful to a Bantu trying to speak Afrikaans than a smart kaffir trying to speak English! I called the fellow 'baas' and, well, it seemed to work because he became very helpful, suggesting that I take a bus to Mafeking and the train from there to Johannesburg, where I arrived the next morning."

Hani remained in the Johannesburg area for four months establishing and renewing existing political and military structures which had collapsed almost entirely at the time. He also set up an intricate system of underground communications. He then moved into Lesotho, using this as a base to return to South Africa on several other occasions. By the time of the 1976 student rebellions, ANC structures had been substantially improved, equipping the organisation to receive the thousands of young people who were offering themselves for military training. "There were no suitable flights out of Lesotho and we had to walk the new recruits back across the Caledon River. Others crossed from Botswana and elsewhere into South Africa and we established a network of escape routes out of the country."

Hani was living a dangerous existence. An attempt was made on his life in 1980 and a year later his car was blown-up at his house on the outskirts of Maseru. He caught the person who was injured while setting the bomb, established that he had been trained by the South African Police in Bloemfontein and handed him over to the Lesotho Police. He returned to Lusaka in 1982 and was appointed Army Political Commissar and Deputy Commander of Umkhonto we Sizwe. A major task for which he was responsible was the ANC's political programme within the army, ensuring that its cadres carried out the *political* objectives of the movement. By 1987 Hani was Chief of Staff of Umkhonto we Sizwe, having already been elected to the National Executive of the ANC in 1975 (at the age of 32). As Chief of Staff he took full responsibility for the daily operations of Umkhonto

122

we Sizwe, being answerable only to the President of the ANC, Oliver Tambo, and Army Commander, Joe Modise.

By the mid-1980s when political and military activity were intensifying inside South Africa, our structures in the major centres like Johannesburg, Cape Town, Durban and elsewhere were well established. People were ready to accept us, shelter us and assist us in our military operations. There was an unprecedented growth of Umkhonto we Sizwe and we established training camps inside as well as outside the country. Every political breakthrough we had resulted in further recruits for military training and soon we had more recruits than we could possibly train. Most of our youth were sent to schools and universities to acquire an education. A negotiated settlement was also beginning to be seen as a possibility. The expectations of the military cadres were at the same time very different. They had a vision of marching victoriously into Pretoria. The political and ethical nurturing of our recruits was crucial. We realised that one day these young people were going to be asked to return to civilian life and be responsible citizens.

Giving expression to the sense of political and social responsibility which rested on his shoulders as Commander-in-Chief of Umkhonto we Sizwe, Hani recalls his early decision to undergo military training himself.

I remember the deep sense of frustration in the country at the time, not dissimilar to the situation within which our more recent recruits found themselves. I left in 1962, two years after the Sharpeville massacre and the banning of the ANC.

Still under some influence of the Church, I was disturbed and challenged by the open hostility of Church leaders to armed struggle. They were downright insensitive to black frustrations and despair and narrow in their understanding of violence and who was responsible for it. I realised that the Church had throughout history condoned a defensive military action as well as providing theological justification for the right of the oppressed to resort to military action to remove a tyrant. 'So what the hell was going on?' I asked.

Well, that was a long time ago. I am at peace with myself and, I believe, I stand in continuity with Christian teaching on war in saying that under certain circumstances military action is morally justifiable. Umkhonto we Sizwe was formed after the ANC was banned. Its actions were politically responsible and its officers and soldiers answerable through the Commander-in-Chief to the political leadership of our organisation. We scrupulously sought

123

to avoid the loss of civilian life and for a long time refused to target the lives of police and soldiers. Bombs were placed at installations, buildings, power stations and sub-stations. At no point were orders given to place bombs at people's homes or in public buildings. But then came 1976, the slaughter of our children and the intensification of repression. A hardening of feelings followed.

I still felt that we should avoid allowing our morality to be lowered to that of the enemy although they were killing our kids, old people, civilians and everyone who got in their way. However, as their total onslaught intensified, I found it more and more difficult to maintain the demarcation between military and civilian targets. We tactically decided to intensify our armed attacks, but again carried out reconnaissance to ensure the minimum loss of civilian life. We were not always totally successful, but you need also to remember that attacks on farmers in the Northern Transvaal were attacks on people who were themselves heavily armed and often working in the closest co-operation with the South African security forces. Indeed they were often an extension of the army and police forces.

This much cannot be denied: Comparatively speaking the civilian casualties that occurred as a result of our military strikes were minimal. We resolutely refused to wage a terrorist war — taking war into supermarkets, cinemas and the like. Where such isolated incidents occurred, they were without our authorisation. My conscience is absolutely clear on that one. But war is a terrible thing. Where indiscretions and unnecessary violence occurred we tried to take the circumstances and emotions of the person into account, but disciplinary action often followed. Our people did not behave like the Barend Strydom's of this world. By and large they were driven by a moral cause, even when their emotions got the better of them.

Take Andrew Zondo, for example, the young man who placed the bomb in the Amanzimtoti shopping centre. He was not ordered by us to do so — he stated in his trial that he acted on his own incentive. I cannot support his actions, but the story he tells of what drove him to this desperate act is a moving account of human compassion.[1]

After the bombing of a golf-club bar in King William's Town and a restaurant in Queenstown by the Azanian People's Liberation Army (APLA), and in the wake of a declaration of war against all whites by APLA, Hani issued a statement on behalf of the SACP (7 December

---

1. For an insight into the motives and actions of Zondo consult Fatima Meer, *The Trial of Andrew Zondo: A Sociological Insight* (Johannesburg: Skotaville Press, 1987).

1992). It was described by the *Cape Times* (which did not print the statement) as the strongest of all condemnations to have been made of the incidents. It reads:

> . . . I would like to express an unambiguous condemnation of the recent acts of terror in King William's Town and Queenstown.
>
> The struggle for national liberation has never been a struggle directed against whites simply because they are white. It is a struggle against a system of·oppression, it is a struggle against apartheid. The SACP and the broader ANC-led alliance have always been absolutely consistent about this.
>
> We are mobilising our people for democratic elections that will mark a major step towards dismantling the apartheid state. Acts of anti-white terror can only serve to provide pretexts to those on the other side who want to provide a race war to delay majority rule.

## Detention Camps

Having sought to stress the ethical ingredient of the armed struggle, Hani emphasises that the ANC has not been without moral fault. He raises the issue of the internment camps. "I am not for one moment suggesting that we have been ethically above reproach. There have been injustices and wrongful deeds committed in our name. The detention and torture camps are among them.[2] I have been a vocal and persistent critic of such action, as have several other members of the National Executive of the ANC. We have repeatedly argued that we could not morally demand that the regime release our political prisoners while we continued to detain people without trial." Insisting that the behaviour of the ANC at the same time be placed in its correct context, he continues:

> Our people were targets of assassination, our people were being poisoned, our camps were being destabilised by agents of the South African regime and there was an urgent need for us to get to the bottom of this. There were spies and government agents working among us. We at the same time recognised that in any movement or government, the security forces should be given clear political directives and that they obey these directives.
>
> Things came to a head after the 1984 mutiny, after some of our cadres began to question what they were doing fighting in Angola, rather than being allowed to take the fight into South African territory. . . I was initially in favour of dialogue with the

2. See *Work in Progress*, No 82, June, 1992. Also *Monitor*, December 1990. Interviews with Hani appearing in these publications have been drawn on to supplement my own interview.

mutineers. But I reached the end of my tether when they killed several key commanders in one of our camps called Bango, taking control of the camp. We had no alternative but to recapture the camp and assert authority. Lives were lost on both sides in the process. This was very sad because the rebels, like us, were members of the ANC, fellow South Africans, fighting for the same cause. At this point I withdrew and was not a member of the tribunal set up to try the mutineers. The outcome was the decision to execute 18 or 19 people. I rushed back to Lusaka and asked the leadership to stop the executions... The leadership, in all fairness, intervened but by that time comrades had already been executed.

Insisting that he has never in his life supported executions or capital punishment, Hani states: "I am a soldier. I think we must fight, but once an enemy is defeated, I've never believed that you execute them. Do something else, punish them, but do not kill them. They're already defeated, at your mercy, if you like."

Referring to security force agents responsible for acts of terror and violence against him and others in Lesotho, he continues: "Some people find it difficult to accept that I should be ready to forgive people who have been guilty of the most heinous crimes against us. On one occasion, we captured a fellow who had led a raid against us. I had no personal grudge against him and understood why he was working against us. He was trying to save himself. Had he refused to obey orders he would probably have been killed. His commanders were ruthless. He eventually came to realise the folly of his ways, and he has been released by our people. I still maintain contact with him. I feel very passionate about justice in our ranks and in a future South Africa. We simply must build a more humane and caring society."

Hani spoke of the complexities involved in building a new police force and army out of the existing security and military operations of the government, the ANC, the PAC and other armies in the country. "A new democratic state will have to sit down and draw up a code of conduct for a security force worthy of a democratic South Africa. I'm not convinced that those who served the National Party government in a brutal manner would be the best sort of people to continue the role of serving a democratic country. Within the ANC there are also certain people whom I would oppose as part of a new security force." He further insists that it is the responsibility of ANC leadership to ensure that all outstanding allegations of torture and abuse are fully investigated. "We need to know so that we can build a new society on the basis of justice. Never again in this country should we give unchecked powers to the security forces. We must ensure that the sort

126

of thing that happened to a limited extent in the ANC and extensively within the security forces of the regime is eliminated from a future democratic South Africa."

## Marginalised Soldiers

Speaking of the calling of the Church to care for the poor and marginalised in society, Hani sees returning soldiers as being in need of special attention. "All concerned citizens should be particularly concerned about the plight of those who are returning home to virtually nothing. The discontent, unhappiness and sense of rejection being experienced by many within the ranks of the Umkhonto we Sizwe is a matter that ought to concern all of us. A future society will pay the price of this discontent in the long run if nothing is done about it." Hani describes the milieu within the ranks of returned exiles and soldiers:

> Exiles and soldiers who had expected to return home as conquering heroes are standing in the unemployment lines. We have limited time on our hands to redress this situation and must ensure that a democratic South Africa does not forget, or marginalise, those men and women who sacrificed everything in order to fight against apartheid and bring about democracy. Many are without education and without the kinds of skills necessary to earn a living. Unless we face up to the fact that we are in a post-war period of reconstruction, in which we are obliged to provide facilities and incentives to demobilised soldiers, we are in trouble. An increasing number of people will become quite cynical about government and society as a whole. This will be an explosive situation, likely to lead to open rebellion.
>
> The present government is unlikely to do anything about this. They see this discontent as working in their favour, as an option for destabilising the ANC. In so doing they are cynically playing politics not only with the lives of these people but with the future state of the country. An interim government will be forced to deal with this matter and a future government can only fail to do so at its own peril.

Concerned to mobilise every sector of civil society in this exercise, Hani returns to the Church. "The task of the Church is to care for people, to empower the powerless and draw those who are rejected and marginalised into mainstream society. There is a huge pastoral task awaiting the Churches. The state will need to devise ways of enabling and facilitating the Churches and other religious organisations to do so. We need a massive co-operative exercise which mobilises people across the nation to fight poverty and empower people — both civilians and returning soldiers."

## The SACP

I observe that we have spoken at length about many things, but little about the SACP. As General Secretary of the SACP, how does Hani see its standing in the country and what is its future role?

> There is deep emotional support for the SACP among rank and file South Africans. At any rally anywhere in the country the Red Flag in treated with respect and the Party is greeted with thunderous applause. The residual memory of Party involvement, since the beginning of this century, in workers' struggles, in the promotion of women's rights and in the advancement of non-racism, is a reality which all the government propaganda against us has never been able to destroy. At this level the record of the Party is more impressive than that of the ANC, the Church, the Mosque or anyone else. . . The task of the SACP is to mobilise workers and others committed to rights of workers and the oppressed, drawing them into the ANC-led alliance, ensuring that where decisions are made at present, or in a future government, the concerns of the marginalised are addressed. This, I regard as a major contribution to nation-building.

Hani further regards the sense of commitment which communists bring to their task as a national asset. "Communists have in the past made a major contribution to the growth and consolidation of the ANC, and they continue to do so. This worries certain people, who suggest that the ANC is too much under the influence of the SACP. Now, first let me say that any suggestion that we either want to, or are able to, subvert the ANC is total nonsense — our commitment is to serve the ANC-led alliance and to serve the poor, it is not to gain power. The prominence of communists in this alliance is entirely due to the level of hard work and dedication which we bring to any task to which we commit ourselves. We expect a high level of discipline from our members, reminding ourselves that a commitment involves example not mere talk."

Hani clearly sees no need for the SACP to distance itself from the ANC neither to facilitate the election of the ANC to government nor to serve its own ends. "The majority of voters will not be swayed by anti-communist propaganda. Party members, in turn, recognise that their task is to promote an ANC government. Our active membership in the country is growing but is not based on mass in the sense of signing up members for the sake of swelling our numbers. There is an important sense in which we are a vanguard party, promoting ideas, values and programmes in the broader community. The ANC is a mass-based organisation. The two organisations serve one another. At the same time I believe that after the election of a new democratic government which will be subject to the demands of the people, the majority of whom are poor and marginalised, the significance of the SACP as a vehicle through which the voices of the workers and the poor are heard will grow in popularity. The ANC is a multi-class, multi-constituency movement. This is necessary and the way it must be. The Party has a more specific constituency. We are serving the democratic cause as a whole by ensuring that the concerns of our constituency are promoted in the best and most vigorous way possible, fully recognising that not everyone will either agree with us or have reason to support us."

## Religion Revisited

Lamenting the anti-religious mind-set that has prevailed in dominant communist ideology as well as the anti-communist hysteria in religious organisations, Hani argues: "One of us has got to cross the Rubicon. We need to cross it together. There is much we can learn from one another and there are certain obvious ethical values that bind us together. There is much in contemporary theological thinking that makes a lot of sense to me and Marxist thinking leaves space for religious praxis. I really believe that we are in some ways natural allies. We need to explore areas where we can co-operate and openly debate our differences."

Hani enjoys speaking about his early fascination with religion. "I left my religious home for reasons that I continue to think have been valid. The Church failed to live up to its own theology. My task was not to try and reform the Church. If I thought it was, I would presumably have been a priest. It was rather to share in the struggle of our people for the very dignity of which the Bible speaks. I have travelled a long way since then, but recognise the need to revisit that home. As I see it there is no proof for the existence of God, but I accept that the debate is not closed. I certainly could not be a priest today. I am an atheist. But I see religion as a philosophy, like other secular or materialist philosophies, engaged in the important task of grappling with and seeking to unveil the mysteries of the universe. Perhaps I understand religion better than I did when I was most at home within it. Religion has a contribution to make to the building of a greater and better society."

129

PHOTO ACKNOWLEDGEMENT: Mayibuye Centre, UWC and *Father Huddleston's Picture Book* (Kliptown Books)

# TREVOR HUDDLESTON

*Makhalipile — The Dauntless One*

I meet Archbishop Trevor Huddleston at
Bishopscourt during his first visit to South Africa
since being recalled to England by his Church in
1956. The interview ends with an ageing
Huddleston, cane in hand and purple vestock,
nostalgically reflecting on the portraits of the former
Archbishops of Cape Town hanging in the
drawingroom.

Among the portraits is one of Geoffrey Clayton, Archbishop of Cape Town from 1949 to 1957. "I had my differences with that old man," he observes, pointing upward over his shoulder.

The Church's engagement in the fight against apartheid is almost synonymous with the life and work of Trevor Huddleston. Often referred to with a measure of pride by Christians wanting to promote the image of the Church as an agent of struggle, the image is both institutionally strained and yet theologically correct.

Huddleston ascended the rungs of the ecclesial ladder to become Archbishop of the Indian Ocean, which located him in Mauritius. "Nothing humble about the Church," quips Huddleston. "Like Britannia, it aspires to rule the waves!" Yet, despite his clerical status, Huddleston still regards himself as standing *outside* the Church establishment. "I am somewhat strangely Anglican; I actually hate the establishment of the Church with a passion. . . My theology at the same time tells me that what I stand for is what the Church is supposed to be." Years earlier, at the height of the resistance to the forced removals in Sophiatown, he observed: "The hardest thing (in life) is . . . to stand by the principle to the end — and having done all, to stand." Reminded of these words which he penned in *Naught for Your Comfort* twenty-five years earlier, he smiles. "I now have a stick but I am still standing. There were times when it seemed as though that was all that was possible for anyone to do."

Perhaps the most prominent member of the Anti-Apartheid Movement anywhere in the world, Huddleston of course did more than 'stand'. He acted. He did so with determination and expectation, in the belief that obstacles are there to be overcome. "I have always maintained that apartheid would be dead long before me. I am now very near the end of my life, so the South African government, the ANC and everyone else concerned better get on with it so that my prophecy can be fulfilled. All I need is another two or three years. If the Almighty denies me this time I shall certainly have a word to say to Him." He smiles: "I still find it difficult not to think of God as a 'Him'. I shall have to work at it."

## Learning to Love and to Hate

Huddleston speaks, with deep affection, of the relationships he forged with the people of Sophiatown during the seven years in which he ministered there:

132

In addition to my responsibilities as a priest, I was expected to trace husbands, wives, brothers, sisters and other family members who were arrested because of violations of the pass laws and other pieces of apartheid legislation. Many were, in turn, caught up in petty crime, gangsterism and alcoholism. My mission was to rescue people, knowing that each one of them is a child of God — filled with enduring vitality and infinite gifts. The gospel is about directing and sometimes redirecting these resources in a creative and responsible manner.

I was awakened to the plight of black people in South Africa. They lived with danger every hour of the day and every day of the week. I came to recognise apartheid as an intolerable evil. I saw it as a crime against humanity, an evil, a demonic power which violated the image of God in people. In this sense it is a blasphemy, needing to be eradicated at almost any cost.

My time in Sophiatown taught me what it meant to love and to hate. The problem is that some Christians seem to think that in order to be spiritual they need to eliminate passion from their lives. People need to know what it is to love and to hate, to show pity and to weep, to laugh and to triumph. The tragedy is that by withdrawing from the rough and tumble of life where passion flows, the Church has been unable to teach its followers to be passionately human.

The people of Sophiatown called him Makhalipile, which means the dauntless one. Fearless in his stand against the wrath of the state, his willingness to risk himself in parts of Sophiatown where few felt entirely safe won the respect of virtually everyone. "Father Huddleston walked alone at all hours of the night where few of us were prepared to go," Nelson Mandela told me when I spoke with him about Sophiatown. "His (Huddleston's) fearlessness won him the support of everyone. No one, neither gangster, tsotsi nor pick-pocket would touch him. Their respect for him was such that they would not have tried — and if they did it could have cost them their lives. His enormous courage gave him a quality that commanded the respect of the place."

Was Huddleston a 'political priest'? "Yes, I suppose I was in the sense that soon after my arrival in South Africa I came to realise the extent to which institutionalised racism or apartheid is incompatible with the gospel. My calling was, however, pastoral. My commitment was to care for the souls and lives of my people. The fact that this placed me at loggerheads with the government said as much about their system as the gospel I preached."

The fact that the institutional Church was reluctant to provide him with the kind of support he had hoped for, elicited his wrath and despair at times. This led to open clashes between him and other clergy; not least with Archbishop Geoffrey Clayton, who regarded Huddleston's views and actions, especially in relation to the Bantu Education Act, as excessive. Huddleston's views have not changed.

> I am still convinced that the Bantu Education Act was the most iniquitous of all apartheid laws. It sought systematically to destroy the potential and therefore the image of God in innocent children. I still believe that if only the Churches had dug their heels in and spoken with a single voice the horrors of Bantu Education could have been curtailed. Instead, there was a whispering within the Church against those of us who opposed the bill. This convinced the authorities that the Church would capitulate. They were right.

For him the witness of the Church sank to an all time low when a banning order, under the Suppression of Communism Act, was served on Oliver Tambo, a graduate of St Peter's College and a faithful worshipper at the Church of Christ the King in Sophiatown. "The Church's silence, indifference and submission were deafening," recalls Huddleston. His words, published in the *Observer* under the rubric "The Church Sleeps On", have haunted the Church ever since. In the article he quoted G. K. Chesterton's "The Ballad of the White Horse":

> I tell you naught for your comfort
> Yea, naught for your desire,
> Save that the sky grows darker yet
> And the sea rises higher

"The Church sleeps on," he wrote. "The Church sleeps on — though it occasionally talks in its sleep and expects (or does it?) the government to listen." Huddleston recalls that Clayton was very angry. "He disapproved of my outspokenness, believing that my antics were making white South Africans ever more intransigent."

Probing the character of the imperious Archbishop and his relationship with this troublesome priest, Alan Paton suggests that Clayton did not really trust anyone's wisdom except his own. The Church was for him the creation of Christ, and he would have preferred Huddleston to limit his criticisms to people who failed to live up to his expectations. "In one particular sense," Paton explains, "Clayton

134

*was* the Church." He took Huddleston's criticisms personally. Distrust eventually became incompatibility. "What Clayton thought of the young prior," writes Paton, "apart from the recognition of his energy and devotion, is one of the secrets of the grave. It is improbable that he would have taken him as a holiday companion. As Huddleston became more and more of a public figure, and more and more the subject of public controversy, Clayton began to withdraw from him."[1]

Recalling those days, Huddleston states: "The Church which I was involved in at the time quite frankly lacked passion. It was too cautious, too discreet and too moderate." Correcting himself, he puts his case differently: "It was the leadership of the Church, which was invariably removed from the squalor of black township suffering and rural starvation, that was too cautious, too uninvolved and too passive." Asked how, given his convictions, he managed to survive and even prosper within the leadership circles of the Church, he responds: "By prayer. By clinging to a vision of what the New Testament requires the Church to be. By mixing with the poor who in their suffering instinctively understand the message of the poor man Jesus. If, on the other hand, I were to have taken the social reality of the institutional Church too seriously, I would have become a total cynic."

Huddleston is visiting Bishopscourt for the first time in more than thirty years. What is his view of the Church today? "Oh, things have changed. During my time in Sophiatown no-one had heard of liberation theology. The Church hierarchy was white. The voice of Africans was scarcely heard within the Church. So, while the Church is still not what it is required to be, neither is it what it once was . . . Desmond (Tutu), Frank Chikane and others have done a great deal to sensitise the Church to the contextual demands of the gospel."

Convinced that it is important to take sides in the struggle for a democratic South Africa, he stresses the need for the Church to learn again what it means to love the poor and to hate material greed. "The Church is simply too moderate and lukewarm. There is not enough fire in the belly."

Our conversation turns to the theological legitimacy of armed struggle.

---

1. Alan Paton, *Apartheid and the Archbishop: The Life and Times of Geoffrey Clayton* (Cape Town: David Philip, 1973), pp.121, 143, p.242.

The Church has never had too many problems with armed struggle. Just War theology is a tried and tested part of our tradition. Christians have through the centuries gone to war against the aggressor. Our churches are overflowing with monuments and flags mourning the death of soldiers and celebrating military victory. . . As far as I am concerned there is more or less an open and shut case for interpreting the eventual resort to armed struggle by the ANC as an act of just war or rebellion. . . There is nothing wrong with pacifism. My problem is those who condemn the oppressed masses who rise in rebellion, while condoning the violence of the system by their silence. The irony is that many of those who have shouted loudest against Umkhonto we Sizwe, have also opposed economic sanctions and other non-violent attempts to bring the tyrant to book. . . Christians are obliged to condemn defensive violence and armed struggle as a last resort against the oppressor less harshly than they condemn indifference to those who suffer; if only because the latter can never be an expression of love.

## A Socialist and a Christian

Born into a privileged and religious home in Bedford, England in 1913, his education at Christ Church, Oxford coincided with the great depression of the 1930s. "It was here, from my position of privilege, that I observed the marches of people in and around Oxford demanding food." Attending the Anglo-Catholic Summer School of Sociology where he was required to wrestle intellectually with the relationship between theology and socialism, he became convinced that the New Testament story of Jesus and the fundamental principles of socialism were somehow related. "The School was thoroughly Anglo-Catholic in its ethos, while totally committed to social issues in the wider sense." Attracting a range of distinguished scholars, the school was for Huddleston "the socialist womb that gave me birth". Here he met the famous communist priest Conrad Noel who "hauled up the Red flag every All Saints' Day," recalls Huddleston. A devout high Anglo-Catholic churchman, Noel was firmly committed to the working-class movement. He introduced Huddleston to the writings of Marx and Engels, encouraged him to read the fathers of the Church and taught him to inwardly digest the Christian socialism of Charles Gore (a founder member of the Community of the Resurrection which Huddleston would later join). "I was like a babe in the woods, required to make sense of complex economic and political theory on the one hand and erudite Christian doctrine on the other. . . Conrad

136

Noel helped me put the two together. For me, Christianity and socialism have ever since gone together — forming a unity which makes sense in a manner that does not make sense when considered apart. Socialism provides an economic programme, the gospel empowers, and together they constitute a vision. I am convinced that to be a Christian is to be a socialist, and I like to tell my socialist friends it will do their souls good to read the New Testament story of Jesus." In 1939 Huddleston entered the Community of the Resurrection. It was here that he discovered a disciplined spirituality that has remained essential to him. "It is the engine that drives my life."

## Spirituality

In an essay entitled "Huddleston: A Sign", Nadine Gordimer tells of a photograph which hangs above her work desk. The photograph was taken by David Goldblatt at a Newclare squatter camp in Johannesburg in 1952:

> It is a night scene, lit only by a tin brazier. The light from lozenges of incandestine coal brings forward out of the dark a pair of gaunt, tightly-clasped hands, the long fingers tautly interlaced, making a great double fist. They are the hands of a white man. Above them there is darkness again, until the furthermost reach of light leaps on the bright white clerical collar, and, more softly, brings from oblivion the three-quarter face. There is a pointed ear standing alertly away from the head and lean jaw, and the tendon from behind the ear down the neck is prominent and tense. The ear is cocked intently and the eyes are concentrated.
>
> The man is the young Father Huddleston. He is listening to and looking at someone you can't make out. . . But the man, the black man, is there; he is there in the extraordinary, still, self-excluding attention of the young priest. . .
>
> I have no religious faith, but when I look at that photograph of a profoundly religious man, I see godliness in a way I can understand deeply, I see a man in whom prayer functions, in Simone Weil's definition as a special form of intelligent concentration.[2]

A deeply devotional person — almost mystical at times, Huddleston's

---

2. " . . . prayer consists of attention. . . Not only does the love of God have attention for its substance; the love of our neighbour, which we know to be the same love, is made of this same substance. . . The capacity to give one's attention to a sufferer is a very rare and difficult thing; it is almost a miracle; it is a miracle. . . Warmth of heart . . . pity, are not enough." Simone Weil, *Waiting for Godot.* In Nadine Gordimer, "Huddleston: A Sign," *Trevor Huddleston: Essays On His Life and Work,* edited by Deborah Duncan Honore (Oxford: Oxford University Press, 1988), pp.5—6.

spirituality is directly related to his engagement in life. "For me not to pray is to take life less than seriously. It is to be superficial and shallow. In prayer and devotion I concentrate my mind on the problem before me. In so doing I seek to discern the presence of God and understand the will of God in relation to my engagement in life. To neglect prayer is for me irresponsible; it is to cut myself off from that energy which enables me to engage life. Prayer is the pith and marrow of my existence." In accordance with his vows, Huddleston celebrates the Eucharist daily, meditates and prays four times a day — in the morning, at midday, in the early evening and before retiring for the night. "Although not legalistic regarding specific times, I have not often failed to honour this discipline. I feel totally ill at ease if I neglect my devotions."

> Doctrinally I am a fairly conventional Anglo-Catholic. I regard the doctrines of creation and the incarnation as central to all that I believe. In essence I believe this is God's world. The more I think about it, the more am I convinced that there are natural and moral principles that hold the world and humankind together. Either we learn to conform to these principles, which in sum require us to live in mutual respect and concern for one another and the natural environment, or we will destroy one another and the world in which we live. The choice is ours. Through the incarnation God has, in turn, endowed all of humankind with divine dignity and infinite value. This means that everyone — however wretched, despised or rejected is of infinite value. This is the marvellous contribution which religion makes to the human rights struggle. It is to boldly declare, that any attempt to marginalise people, reducing them to an underclass status or regarding them as expendable in the interest of some or other ultimate cause, whether Verwoerd's apartheid or Stalin's brand of state socialism, is tantamount to blasphemy. To subordinate people is to subordinate God.

In brief, Huddleston's spirituality is a people-oriented spirituality. It emerges out of his understanding of the ministry of Jesus, which focuses his attention on people. "It's all very simple really. My spirituality is grounded in the New Testament teaching which tells us that it is not possible to love God without loving people, and the example of Jesus shows us that we must begin by loving those who are most in need of love and human dignity. Prayer is a meditation on the meaning of love and what it requires of each of us in a given situation. It is to empower us to go and do what needs to be done. It is also to receive forgiveness and to try again when we fail to do the loving thing."

138

Huddleston is slightly ambivalent about institutional worship. He regards formal worship and the liturgy of the Church as an important ingredient of his spiritual life. "I cannot see how people can live without the liturgy," he argues. "Yet even after I became an archbishop I was unable to regard this as the sum total of fulfilling my vocation. There is more to the Christian life than 'going to church'. If worship does not drive us into the world to heal the sick and liberate the oppressed it is sheer escapism. The Church is called to be an instrument of God's creative and redemptive work in the world. If it ceases to be this, becoming preoccupied with doctrine, Church order and the niceties of worship alone then, as Father Michael Scott (a fellow priest, declared a prohibited immigrant in 1950) used to like to remind us, 'the salt would have lost its savour and be fit only for the dung heap'."

## From Mirfield to Sophiatown

Huddleston has perhaps always had a bent in favour of the working-class and the poor — taking on himself a lifestyle of simplicity and poverty. "Like Jeremiah, this is more or less how I came out of my mother's womb."

During his university vacations, while at Oxford, he worked with the hop-pickers in Kent. He spent time with the under-castes of Hindu society in India and Ceylon (Sri Lanka) and, after ordination to the priesthood in 1937, he worked as a curate in the working-class area of Swindon in Kent. Here he met and "immensely liked the railwaymen of England". In 1939 he joined the Community of the Resurrection, with the mother house being moved from Pusey in Oxford to Mirfield in the industrial North of England, in order to be in closer proximity to the poor. Founded to reproduce the life of the early Church as recorded in the Acts of the Apostles, it required the vows of poverty, chastity and obedience. "To talk of these vows in terms of 'calling' and 'vocation' misses two very important ingredients of what they entail. The one is *freedom*. The freedom to take hold of life and do something about it. It is to seize the moment. The other is *perseverance*. It is to persevere in the work of living and not give up. It is to refuse to either grow complacent or to capitulate before the enormity of the task before one. It is to hang in there."

In 1943 Robert Raynes arrived as the new superior of the Community of the Resurrection in Mirfield, having served for several years in Sophiatown. One of his first tasks was to appoint Huddleston to his former parish. "It was wartime you know. The convoy in which I was travelling was bombed off Portugal. All very exciting!" Arriving at his parish located in an exposed and exploited black township outside of Johannesburg, Huddleston saw within it something which, "only those who knew and understood its complexity could ever understand, let alone love". Speaking of the human suffering involved in the destruction of Sophiatown, he continues: "It was torn to the ground and its people resettled in what is today Soweto, to make way for the white suburb of Triomf (Afrikaans for Triumph) — that disgusting expression of satisfaction at having destroyed the homes of African people. I recall reciting to myself a line from one of Robert Brooke's poems: 'Something which cannot be built again so easily or so fair'."

Huddleston knew the dark side of Sophiatown. "It was a place where human suffering, iniquity and gangsterism abounded." Thinking for a while, he continues:

> You need to understand, for me there was a certain ecstasy in the agony of Sophiatown. I loved that place more than any other in my life. When Sophiatown was obliterated South Africa lost more than a place, it lost an idea. Sophiatown was a remarkable community of people who amidst the chaos of suffering thrust on them by racism and greed, had learned what it meant to triumph over the most adverse odds. Given the freedom, the resources and the opportunity, Sophiatown could have built on the goodwill and creativity that characterised so many of its people, to make a lasting contribution to a better South Africa. By destroying Sophiatown the sense of community which was its characterising mark was destroyed. People's initiative was killed and their hopes shattered. As a consequence social problems multiplied, while the wisdom and hidden beauty of the place was undermined. What held Sophiatown together was the belief that people, however poor and exploited they may be, have the right to live where they like, to build themselves a home, to be themselves and to sustain one another. Take that away and you have social chaos. . . Think of the musicians, poets, artists, writers and the like that came out of Sophiatown. In killing that place the government killed a certain creativity, an African idea of what it means to be human. . . Yet, thank God, such ideas can never be totally extinguished. Such ideas need to be raised from the ashes of the many Sophiatowns of this country, because these are the ideas that we may yet need to put the country back together again.

Huddleston's ministry in Sophiatown ended in 1956, a year after he was given the *Isitwalandwe* award (the ANC's highest honour) at the Congress of the People — the only white person ever to have received

140

this distinction. The reason his Church recalled him has never been clear. Speculation abounded and some still wonder exactly who was behind the decision. "All I wish to say is that this decision was the most demanding test of my vow of obedience I have ever been asked to face," Huddleston observes as he looks back on those tumultuous days. The government was delighted to see him go. The people of Sophiatown, mourned his departure. The Bishop of Johannesburg, Ambrose Reeves (who was himself expelled in 1960 for his role in exposing the Sharpeville massacre) and a small group of priests and friends, including parishioners who could get time off work, were at the airport to bid him farewell. "I stood at the entrance to the plane and waved my farewell. I thought my very reason for existence was being taken from me. . . I had come to South Africa and in a short while the cause of the victims of apartheid had become the all consuming passion of my life. 'Was there anything else worth living for?' I asked myself."

Huddleston personifies the outrage which every decent human being ought to experience when confronted with the realities of apartheid. The tragedy is that too many whites have protected themselves from this reality, while others regard it as beyond their dignity to act with too much outrage.

## A New Task

Huddleston, the dauntless one, soon found there was every reason to exist. The opening scene of this new phase of his life was the publication of *Naught for Your Comfort* shortly after his return to Britain. It was a desperate and enduring cry to the world to heed the extent of the apartheid monster; a book that today still reads as one of the most moving personal testimonies to the iniquities that marked a period of South African history that must never be forgotten. Together with Julius Nyerere, Huddleston was the main speaker at the launch of the Boycott Movement (later to be known as the Anti-Apartheid Movement) within months of his return. He threw himself into the work of the movement. Almost forty years later, he looks back, observing: "I had the honour of being the first to propose a cultural boycott, cultural sanctions, and I did that as long ago as 1955. I only hope that the lifting of those sanctions is not premature." Among the most formidable advocates of economic sanctions and the armed struggle, he tirelessly gave new expression to the cause for which he had fought during his years in South Africa.

After spending time as the Master of Novices in the Order of the

Resurrection, he was appointed Bishop of Masasi in Tanganyika (Tanzania) in 1960, sharing in Nyerere's vision to provide for the needs of the poor through his *Ujamaa* programme. In 1968 Huddleston returned to England as Suffragan Bishop of Stepney in the East End of London where he came face to face with a different kind of racism — against Asian immigrants. In 1978 he was elected Archbishop of the Indian Ocean.

## Returning Home

"South Africa is in a very real sense home to me. It was suggested to me that I be buried in Sophiatown. I only hope nobody objects to restoring that honoured name to the place. Provided they do that, to be buried there is quite appealing."

"My night on the flight home contained little sleep. I saw the African sun rise and I returned to my place of departure — unforgettable and unforgotten." Explaining that he did not often fail to begin his day without the Eucharist, he saw this particular day as different. "The love of God which I usually celebrated in the sacrament of Holy Communion, I this day experienced through the human communion of friendships restored. As I embraced Nelson (Mandela), Walter (Sisulu), Oliver (Tambo) and the others who were at the airport to meet me I discovered yet again the extent to which the love of God is radiated and communicated to us through people, through struggle and through the celebration of just victory. When I thought about this a little later I realised that I had indeed started my day with a Holy Communion. This celebration I shall never forget. Theology, liturgy and the sacraments are means of God's grace to us, but God's grace is never limited to such ecclesial things."

## Into the Future

How does he see the future in South Africa? What are his fears and for what does he hope? "I have seen, witnessed and shared in a range of experiences and events during these past weeks," he replies. "I have experienced hope and I have known despair. My visit has brought back memories and echoes from the past. It has also introduced new visions and forebodings. All this reverberates in my mind as my visit comes to a close."

> My fear is that the country could be engulfed in violence. The burden of past oppression, exploitation and apartheid divisions has sown fear, suspicion and anger. There are also forces at work which are ready to promote and exploit these realities. I fear petty

142

Bantustan leaders who owe their existence to apartheid; who are reluctant to surrender their power. There is the right-wing. There is also the question whether the National Party will ultimately settle for genuine democracy, bearing in mind that some of its leaders have in the past shown a capability for corruption that makes some of the worst black leaders of this continent look like paragons of virtue. De Klerk has no more than three years before a freely-elected, non-racial, non-sexist, democratic parliament must be in place. To delay beyond that could be too late.

When, on the other hand, I look at the progress we have made since I left South Africa in 1956 and the advances made since Nelson Mandela walked out of prison, then I have hope. Now, hope is not the same as optimism. Optimism is transitory, hope endures against all adversity. Theologically, hope is the sure and certain knowledge that this is God's world and that God's righteousness will prevail. . . We are looking for irreversible change, and international and internal pressure must continue until that happens. We are all both sinners and people made in the image of God. We are capable of doing both the wrong and the right thing. My theology and politics intersect at the point of devising a strategy to ensure that right triumphs over wrong to the extent that this is possible in this world. On balance I am mildly optimistic that within a few years there will be a democratically elected government in South Africa — if only because all the major players realise that it is in their own interest to settle now rather than later.

Asked if he had one last request to make of God what it would be, the two sides of Huddleston's character emerge yet again. "If I were to know that I were to die tonight and were given a personal request, it would be that I go to heaven, there to be united with God and the people I love. If it were a last request of God for South Africa, it would be for a Constitution that eliminates all forms of discrimination and takes care of the poor."

Huddleston returns to the role of the Church: "I have positively no doubt that God's first and foremost expectation of the Church is that it care for the poor and exploited. That is the basis of all that I read in the Bible. My most earnest and sincere prayer is that the Church will rise to this calling. Should it fail to do so it is likely to be thrust aside by history. God is quite capable of finding an alternative agency through which to work."

He recalls the ups and downs of his 79 years, observing: "You know, I actually become more radical every moment that I live."

PHOTO ACKNOWLEDGEMENT: Mayibuye Centre, UWC

# NELSON MANDELA

*Liberation Not Power*

"I have fought against white domination, and I have fought against black domination. I have cherished the ideal of a democratic and free society in which all persons live together in harmony and with equal opportunities.
It is an ideal which I hope to live for, and to see realised. . . If needs be, it is an ideal for which I am prepared to die."

Famous words. Words spoken by Nelson Mandela from the dock before being sentenced to life imprisonment in June 1964. Having already been in prison since November 1962, he would have a total of more than twenty-seven years imprisonment behind him when again he addressed the nation. A huge crowd gathered on the Grand Parade in Cape Town to celebrate his release on 11 February 1990. He used these same words, saying that they are as applicable today as they were in 1964.

His enemies robbed him of the best years of his life. They also failed in their mission. Mandela became the world's best known and most respected prisoner. Now free (although still without a vote in the land of his birth) he is devoid of all bitterness, introversion and despair.

## Religion

Mandela's imprisonment is a kind of religious symbol; it is a summary of his 'bottom-line' values, the things that he considers worth dying for. I am keen to discover what sustained him during those long years, enabling him to emerge from isolation with the gentleness, strength and continuing resolve that characterise his person. Having spoken for some time, the question of religion emerges. "The relationship between a person and his or her God is a deeply intimate and private matter. It is not a matter I usually regard as open for public discussion. . . There is a sense in which, for me, it is a matter beyond articulation. It is an experience I do not fully comprehend." Does he regard it as important to endeavour to comprehend this reality? "I think it is more important to live in accordance with one's deepest values and convictions, whether religious or otherwise, rather than to fully understand them. But yes, I suppose all of us try to some extent to make sense of what drives us."

As he is not ready to say much more about this understanding, I ask whether he thinks religious belief is an important ingredient of life. Is it important for his life? Does it contribute to the well-being of society?

> Yes, I certainly recognise the importance of the religious dimension of my own life. More important for me, however, is the significance of religion for countless numbers of people I meet both in South Africa and around the world. Religion is important because at the centre of the great religious traditions is the pursuit of peace. South Africa needs peace, the world needs peace and I

146

am convinced that if we were to put into practice the central tenets of Christianity, Judaism, African traditional religions, Buddhism, Hinduism, Islam and other faiths — all of which have a lot in common — there would be peace in the world. . . I have no problem with religious belief. My problem is that all too often people fail to act on what they claim to believe.

Religion is about mutual love and respect for one another and for life itself. It is about the dignity and equality of humankind made in the image of God. This is a God who, if I understand the Bible correctly, requires us to be engaged in the actual fight against evil, poverty, disease, illiteracy, the lack of housing and other social ills in society. I have enormous respect for religious people in our country who have been at the forefront of our struggle. They live their faith and I deeply respect the faith which they proclaim. I think of people like Michael Scott, Trevor Huddleston, Archbishop Tutu, Frank Chikane and many others.

Having spoken of the contribution of religious people to the history of the African National Congress — people like the Rev John Dube (first president of the ANC), Chief Albert Luthuli, Canon Calata, Z. K. Matthews and others — Mandela speaks of the ministry of chaplains he met on Robben Island. "Most of these men understood my convictions; some of them shared my values." He mentions Father Alan Hughes of the Anglican Church: "He was always willing to share pieces of information denied to us on the island. He helped us keep in touch with the wider community, locating his religious message within the broader context of life. His religion was an impressive spiritual understanding of life — never something separate from it." He remembers Rev André Schäfer of the NG Kerk in Afrika, "as being hostile towards us at first, but later becoming one of the best liked chaplains". Mandela was particularly intrigued with the historical and scientific information which Schäfer wove into his sermons. "I remember him telling us of astronomy confirming the appearance of a particularly bright star or cluster of stars in the heavens at the time of Christ's birth. . . The way in which he integrated natural phenomena and historical events with religious stories and ideas provoked numerous discussions among the prisoners in our block." Mandela speaks too of Theo Kotze, who was a Methodist chaplain for a while. "The government regarded him as being too political, and he was prevented from visiting the island." Mandela emphasises the ecumenical approach of the chaplains who came from different denominations of the Christian Church and ministered to all "without ever asking who belonged to what Church

147

or religion. I never missed a service and often read the scripture lessons. . . Come to think of it, I was quite religious". Equally important for him were the religious services provided by other faiths: "I particularly enjoyed the visits of Imam Abdurahman Bassier with whom I had long conversations, remembering that it was Maulvi Cachalia who first outlined to me the basic tenets of Islam many years earlier. It was an enriching experience for me to gain a deeper knowledge of a religion other than my own." He knew of the existence of a kramat on the island, said to be that of Tuan (or Sheikh) Mantura. "The religious convictions of people like the Sheikh move me quite deeply. It was his faith that drove him to resist Dutch imperialist designs in South-East Asia, for which he was exiled and imprisoned on Robben Island in the mid-1700s. That kind of religion must be taken seriously." Mandela wrote to Sheikh Omar Gabier in March 1985 of his visit to Sheikh Mantura's tomb: "I literally harassed the commanding officer of the prison for permission to visit the kramat. Permission was finally granted only in 1977. That was a day which I will not easily forget. Symbols and monuments, especially those which represent great movements or national heroes, can move one beyond words. My fellow prisoners and I spent more than an hour at the shrine and came away feeling proud and happy that we were able to pay our respects to so great a fighter for justice."

After being moved to Pollsmoor Prison Mandela missed the variety of worship to which he had become accustomed. At Pollsmoor, prisoners were only allowed visits by representatives of the specific Church or religion to which they belonged. "This was a source of great disappointment to me. It turned out, however, that it was also an occasion for me to develop a friendship of great importance with Rev Dudley Moore, the Methodist chaplain. He visited me on a frequent basis and I received Holy Communion from him regularly. To share the sacrament as part of the tradition of my Church was important for me. It gave me a sense of inner quiet and calm. I used to come away from these services feeling a new man."

Would he then regard himself as a religious person? "No, I am not particularly religious or spiritual. Let's say I am interested in all attempts to discover the meaning and purpose of life. Religion is an important part of this exercise." Does he believe in a God? "As I have said, the relationship between a person and God is personal. The question concerning the existence of God is something I reflect on in solitude."

I am about to change the subject when Mandela quotes a verse from the same poem (written by Tennyson) which Govan Mbeki quoted in an earlier interview. He too tells me that Alexander Kerr, the rector of Fort Hare University during their student days, often quoted these words:

> Strong Son of God, immortal love,
> Who we, who have not seen thy face
> By faith and faith alone embrace,
> Believing what we cannot prove.

I tell him that Govan Mbeki recalled these words in the same way, insisting that he is an atheist. "Oh, no!" he volunteers, "I am not an atheist. Definitely not."

## Prison

A lot happens at a personal level during twenty-seven years: there was the death of his aged mother Fanny Mandela in 1968; the death of his son Tembi a year later, the detention and torture of Winnie Mandela; her banning and banishment to Brandfort; news of an attempt on her life; the burning of his Soweto home and much more. There were decisions to be made and moments of joy in which he could not share directly: the education of children, the birth of grandchildren. "These are the things that made me most aware of isolation," he observes. "One of the greatest joys after my release was the privilege of closing the front door and sharing privately in the decisions which any family person is required to make. In some ways the violation of this right was the most painful part of my years in prison."

Mandela talks about prison: "Work on the island was very demanding, but it had its own sense of joy. The rock formations, the sea, the wind, the fresh air, and the bird life; that were part of the island, kept us going."

> You know, just to look at the sea and to consider its width and sometimes to test its depth along the edges of the island, insofar as we were allowed, was for me more than a physical experience. Isolated from society, I was able to become one with nature. I watched the tides come in and go out. There was the movement of ships. I considered the rock formations. I enjoyed the elements even when they were harsh, and I looked forward to the changing seasons. Nature came to be very important for me. It sustained, invigorated and inspired me.

Nature was important but so were people. He speaks of the deep personal bonds which he forged with others in prison, especially with other Rivonia trialists. He has a special appreciation for the discussions he had with Fikile Bam and Neville Alexander, who were members of the National Liberation Committee at the time. "Politically we differed but intellectually those fellows enriched me," he notes. He remembers working in the quarries and elsewhere on the island with fellow prisoners with whom he had no opportunity to meet in other circumstances. "We talked as we worked — those were tough but formative years which we spent together. Sometimes we became so engrossed in conversation that the guards regarded us as neglecting our work."

How does he feel about the guards and other prison authorities? "Of course there were some unpleasant characters, but also some essentially good people. . . I still keep in touch with some of the warders." It was on Robben Island that he first met Lieutenant James Gregory, of whom he speaks with respect, and Warrant Officer Swart, who was then an ordinary warder. Mandela again met up with Swart at Pollsmoor Prison and, when later he was sent to Victor Verster Prison, Swart was appointed to cook for him. "I enjoyed a most pleasant relationship with that fellow. He was without any racial or other prejudices. Just a good human being."

"We have got to learn to live together, to transcend our prejudices, to resolve our differences amicably, to respect one another and together to reach towards co-operation and attainable common goals. Those are some of the things that I learned in prison. I think religion, when it is taken seriously, can help us attain these goals."

## Leadership

Mandela speaks of his understanding of political leadership: "Leaders are important but history is ultimately not made by kings and generals. It is made by the masses — workers, peasants, doctors, professional people and the youth. If a leader ignores the masses he or she is ultimately compelled to resort to tyranny to remain in power. Leaders at the same time have an obligation to lead; they are required to move their people forward, from where they are at a given time, to where they are required to be. This what makes the relationship between leaders and the people so complex."

Mandela is a man of the people. His popularity as a leader is self-evident. He is also his own person. He refuses to reduce his vision and insights to those of his constituency — even if this would produce certain short-term political gains. We saw this in the United States when he refused to condemn the Arafat-Castro-Gadhafi trio, even when the liberal establishment courted and tried to seduce him into doing so. He has defended the Palestinian Liberation Organisation in the face of Zionist attacks, both at home and abroad. Having lured and courted the Muslim community in the historic Bo-Kaap during a visit to Cape Town in 1992, he shocked his audience by insisting that he recognised the right of the State of Israel to exist.

It is precisely this ability to withstand the manipulation of others that enabled Mandela to walk out of Victor Verster Prison with his head held high. He refused to succumb to the threats and rancour of the state. He is equally impervious to the charm of some of the most seductive lobbies.

## The School of Life

How does Mandela account for these values? "My values and my life have been shaped by the circumstances and the history that I have lived through. Like anyone else, I am a consequence of the rough and tumble of my context." Mandela's life has been an eventful, demanding and fearful one. And yet, he insists, "I consider myself extremely privileged to have lived through these times. Given the realities of history which cannot be wished away, I have few regrets. . . Although, I wish there had been less suffering and death for our people."

Mandela was born in the small village of Qunu in Transkei, into the Tembu royal family, on 18 July 1918, to Chief Henry Mgadla Mandela (chief councillor to the Paramount Chief of the Tembu) and his fourth wife, Nonqaphi Nosekeni. Although groomed to become a chief, he recalls his household chores, which included herding cattle and helping to plough his parents' fields. Above all he recalls with fascination the stories about the great leaders of his people. He told the court during his treason trial:

> In my youth in the Transkei, I listened to the elders of my tribe telling stories of the old days. Amongst the tales they related to me were those of wars fought by our ancestors in defence of the fatherland. The names of Dingane and Bambatha, Hintsa and Makana, Squngathi and Dalasile, Moshoeshoe and Sekukhuni, were praised as the pride and the glory of the entire African nation. I hoped then that life might offer me the opportunity to serve my people and make my own humble contribution to their

*151*

freedom struggle. This is what has motivated me in all that I have done in relation to the charges made against me in this case.

Whilst attending the local mission school, Mandela had been given history books which told different stories. These were the stories of white heroes and black people who were seen to be cattle thieves and trouble-makers. While questioning these stories at school, he had continued to hear stories of more recent events at home. He was told how in 1921 the police massacred 163 men, women and children who had gathered under the prophet Enoch Mgijima, refusing to leave the village of Ntabelanga near Bulhoek. He had further learned of planes being used to bomb the Bondelswarts people in the mandated territory of South West Africa (now Namibia) because they refused to pay a dog tax. These were events lodged in the memory of the young Mandela whose political awareness was beginning to be formed. By 1930 his father was an ill man. Realising he was dying, Mandela's father presented him to David Dalindyebo, the acting Paramount Chief of the Tembu, who took responsibility for the twelve year old boy's education and upbringing.

Having matriculated at the Healdtown Institute in Butterworth, Mandela studied at the University of Fort Hare but, after leading a student boycott of the SRC election in his third year, he was suspended. Returning home to Dalindyebo's Great Place, Mqekezweni, Mandela was told by the Paramount Chief to accept the college ultimatum and abandon the boycott so that he could complete his studies. Almost ready to obey and hoping to avoid an arranged tribal marriage, he fled to Johannesburg where he was employed as a mine policeman. He was traced by relatives, but he eventually managed to persuade his guardian that it would be better for him to remain in Johannesburg to study Law. He found a room in Alexandria (a sprawling black township on the north-east edge of Johannesburg), completed his BA degree through the University of South Africa and studied Law at the University of the Witwatersrand. He met and established a life-long friendship with Walter and Albertina Sisulu, and eventually opened the first black legal partnership in South Africa with Oliver Tambo.

Mandela became National Secretary of the ANC Youth League. In 1949 it took control of the ANC; which resulted in Dr A. B. Xuma being replaced as President by Dr James Moroka. Mandela was elected to the National Executive, became Youth League President in 1950 and in 1952 he became President of the ANC in the Transvaal and Volunteer-in-Chief in the Defiance Campaign. In the same year he was charged under the Suppression of Communism Act and given a nine-month suspended sentence, while being banned for six months from leaving the Johannesburg area. Thereafter a series of banning orders was imposed on him for the next nine years. Elected Deputy President of the ANC, he was prevented from attending gatherings. This resulted in most of his work being done with small groups of people and in a secret manner. He was involved in the planning of the 1955 Congress of the people in Kliptown and he attended the event in disguise. In 1956 he was arrested with 156 other political activists and charged with high treason. All were eventually found not guilty. In the wake of the Sharpeville massacre, on 21 March 1960, the ANC and the PAC were banned and on 16 December 1961 Umkhonto we Sizwe was formally launched, with Mandela as Commander-in-Chief. He illegally left the country to address the Pan African Freedom Conference in Addis Ababa, seeking to rally international support. Having returned to the country, he was dubbed the Black Pimpernel by the media as the police tried to hunt him down. Disguised as a chauffeur, driving his white 'boss' (in reality the dramatist Cecil Williams) from Durban to Johannesburg, he was arrested on Sunday 5 August 1962. On 7 November of the same year he was sentenced to five years imprisonment, for incitement to strike and leaving the country without a passport, and sent to Robben Island. In January 1963 the police raided Lilliesleaf in Rivonia, outside of Johannesburg, arresting the nucleus of the Umkhonto we Sizwe high command. In October Mandela was brought to trial together with Walter Sisulu, Govan Mbeki, Ahmed Kathrada, Rusty Bernstein, Dennis Goldberg, James Kantor, Andrew Mlangeni, Elias Motsoaledi and Raymond Mhlaba. They were charged with sabotage and attempting to violently overthrow the state.

Admitting to involvement in sabotage and making plans for guerilla activity, Mandela told the court:

> I admit immediately that I was one of the persons who helped to form Umkhonto we Sizwe, and that I played a prominent role in its affairs until I was arrested in August 1962 . . .

> We felt that without sabotage there would be no way open to the African people to succeed in their struggle against the principle of white supremacy. All lawful modes of expressing opposition to this principle had been closed by legislation and we were placed in a position in which we had either to accept a permanent state of inferiority, or defy the government. We chose to defy the law. We first broke the law in a way which avoided any recourse to

violence; when this form was legislated against, and when the government restorted to a show of force to crush opposition to its policies, only then did we decide to answer violence with violence.

In June 1964 Mandela and the other accused (with the exception of Rusty Bernstein who was discharged) were found guilty of sabotage and sentenced to life imprisonment. Dennis Goldberg (the only white among them) was held in Pretoria and the others were flown to Robben Island. Mandela was eventually moved to Pollsmoor Prison and then to Victor Verster Prison after being treated for tuberculosis in the Tygerberg Hospital and the Constantia Clinic in 1988. He was released from prison on 11 February 1992.

## Armed Struggle

"The time comes in the life of any nation when there remain only two choices — submit or fight." Words included in a statement released on 16 December 1961 when the first explosions were detonated by Umkhonto we Sizwe. "The decision was extremely painful to me," Mandela recalls. "I had realised for some time that the need to resort to arms may well be forced on us. I was particularly fearful that events which ultimately led to the Sharpeville massacre could be the turning point. We had planned an anti-pass campaign which we wanted to be as non-violent as possible. I was at the same time fearful that some people were courting martyrdom. The PAC did not support our plans. Be that as it may, the events that followed revealed the government for what it was in all its naked brutality."

The acts of sabotage and terror that followed, disturbed Mandela. The first sabotage explosion occurred on 18 October 1961; it was the work of the National Liberation Committee, which later called itself the Armed Resistance Movement, made up largely of radical whites drawn from the Liberal Party. The PAC's Poqo, which adopted a strategy explicitly designed to kill whites and collaborators, was inspired by a vision of a spontaneous mass uprising — believing this could be sparked by the heroic actions of a few cadres. Mandela was extremely critical of their activities. "I believed Poqo lacked organisation and discipline. Its reckless promotion of violence, if it succeeded, could have engulfed the country in flames." A further group, the Yu Chi Chan, with roots in the Non-European Unity Movement, also focused on sabotage.

In this contect Umkhonto we Sizwe's first explosions were set off simultaneously in Port Elizabeth, Johannesburg and Durban.

154

We planned our focused acts of sabotage in the hope that they would force the government to face the gravity of the situation and negotiate a settlement. It was an attempt to prevent civil war.

We were concerned to control and discipline the armed rebellion in the country. We wanted to minimise the loss of life. We wanted to limit the possibility of blacks and whites killing one another in a bitter racially-based civil war. That would have further violated the racial harmony that stands central to ANC policy.

Well, it did not work. The government resorted to a 'gloves-off' policy to crush the ANC. Our restort to armed struggle beyond sabotage was forced on us. This was a defensive strategy and it continues to be such. That is why after thirty years we suspended the armed struggle. The possibility emerged to sit down with government representatives and to negotiate; something which the ANC consistently asked for since its founding in 1912.

I hope it will never be necessary for us to resort to an armed struggle again, but if there is complete deadlock in negotiations and we are convinced that we can make no further progress at the negotiation table, we will return to armed struggle. There should be no doubt about that. . . It will, however, occur only if every other method has failed.

Our commitment to liberation is without qualification. We will do what needs to be done. We are determined to break the monopoly of power by a minority of less than 15% of the nation. Those days are gone. We will settle for nothing short of true democracy.

We discussed the ongoing violence in black townships. "The primary cause of this violence is clear," he observes. "It is the consequence of decades of apartheid. I am at the same time on record in Natal as having told the people to throw their weapons into the sea, and have repeatedly appealed to ANC members not to respond to agent provocateurs . . ." Referring to the Boipatong massacre, he says: "The government needs to understand that it cannot continue to murder our people and expect no response from us. We refuse to negotiate with a government that murders our people. The full story of a so-called 'third force' as well as security force action against innocent people needs to be disclosed and sooner or later that will happen . . ."

Insisting that the ANC continues to be committed to a negotiated settlement, Mandela stresses that the behaviour of the government within the negotiation process will determine how the ANC is to respond in the future. "Mass action is a powerful weapon and we are ready to use it where and when necessary. If need be we will use it to bring the country to a standstill."

Does he see the threatened violence of the extreme right wing as a matter of concern? "Yes, I am concerned. I don't, however, have any sleepless nights over their threat of military action. They can ultimately be of no more danger than the Ossewa Brandwag was during the war years. Once we have a democratic government in place, the size of the right-wing groups will be seen for what it is. I, at the same time hope and believe that at least some within their ranks will face reality and share in the building of a new nation."

## The South African Communist Party

Asked whether he regards the alliance of the ANC with the SACP as a problem among potential voters, Mandela is quick to reply: "No, not at all. I am prepared to defend the alliance to anyone. During World War II Roosevelt, Churchill and De Gaulle established an alliance with Stalin in order to fight fascism. That alliance changed the course of history. On the same basis the ANC made an alliance with the SACP to fight racism and white domination. The calibre of the leadership and members of the SACP is at the same time such that more and more people, who are not communists, understand why there is a relationship between us. The ANC and the SACP share a common commitment to rid this country of all vestiges of apartheid and to see the emergence of a just and democratic non-racial and non-sexist society."

Responding to the accusation that the SACP controls the ANC, Mandela tells of an encounter he had with members of the government: "I like to humour them a little. They were obliged to concede that they had failed to dominate us at Codesa and elsewhere. In fact they had been obliged to submit to our proposals on a number of issues. 'If you have not succeeded in manipulating us what makes you suggest the SACP is able to do so? Are your powers of persuasion that inferior to theirs?' They didn't like the point. The ANC shares the views of the SACP on a number of issues. We differ on some issues. Ultimately we are each in control of our own organisations."

Will the ANC go into an election with the alliance intact? "Absolutely. I would defend that to the hilt. Despite the propoganda of the state, we will win an election with the alliance intact."

## His Regrets

Asked about his present anxieties and sorrows, Mandela speaks of the ongoing violence in black townships and rural areas. He also mentions the political divisions among black people. "My vision is that all the freedom fighters in this country, no matter what their political persuasion, work together for a greater South Africa. I have done my best to bring this about and regret having failed in my task. I will, however, continue to strive for that unity and hope that one day the PAC, AZAPO and other such organisations will work together. That will be a fulfilment of a life-long dream."

I recall the visits I made, as a Methodist minister, to Robert Sobukwe when he was in Groote Schuur Hospital in 1977, mentioning an occasion when Sobukwe said to me: "If Nelson Mandela and I could spend only a few hours together the divisions between us would be resolved." Mandela comments: "I am sure. I fully support that statement. He was a remarkable man. . . I regret deeply that he died before I was released from prison." Does he think that historic divisions between the two organisations could be transcended? "That's more difficult to answer. I like to think that this too will one day be possible."

I enquire about his separation from his wife and he refers me to the press statement he made at the time when the separation was announced. Expressing an understanding that some within the religious communities would be concerned about the breakdown of his marriage, he adds: "Comrade Winnie is a very strong, intelligent and resourceful person. I very much regret that our marriage has broken down, because she gave me so much support during the years I was in prison. For reasons that I do not want to go into, it is absolutely imperative that we should separate, but I still have my respect for her."

## The Future

Although the most prominent of ANC leaders since long before his imprisonment, Mandela was not elected President of the organisation until 1991, when he succeeded the ailing Oliver Tambo.[†] Suggesting that he is commonly regarded as State President in waiting, I ask about his hope for the future. "I am a politician and politics is about power. Obviously I would like to see an ANC government. My primary hope and commitment is, however, that the people of South Africa will be victorious in their quest for justice, freedom and self-dignity. My principal concern is, therefore, not victory at the polls. It is the political and economic freedom of our people. That is more important than who wins the first or any later election. My final commitment is to liberation, not power."

---

[†] Oliver Tambo died on Saturday, 24 April 1993.

PHOTO ACKNOWLEDGEMENT: Mayibuye Centre, UWC

# GOVAN MBEKI

*Promoting the Human Project*

Mbeki insists he is a "committed Marxist" and "definitely an atheist". He is also, in a certain sense, a spiritual kind of person.

Reflective in his desire to unravel the meaning of human existence, his passion is to transform society into a more tolerant place within which people can give expression to their humanity. "I am convinced," he states, "that life ought to be more than a grim battle for survival. Life must include the joyful pursuit of a fullness towards which all awakened people are compelled to reach." Asked to explain what it is that drives him as a person, he responds: "It is the human project. I am busy empowering people to be makers of their own future." He chooses his words carefully:

> Life is about freedom. Where there is freedom there is life. Where freedom is denied, rebellion and revolution are inevitable. Where people, on the other hand, are afforded the opportunity to be free and explore the implications and the restraints of freedom — and there are restraints if everyone is to be free — life consists of a series of events within which human beings have the opportunity to realise their full potential as people, and to share in a creation of a better tomorrow.

As he speaks his large and lean frame, white hair and casual but neat attire constitute a commanding presence. His lived experience and remarkable intellect, together with a warmth of personality and readiness to converse, give one the sense of being in the presence of one who is at once both a wise elder states-person and a benevolent teacher.

An intellectual and an activist, Govan Mbeki's conversation soon reveals a broad, classical education. The product of an early twentieth century missionary education at the Methodist Church's Healdtown Institution, near Fort Beaufort, it was here that he acquired a profound love for Latin and classical literature. This developed further at university and it continues to come to expression in illustrations and the odd turn of phrase to which Mbeki resorts as he speaks about the long and eventful years that constitute his life. Anything but an ivory-tower intellectual, his learning is grounded in the rough and tumble of tough and demanding events.

His reflective character (the spiritual and intellectual side of Mbeki) must at the same time be understood in relation to a person who realises that the immediate demands of life often require no more than the simplest and most instinctive will to survive. Indeed, he argues, "unless people are released from their desperate quest for mere survival they cannot begin to understand the higher implications of freedom, which include mutual respect for one another".

Ever concerned about the lot of the vast majority of people, he points out that "the fight for survival is all that many oppressed people in South Africa have been able to address themselves to since the beginning of the colonial period, and more especially since the advent of apartheid in 1948". It is this reality that drove Mbeki, school teacher, author, journalist and political organiser to become a founding member of the High Command of Umkhonto we Sizwe when the African National Congress resorted to armed struggle. "Historical circumstances and the obstinacy of the regime left us with no alternative but to fight."

The complexity of human existence, which he sees as involving survival and freedom on the one hand and intellectual reflection on the other, is vividly portrayed in two images on which an ageing Govan Mbeki likes to ponder. The one is his personal quest for survival extending from an attempt to escape arrest at Lilliesleaf Farm in Rivonia on 11 July 1963, through 24 years of imprisonment until his release in 1987. The other is the intellectual and moral importance of the story recorded in classical Greek literature of Odysseus navigating his ship between Scylla and Charybdis. Mbeki frequently reflected on this story during his early days on Robben Island. The mundane will to survive and the intellectual quest for perspective on the harsh realities of life are two inter-related dimensions that constituted the person of the young revolutionary sent to prison for life in 1963. To fail to appreciate the pathos which fuels either of these images, is to fail to appreciate the richness of the older Mbeki's outlook on life.

## Two Sides of the Revolutionary Mind

"My only concern was to get away. The adrenalin was pumping hard. I almost managed to escape." Mbeki's reflections on his Rivonia arrest constitute the opening chapter on a story of harshness, loneliness and brutality. It clearly cut deep into his character. "We had already decided that this ought to be our last meeting at Lilliesleaf. But it was already too late. A dry cleaners' van came up the driveway and made its way to the main house where Arthur Goldreich was living. Watching from the cottage where I was staying I soon realised that something was amiss. Suspecting it might be the police I jumped out of the window and was about to round the corner of the house, aiming to reach the long grass a short distance away, when the command came to 'Stop!' I heard the revolver being cocked,

I turned around and I knew that a certain phase of my life had come to an end. The other chaps, Sisulu, Kathrada, Goldreich and the others had also been arrested."

There is a gentle smile on Mbeki's face as he revisits the event. "Such moments have a way of reducing one to the basics of life — the will to escape and survive. At the same time, my commitment to the struggle thrust itself into my consciousness. It was a commitment which sustained me and others in the years ahead."

He speaks of the winter's day on which he and the others arrived on Robben Island on 13 June 1964. "The place was desolate and windswept. The reality of what lay ahead suddenly dawned on me. We had gone to jail for refusing to believe that life was mere survival. It was now going to take an extraordinary effort to both survive and triumph over these new circumstances. At the same time I instinctively knew that our belief in the moral and political integrity of our struggle would enable us to rise above the challenge. Even when the most brutal prison wardens tried to reduce us to animals, we knew that both right and history were on our side."

By nature a gentle and thoughtful person, the harshness of the years that followed challenged Mbeki to think deeply about the possible source of the hostility which drove some of his warders to the degree of aggression which he experienced. He recalls them trying to drum into his head the fact that his jail sentence was for life.

> *"Julle gaan in the tronk vrek!"* ("You will die in prison!") one of the more determined warders liked to remind me. This particular warden managed to generate a particular hatred for me. He would speak to me as though he were talking to a dog. When once a more senior official was speaking to me about my studies, suggesting that by the time I got out of jail I could have earned a doctorate, this tormented fellow butted in: "The only way he will get out of here is feet first!" I looked at the pitiful chap. His entire life seemed to be bound up with prison and a need to torment and abuse prisoners. "If I come out of here feet first," I told him, "so will you, and one day when there are no more political prisoners for you to depend on for your existence you will presumably have no reason to exist." I don't think he even understood what I was talking about. What a miserable understanding of life the poor fellow had.

The captivity of the warden seems to function for Mbeki as a metaphor of the bondage within which people are entrapped, while persuading themselves that they are free. "The prisoner," he continues, "who knows that he or she is in jail is often more free than those

162

who are weighed down by their own invisible chains. Rousseau was right: 'born free, humankind is everywhere in chains.'"

Memories, history, dates, incidents and people are all part of the story Mbeki tells. With equal ease he speaks of literature and almost instinctively he is back in the classical period, as he locates his experiences within the context of the history of intellectual ideas. "In times of anguish I have often thought back," he says, "to writers like the Roman historian Livy and especially the Latin poet Ovid who wrote of his experiences in exile. I have also found myself returning again and again to Greek mythology and the story of Odysseus steering his ship between Scylla, the giant rock in the Strait of Messina and the whirlpool of Charybdis." He carefully, almost with fascination, explains how before the advent of the compass this was accomplished by fixing one's course on the appropriate star, in order to pass between the rock and the whirlpool en route to the spices and wealth of the East.

> The person who goes to prison, driven by a great ideal is prepared to pay what price is necessary to see that ideal realised. He or she is really like the navigator of an ancient ship, with eyes set on a star. . . There is an objective before which all else, wild seas and treacherous winds, are regarded as mere obstacles to be overcome.

> You fix your eyes on a goal, on an horizon, and deviate not until you have reached it. You know that whatever problems may appear in your pursuit of that goal, must simply be overcome. There is no alternative. Whatever cost you may be required to pay, you are ready to pay, because the goal for which you are reaching is clearly before you and important enough to be your guiding star. Lose sight of the star and you are bound to deviate. Keep it firmly in your mind's eye and whatever challenges appear before you can be met.

> I repeatedly reminded myself of Scylla and Charybdis while in prison, and kept my eye on the star. My contact with other political prisoners, both my contemporaries and those younger comrades who joined us, had a way of making the star ever clearer to me. We sustained one another and the star became ever brighter.

Mbeki explains the nature of the star. "In a word, the star is a star of freedom," he says. He insists that the deep-seated restlessness in the masses, together with the instinctive and experiential knowledge which they have of their oppression, is not sufficient to enable them to

*163*

clearly understand the reasons for their oppression. "Ask the average black person why he or she is oppressed and the answer is, 'Oh because whites don't like us — they don't pay us enough money'." It is the task of political leadership and activists to reach beyond this initial sense of oppression, he explains. It is to enable people to understand what underlies the attitude of so many whites to blacks and the nature of the economic basis of white wealth and black impoverishment. "When black people begin to understand this process," he argues, "then the simple black-white divide that underlies their understanding of South Africa begins to change. It is then that oppressed people begin to realise the importance of a non-racial struggle; of the complex structural economic factors involved in apartheid and the need for the building of political alliances which transcend race, class and gender."

Remembering again his time in prison, he talks of how he used to think of the days of slavery. He imagined how individual slaves must have felt that slavery would never end. He thought of the slave uprisings in Rome of which he had read and the history of slavery in South Africa. Stressing his belief in the movement of history, he reminds us that time has a way of making a mockery of the stern promises and threats of any one age. He repeatedly reminded himself that apartheid too would end — insisting that it simply had to happen in his own life time. "I always told myself I would see a democratic, non-racial South Africa. I am an old man today, but now fully expect to see this happen before I close my eyes in death."

Mbeki recalls the loneliness of his prison cell. Frequently he was punished for what was regarded as insubordination to a warden or because he was part of an act of prisoner resistance. He would be sent into isolation — sometimes away from the Island. On one occasion he was sent to Colesberg for ten months. On another occasion he spent a month in a Uitenhage prison cell. "It was disorientating, I never knew what they were planning to do." He vividly describes the loneliness of the isolation cell. "It is empty. You have only the blanket which you fold and make into a bundle and the mat on which you sleep. In the morning, as part of your punishment, you are ordered to place the blanket and mat outside of your cell. You have nothing to read, except the Bible. I became tired of reading it. I was in this kind of isolation for three months on one occasion and for several shorter spells on other occasions. My life consisted of cold, grey concrete, iron bars and my thoughts," Mbeki says quietly. "If you are not prepared for it, you can go off your head. But we were prepared and this was what sustained us. We knew *why* we were in jail."

Did he ever doubt the stand that he had taken? Was there ever a time during his imprisonment when he felt tempted to compromise, to simply do what was necessary and to get out of jail? "Never!" comes the adament reply. What did he make of P. W. Botha's conditional offer of release if he forswore violence? "We treated it with the scorn it deserved. It made a mockery of the history of our struggle — the integrity of which had sustained us for years in prison. It was absurd for Botha even to have thought we might respond positively. If anything, it reminded us of the extent to which Botha was out of touch with the reality of our struggle."

## A Teacher at Heart

Mbeki was a teacher from 1937 until 1954 when he became editor of the newspaper, *New Age*. Twice during this period he was dismissed for his political activities. "I've done many things in my life, but at heart I am a teacher." His commitment to the profession is clear as he speaks about the process of enabling people to understand. "You get into a classroom. The students ask you a question. You answer them. You sometimes see blank expressions on their faces. You explain your answer in more detail, you illustrate your point by referring to a concrete example and eventually the 'penny drops'. You see faces beginning to brighten up and you realise how fulfilling your vocation as a teacher really is. And where there are some who still do not understand, it is your task to spend more time with them. It is your obligation to ensure that they understand the point you are trying to impart." He emphasises the importance of enabling people to understand the social, political, economic, cultural and religious dimensions of their oppression, pointing out that political education is a complex and varied exercise, which includes a knowledge of history, an ability to analyse the prevailing situation and above all lived experience. "When that happens the simple awareness of oppression gives way to an intensified desire to be free. The star of freedom appears before their eyes. They become committed to the struggle for liberation." He pauses. "This is at the same time a struggle to be human. It is a struggle to be a subject of one's own history. It is the process of being a person — not someone else's boy!"

Deeply interested in the 1976 Soweto school rebellion, he argues that even where formal education was as poor as it was, the reality of oppression was such that even the most limited amount of political conscientizing could mobilise a whole generation of students in revolt. "People were always aware of what Bantu education was intended to achieve. Then, as a result of a series of events it was as if the scales fell from the eyes of our people, they gained a vision of what needed to be done, and South Africa has not been the same since."

> Even Bantu education and all that Verwoerd conceived in his grand plan of apartheid could not kill the instinctive human will to be free. Even when oppression and the social engineering of apartheid was most intense, ordinary people, badly educated students and parents who had been bullied and seemingly beaten by the structures of apartheid oppression, knew that it was in their capacity to be free. All that was needed was resolve, vision and organisation.

> The seed of freedom is located within the depths of every human being. It is our task to nurture, water and cultivate it. When that happens the seed sprouts, breaks through even the hardest ground, blooms and bears fruit.

> Education, whether in its institutional form, whether political or at the level of people's education, that does not enable people to realise their full potential as people and to be free and responsible human beings is simply the impartation of knowledge. . . Knowledge is important . . . but education involves more than the impartation of knowledge. It has an empowering and transforming character about it.

## What About Religion?

I suggest to Govan Mbeki that his obvious concern for people to realise their full potential as human beings and the pursuit of individual and corporate freedom is what religion is supposed to be all about. He is quick to respond: "I came out of a religious home and lived under the influence of many religious people; my problem is that in reality I have never experienced religion as a liberating incentive. I have experienced religion as a restrictive, incapacitating and limiting activity. The religion I knew in the formative period of my life simply did not address the things that concerned me most. It was moralistic and authoritarian, restricting me in my quest for fulfilment as a person and in the pursuit of political freedom." He vividly recalls Max Yergan, a politically aware evangelical black American representative of the American Young Men's Christian Association, being banned from the Fort Hare pulpit for preaching a dynamic sermon on the text: "I have come that ye may have life and have it more abundantly." The rector found it 'too political'. Mbeki was fascinated by the sermon. "Yergan," he tells us, "eventually felt compelled to leave the church because of his political views. He became a Marxist and then did a full circle, becoming a right-wing anti-communist." For Mbeki religion was authoritarian religion which shunned politics. "I simply came to find humanism and Marxism far more relevant to my needs. I drifted away from the church, finding no scientific or rational basis for believing in God. I am an atheist."

Mbeki speaks at length about his early life and the religious impact of his home, school and university career. He was born on 8 July 1910 in Mpukane, a small village in the Nqamakwe district of the Transkei. His father was a successful small farmer, a devout Methodist and teetotaller. "He would not even drink a glass of water without saying grace!" His mother was the daughter of a Methodist minister. "I attended Sunday School, wrote the scripture exams and remember obtaining 100% for my knowledge of the Bible in standard six." Mbeki's parents chose to name him Govan Archibald Mvunyelwa: "The Govan came from a Presbyterian minister and former principal of Lovedale College who had died 35 years earlier. Mvunyelwa means 'the one for whom people sing'; and Archibald is an additional name that simply slipped in!" He began his schooling in the local Methodist primary school, went to high school at the prestigious Healdtown Institution, a leading Methodist mission school, and then proceeded to Fort Hare University where he first completed his Senior Certificate and later enrolled as an undergraduate, earning a BA degree. He began to show an interest in politics in the late 1920s, acting as an interpreter for his cousin, Robert Mbeki, who was a member of the Industrial and Commercial Workers' Union (ICU), but it was his time at Fort Hare (1932–37) that was formative in his life. By this time he was already questioning the relevance of the Christian faith. "It was the relative silence of the church during the passage of the Hertzog bills in 1933/1934 that was perhaps the final straw for me. My dilemma was not initially with religion per se, but the kind of religion that came to expression in the missionaries with whom I had contact. They simply did not live up to the message that I read about in the Bible. Eventually I lost all interest in religion."

He met Eddie Roux who was spending his honeymoon camping with his wife Win and taking time out to hold outdoor meetings at Fort

Hare and elsewhere. Deeply impressed with Roux's ability to relate Marxist theory to the very issues that he was trying to work out in his own life, Mbeki struck up a friendship with him that would last long beyond Roux's break with Marxism and the Party. He saw the Communist Party engaging in the struggle of the poor and the workers, against the rich and the comfortably off, and in a manner that the church never even approximated. Although Mbeki had already joined the ANC in 1935, he did not join the Party until after the banned Communist Party of South Africa (CPSA) was reconstituted underground as the South African Communist Party (SACP) in 1953. "Roux had started to steer my thoughts in a new direction. I began to read Hegel, Marx, Darwin and others. I also enjoyed poetry and the classics." His favourite authors were Wordsworth, Kipling, Mqhayi, Cicero, Ovid and Vegetius. "It took time, but eventually there seemed to me no good reason for me to believe in God," he continues. "Education can be unkind to religion. My political engagement in turn made the abstract religion with which I was surrounded seem quite irrelevant."

Interested in more recent developments in the study of religion and particularly the liberation theology debate, Mbeki sees God-talk either as escapism or, positively conceived, as a poetic or symbolic expression of a human quest. "I accept the importance of this kind of religious discourse for vast sections of our population. I can only say that it has never been a source of inspiration to me, nor has it motivated me to be politically engaged. The religion I was taught was about a God out there sitting on a throne, with angels to the left and right of Him. I contend that such notions are not only irrelevant to the quest for freedom but undermining of it. There is furthermore simply no evidence to show that such ideas are any more than the figment of human imagination, grounded in an age long gone." In his most distressful moments has he ever thought back to the religious influences of his youth? Was he ever tempted, while in prison, to resort to prayer? "I often thought back to my early days in the Transkei, with affection to my parents' home, with gratitude to my teachers for what they taught me but no, not for decades have I felt the need for prayer or religion in my life. My religion is a thing of the past. It is gone forever."

He recalls Alexander Kerr, rector of Fort Hare while he was a student there, frequently ending his sermons with a verse from one of Tennyson's poems:

Strong Son of God, immortal love,
Who we, who have not seen they face
By faith and faith alone embrace,
Believing what we cannot prove.

"These are words that have stayed with me over the years. Some people of great personal integrity, whose participation in our struggle is vitally important, are believers — people like Desmond Tutu, Frank Chikane, Beyers Naude and others. They cannot prove their faith. Who am I to suggest that their faith is not important? It has motivated them to be involved in the struggle for a better society. That is enough for me." Does he have any sense of life after death or an appreciation for the African belief in the significance of the ancestors for the living? "I dismiss outright any possibility of life after death. I cannot accept notions of ancestral veneration. This is an appealing belief, but without substantiation. When you die you are dead!"

Mbeki wrote a tribute from prison to Ruth First at the time of her assassination, to which he refers. He prefaced the tribute with words from Wordsworth's "We must be free or die".

Comrade Ruth is no more, but to those who would shed tears we say: Weep no more. She lived a full and fruitful life. Her life holds lessons for us, the living: to hold back nothing of ourselves to ensure ultimate victory for the cause of the struggle against fascism. Comrade Ruth dedicated her life to this noble cause, and in thinking of her, let our resolve to bring about liberation of the masses of the oppressed and exploited peoples of this land — whatever the price — be strengthened. She has shown us: "We must be free or die." (*Learning from Robben Island: The Prison Writings of Govan Mbeki.*)

Reflecting on the tribute, he continues: "We must never ultimately trade freedom for life. We must live freely and die if necessary for the freedom of others, without selfishly imagining that we will be rewarded in heaven for so doing."

Does he think religious institutions have a role to play in a new society? "The task of all people and organisations committed to peace, is to share in the humanising project, to help people realise their full potential and make society a better place. My understanding of the Bible is that this is what the church is supposed to be doing. If the church, mosque and other religious organisations commit themselves to this they have a vital role to play."

# After 24 Years in Prison

Mbeki fixed his eyes on the star of freedom. This enabled him to live through 24 years of imprisonment. His goal throughout this period remained the realisation of the fullest human potential of all people. He was prepared to pay whatever price was necessary to see freedom reign in South Africa. When did he come to realise that he was going to be set free? He tells the story with the skill and passion of a village elder:

> One day, which promised to be the same as any other day in prison, the head of the prison simply told me to pack my things. I was being moved to a new section. . . I was instructed not to be difficult, otherwise force would be used. After several weeks I was called into the reception area and measured for a suit. Again I was told nothing, but realised that something was in the air. I cautiously admitted to myself that this could mean I was going to be released, but prevented myself from becoming too expectant. Again there was no further action for a number of days. . . Then early one morning before breakfast, while I was washing my *balie* (bucket) I was called, placed in an ambulance and driven to the quayside where I boarded a speed boat and was taken to Cape Town. I was escorted to a waiting car and taken to Pollsmoor Prison. There I met with Nelson Mandela. He told me that I would be the first of the Rivonia prisoners to be released.
>
> I was eventually placed in a cell of my own. Again weeks passed by. . . Eventually, late one afternoon, a Major in the security police visited me and said I was going to be released, but that he was not able to say precisely when. I was also warned that my behaviour would determine the fate of the other Rivonia prisoners. I prepared myself for a wait of days if not weeks, but the next morning I was awakened at 5 o'clock, placed in a helicopter and flown to Ysterfontein military air base. From there I was taken to Port Elizabeth. A long chapter in my life had come to an end. That was 5 November 1987.

# A New Task

"There is no point in being bitter," Mbeki responds to the inevitable question. "If we are unable to realise our potential as the makers of our own destiny, we simply become the victims of history. Those who imprisoned me should perhaps be pitied. They could not face up to the challenge of the changing process of history. They capitulated under the weight of change and tried to fight against the inevitable in the only way they knew how. Sometimes I still get angry when I think of the long years that could have been better spent. But no I am not bitter. I try not to be."

Mbeki believes his final years can best be spent in political education. He speaks with almost a sense of awe as he recalls the education programme in which he was involved in prison. With obvious affection he remembers Joe Gqabi who was incarcerated in the same section of Robben Island prison as the Rivonia prisoners. "The late Joe Gqabi was an expert in covert communications. He set up an underground network for communications in the prison which was still in operation when I left Robben Island. In addition to the important role it played in enabling us to communicate in a manner that the prison authorities never understood, it also provided a structure for our prison education programme." Mbeki and other senior prisoners insisted that newly arriving prisoners should engage in formal study — for some this meant literacy classes, for others higher education, for some Matric and for others university courses. "When some young comrades were reluctant to study I took them aside and explained that while on the Island the ANC leadership had a duty to function *in loco parentis*. They were told that they were simply required to study." Mbeki set the example by earning a BA Honours degree while in prison, in addition to taking responsibility for large sections of the political education curricula.

In later years prison conditions improved to the extent of allowing the implementation of political education in a more open manner. Mbeki helped design a three year course in political history and organisation, sections of which have since been published as *Learning from Robben Island: The Prison Writings of Govan Mbeki*. The author of many articles in a variety of magazines and journals prior to his arrest, he also authored several books, including *Transkei in the Making* and *The Peasants' Revolt*. His latest book, *The Struggle for Liberation in South Africa*, was published in 1992.

## The Future

Mbeki views life communally. He returns a second time to the hapless warden who seemed to acquire a sense of joy at the thought of a prisoner dying in his cell. He argues that while some are made to suffer in South Africa all will suffer. "The freedom of one person is intrinsically bound up with that of another. We must get apartheid and unnecessary human suffering out of the way so that we can all be free. We must eradicate those influences and drives from society

*171*

which embitter people (like the prison warden) or cause them to be preoccupied with mere survival (millions of South Africans), so that we can learn as a people what interdependence means and why we must all be free in order for some to be free. No white South African can know true freedom and the security of peace while blacks are forced to endure under the captivity of apartheid and poverty. There is a long journey ahead for South Africans before they may fully appreciate this, but it is a journey that must be travelled. To learn tolerance and acceptance of one another, knowing that the violation of someone else's rights constitutes a violation of my rights, is something that will take time. When one member of a family suffers the entire family suffers. When we begin to learn this at a national level we will be a nation. Not before."

Does he have fears about the future? "Well the victory has not yet been won. There can be many a slip between cup and lip." He fears the damage the right-wing can do. He is highly critical of Buthelezi's Inkatha Freedom Party and the activities of some other Bantustan leaders. "Our young people who are determined, committed and brave freedom fighters, often need still to learn from our history of the nature of the goal towards which we are reaching. They must be helped to understand the difficulties and obstacles which still lie ahead of us. I am sometimes anxious that their impatience will not be channeled in a creative manner. But then I remember the remarkable maturity that so many of them have shown in the most demanding situations."

He spoke of the challenges facing the new society. "I sometimes fear the possibility of a bourgeois revolution," Mbeki seems almost to confide. "It would be a pity if our long struggle ended short of a serious commitment to resolving the problems of poverty. These problems cannot be solved by merely replacing the present leaders with a few black leaders. There will be enormous pressures on a democratic government to conform to the patterns of western capitalist regimes. We need to resist this pressure. There is so much talk about the success of the capitalist system, while the problems of illiteracy, the squalor of townships and the reality of ghettos remain in the most successful capitalist countries of the world. We must find an economic vision that goes beyond the vision of the West, while recognising the failure of the Soviet bloc countries."

How does he see the role of the SACP? "It is to work towards the same goal as the African National Congress," Mbeki insists. "This is

172

the common good of all the people of South Africa. It is to remind the ANC of this commitment. It is also to share with others, whether in trade unions, churches or elsewhere, in showing a priority commitment to the welfare of the poor, nudging the leadership of the ANC in the direction of the goal that we all set for ourselves in the early years of this century."

What is his task now that there is the possibility of a democratic South Africa emerging under an ANC government? He returns to the theme on which he dwelt earlier in the interview. "It is to share in the human project. People must be enabled to realise their potential as people and share in the democratic restructuring of the country. This is why I got involved in politics in the first place. It must continue to occupy me in the final years of my life."

PHOTO ACKNOWLEDGEMENT: *South*

# FATIMA MEER

*A Muslim and a Woman*

Fatima Meer reflects on her status as a professional woman in the Islamic community: "The liberating dimensions of the Qur'an are often suppressed by patriarchal control in Islam."

# Indian and Muslim

Fatima Meer espouses many of the values and religious practices evident in the home of her childhood. Born into an 'extended' family in Durban, she is the daughter of Moosa Ismail Meer and his second wife, Rachel Farrell.

At the age of twenty, her father had come to South Africa, leaving his wife Khatija with her family in India. He joined his maternal uncle in Kimberley and it was here that he met Rachel, a fifteen-year-old orphan. They eloped, married and settled in Durban where Khatija joined them with her infant son. Rachel gave birth to Fatima soon thereafter.

> My biological mother was white, being of Jewish and Portuguese descent. My 'other mother' was Indian. I never thought of her as a step-mother. In many ways she was a greater influence on me than my biological mother. I called her Ma and my biological mother Amina-Ma. After her marriage to my father, it was as though her ancestral roots never existed. She was given the Muslim name of Amina. Although baptised a Christian, she became a dedicated Muslim, spoke fluent Gjarati and affirmed the Indian customs of our home. My father, my two mothers and my eight brothers and sisters, as well as some aunts, uncles and cousins all lived happily together as part of a huge family household.

Meer speaks of the early religious influences on her life: "From an early age I was exposed to both ritual and rationalist Islam. Women are not required to attend the mosque, being expected to practise their rituals privately. My two mothers saw to it that I did just that. They made me read the Qur'an, say my prayers and attend Madressa." Her father had a far more rationalist approach to religion and she eventually adopted his outlook on things. "He created a milieu within which it became natural for me to question, on the basis of scholarly work and a careful reading of the Qur'an, many of the imposed practices of Islam. I soon came to believe that there is no contradiction between rational truth and Qur'anic truth. The one must find the other. Neither do I see an essential contradiction between being a modern woman and a Muslim."

Meer's father, who eventually became editor of *Indian Views* in 1910 (a post he held for an astonishing six decades) was highly respected in the Muslim community. He was at the same time regarded with great suspicion by the *ulama* (the Muslim clerics). Meer recalls that he usually attended Mosque only at Eid, and refused to wear the Turkish fez, which was customary Muslim attire:

> He went about bare-headed and promoted public debate on Muslim ritual and practice, questioning the official teachings of the local *ulama* through the columns of his weekly publication and in the daily press. His rationalist interpretation of the Qur'an resulted in a direct confrontation with several leading *ulama*.

> Things eventually got to the point where some of the *ulama* organised a hit-squad to deal with him. The broader Muslim community got to hear about this and they in turn arranged for his physical protection. . . Even at the height of this conflict my father never flinched in his loyalty to Islam as a faith and a moral practice. He insisted that he had as much right to interpret the Qur'an and the teaching of Islam as the *ulama*, challenging them to subject their views to rationalist debate and their interpretation of the Qur'an to critical enquiry.

> The publication of his book, entitled *Muslims and Non-Muslims* caused another controversy, this time on the issue of Halaal food. He argued that meat only became unclean when offered to false gods.

Clearly influenced by her father, she insists that the 'two Islams' of her childhood, never created a serious tension in her life. "My father did not reject Islamic ritual, nor did he criticise those who practised it. He simply asked that people practise their rituals in a thoughtful manner. He taught me to do that and enabled me to realise from an early age that dogmatism in religion is a dangerous thing."

A critical reading of the Muslim tradition was, however, sufficient to enable her to rise above the patriarchal influences of the Mosque. "To the extent that Islam is an empowering faith that enables me to realise my talents and resources, I can do no other than challenge structures which restrain and oppress women wherever I encounter them."

Her concern is to keep a balance between spirituality and rational thought. "We cannot reduce the mysteries of life to our rational understanding of things. But neither can we live meaningfully

*177*

without a thoughtful appropriation of, and response to, religious belief."

## Gandhi and Luthuli

Fatima Meer speaks of two major influences in her spiritual development: Mohandas Gandhi and Albert Luthuli. "I was at high school when India was fighting for its independence, which it finally gained in 1948, the same year that the National Party came to power in South Africa. I became deeply interested in the political develop- ments in India and South Africa, while being engrossed in the impact of the Mahatma on developments. Ma had told me of grandfather's work with Gandhi and I became fascinated with his teaching on *satyagraha* (passive resistance). Meer began to enquire into the spiritual essence of the Mahatma's teaching:

> I came to realise that for the Mahatma there was a spiritual centre that informed all that he did. It was this that made him who he was, and I began to explore the implications for my own life. Spirituality gives us direction and purpose in life, steering us in the direction we ought to go. In brief, the Mahatma taught me to get in touch with my soul. Being a Hindu, he also gave me a respect for other religions.
>
> This introspection is still a very important dimension of my political engagement. When we lose the ability to continually take stock of our inner resources and identity, we are in danger of losing our humanity. Activism for its own sake, is a dangerous thing. We must always ensure that our actions are a consequence of who we are and what we want to do. Too often people lose control of themselves and act against their innermost values.
>
> Gandhi would at times withdraw from the political battlefield because he feared the loss of the spiritual centre of what was happening. He was often misunderstood and criticised for this. I sometimes think we could do with a little more Gandhian reflection in our political activism."

As a result of her involvement in the Defiance Campaign in 1952 Meer met, and came to know, Chief Albert Luthuli, who was President of the ANC at the time. She describes him as a deeply spiritual and disciplined man.

The Chief was a sincere Christian. Very ethical, very upright and very honest. He was always in charge of his actions. In this sense there was a Gandhian dimension to him. Giving expression to his faith in his everyday actions, rather than being overtly pious or ritualistic, he reminded me in some ways of my father. He taught me the importance of disciplined politics.

"There is also, of course, Nelson Mandela," she continues. "He is a giant among people. One simply cannot write a biography of such a man and not be influenced by his life. The magnanimity and generosity of the man provide an example that can only be admired. Throughout the many years in prison, separated from his family and from material comfort, he was a glowing beacon of self-sacrifice for higher ideals."

## Politics

Her political awareness began very early in her life. "Politics has been part of my life since I was maybe five or six years old. In a strange way it was intertwined with the religiosity of my mothers. As a child I used to ask why I could not sit on certain benches or play on swings reserved for whites. They would reply: 'Don't worry. You will enjoy these things in heaven one day.' That answer did not satisfy me for too long. I wanted the necessities and the good things of life in the here and now." As she grew up Meer was exposed to the politics of the Natal Indian Congress (NIC) through her father. She frequently encountered Dr Yusaf Dadoo and Dr G. M. Naicker (two prominent NIC leaders) and became accustomed to the debate and activities of NIC members. Resisters who came from the Transvaal and other parts of the country to participate in acts of civil disobedience in Durban, regularly stayed-over in our home and I learned to respect their willingness to engage in acts of protest for which they were jailed."

Her first political speech was delivered while still at high school in 1946, and she was served with her first banning order in 1951. "Margaret Ballinger was still a member of Parliament in those days and she secured a response from C. R. Swart, who was Minister of Justice at the time, concerning the reason for my banning. He told her that I was banned because I had appeared on a platform with communists and that he had it on record that I had said 'freedom will come slowly but surely'. This made me a dangerous person!" She would eventually suffer a total of twelve years as a banned person. Her passport was withdrawn, she was detained without trial for five months in 1976, her home was fire bombed on two occasions and she survived an assassination attempt. Meer's husband Ismail, who had himself been banned on several occasions, was arrested and charged with treason in 1956.

Suspicious of dogmatic solutions to complex problems, she speaks of the need to question all political dogmas. "My concern with communism is not its socialist ideals. These are noble and quite acceptable to me. My concern is the dogmatic solutions which communists tend to promote in the political arena. I know that not all communists are so inclined but systematised Marxist doctrine does lend itself to *a priori* statements which I cannot accept. I find the teaching of the young Marx quite exhilarating and often use Marxist insights in my own work. My argument is, however, that there are several different ways of approaching a political concern and I rebel when people tell me that I have got to adopt their rules in order to understand things correctly. I am as opposed to Marxist dogma as I am to any unquestioned religious dogma."

## Intolerance

Meer speaks of intolerance as being at the root of South Africa's problems: "Intolerance will yet be the ruination of this country. Our problems are immense and we need to reason together in seeking solutions. The dogmatism of the past must never again be allowed to re-emerge in a different form or guise." Can this be prevented?

There is every sign that intolerance is intensifying and I fear the worst is still to come. There is not likely to be reconciliation, tolerance and acceptance of one another in my lifetime.

We can, however, contribute to the reconciliation process by reminding ourselves that we are actually all part of the one human family. Semantics is important is this regard. Religious people sometimes talk to one another as brother and sister. This language tells us that we belong together, despite any differences we may have.

I fear the Natal violence will intensify. The right-wing Afrikaners show no sign of compromise or tolerance. We could be moving into a period of unprecedented violence, with terror campaigns continuing for years to come. Indians and coloureds are at the same time feeling increasingly insecure as South Africa seems to be defining itself in terms of two races — whites and Africans. For South Africa to prosper it is imperative that everyone be included. We cannot build a new nation without developing a common destiny.

It is this concern that brings Fatima Meer's professional skills as a sociologist and her Gandhian spirituality to the fore. "My commitment to making educational resources available to as broad a section of society as possible is one way in which I seek to contribute to giving people a sense of self-worth, while introducing them to the perceptions and views of others." As director of the Institute for Black Studies at the University of Natal for many years, she has dedicated herself to investigating the needs of the marginalised sections of society. Her studies have focused on indentured labourers, women in industry, the causes of violence in Natal and related matters. She sees her appointment to the Board of the South African Broadcasting Corporation as a further opportunity to create tolerance and understanding in South Africa. "Each individual needs to come to grips with his or her own identity as a person. So I am back with the Mahatma! I am convinced that we need to rediscover the spiritual centre of our lives. I am a Muslim and find no need to look any further for spiritual resources. Others stand in different traditions and need to utilise their religious resources to develop their own human potential. This is where Mosque, Church, Temple and other religious institutions are so important. They can help people to become complete human beings, to rise above their prejudices and to be themselves. . . Religion is really about people. It is about the process whereby people become fully human, which involves discovering the spiritual essence of our being. For theists this is the Spirit of God."

## Andrew Zondo

We speak about her book, *The Trial of Andrew Zondo*, which tells the story of the young man who planted a bomb in the Amanzimtoti

181

shopping centre. "I wrote the book in two days. All of a sudden I was thrown into the life of this young man languishing in prison," she reports.

His Senior Counsel asked me to give evidence in mitigation, speaking about the sociological conditions that contributed to the desperate actions of this young man. Never having met Andrew before, I visited him in prison, went to see his parents who are deeply committed Christians, and slowly began to enter into the soul and the mind of this young man. He was a remarkable person, with a deep and sensitive conscience. He felt a sense of compulsion to do something about the oppressive apartheid system. Experiencing few constructive options he placed the bomb in the shopping centre. In a sense it was all he could do in an awful quest to assert his ability to be more than merely a victim of society — to be a person. Well, people were killed. South Africa is a tragic place. But Andrew Zondo was as much the victim as those who died in the bombing. I am still convinced that the verdict against him was quite unjust. He should not have received the death sentence even by South African legal standards.

Final comments in her book recall Andrew standing in the dock when the verdict against him was read:

The Judge then in measured tones and with all the authority invested in him by the State passed five death sentences in a matter of a minute:

"On count one you are sentenced to death. On count two you are sentenced to death. On count three you are sentenced to death. On count four you are sentenced to death. On count five you are sentenced to death. May the Lord have mercy on your soul."

Whatever emotion the youth felt at that moment, it was barely reflected on his face. But when the Judge paused, Andrew raised his arm in the clenched fist salute and called, "Amandla!" (Power!) The inexorable patriotism in his tone was all the more courageous because of its loneliness. It shattered the numbed formality of the small European court. There was no returning call; this was not a Mandela, this was the lone soldier, nondescript and to be lost in the unwritten pages of history. Most of Andrew's friends had chosen caution over valour and stayed away from that heavily guarded white court.[1]

---

1. Fatima Meer, *The Trial of Andrew Zondo: A Sociological Insight* (Johannesburg: Skotaville, 1987), pp.162–3.

For Meer, the greatest tragedy of South Africa is the destruction of people through the systematic depletion of their humanity.

Is she opposed to the death penalty in all situations? "Yes I am," she responds. "The God of the Qur'an is a merciful God. Specific verses which prescribe death, like all other verses in the Qur'an, must be interpreted contextually. To suggest that everything we read in the Qur'an has some kind of prescriptive legality for all time, makes a mockery of the text."

## The Iranean Revolution

In an outspoken manner Meer supported the Iranean revolution. Her book entitled, *Towards Understanding Iran Today* provides a useful summary of her argument. "There are many things I can criticise in the Iranean revolution and in post-revolutionary Iranean society. What annoys me, however, is the concerted ideological attack on what is conveniently labelled 'Muslim fundamentalism'. So successful was the propaganda campaign against the revolution that the atrocities of the Shah and the exploitation of the poor of Iran by Western business interests were virtually ignored. The Ayatollah and Muslim extremists were blamed for everything. Of course they are not angels. Their rebellion against the existing order in Iran was to my mind, however, not only inevitable, but justified. My concern is to present the other side of the story — the side the West ignores."

Meer argues that the Islamic faith itself was demonised in the process of condemning the excesses of the revolution. This she argues is precisely the kind of ideological intolerance that is destroying the world:

> For me fundamentalism means going back to the basics of something, getting back to the essentials of religion. To ascribe all that has gone wrong in Iran and elsewhere to Islamic fundamentalism is to suggest that at heart Islam is a fanatical, disruptive religion. By implication it means that the West is only prepared to accept a form of Islam which adapts to its demands and standards. This is imperialist jingoism. It smacks of talk of colonialism being for the good of the natives! It must be condemned in the strongest possible terms, because it creates a moral milieu within which it

becomes acceptable to do almost anything to crush the demon. The dispossession of the Palestinian people, the founding of the exclusivistic Zionist State of Israel and the expectation that Palestinians should accept their violation is a case in point. The average person in the West hears of conflict in Palestine and assumes that the Palestinians are to blame.

The history of colonialism and religious proselytism has turned people of different cultures, religions and races into enemies. The anti-Islamic hysteria concerning Muslim fundamentalism tells us that the ravages of colonial conquest are not yet over.

What does Meer make of the Rushdie affair? "I am on record as having condemned the passing of the death sentence on Rushdie. It is totally unacceptable." Meer nevertheless sees the West's handling of the incident to have two dimensions to it. She accepts the condemning of the death sentence. Her concern is, however, that it has also been used to castigate fundamentalists unjustly:

> I accepted an invitation to be part of a Weekly Mail Book Fair in Cape Town, to share in a discussion panel on the Rushdie affair. The anger of the rank and file Muslims in the Cape concerning Salman Rushdie's *Satanic Verses* was, however, such that the Muslim Judicial Council (MJC) called for a boycott of the Book Week. I realised that their passion was charged with faith and that it was a passion that they shared with the vast body of Muslims throughout the world — people who are largely impoverished and oppressed. Such people live and survive by their faith and I felt that I could not isolate myself from them through ivory tower intellectualism. Deliberately to undermine faith goes contrary to my moral intellectual standards. I have always claimed my identity among the oppressed and that is where I again chose to locate myself.

Some have suggested that Meer has become more supportive of Islam and more tolerant of the *ulama* than she was in the past. "I don't think this is the case," she insists. "I am the Muslim I have always been. I am ready to be critical of my religion where and when this is necessary. There are, however, developments in the West which ideologically link capitalism with Christianity. These developments have replaced a capitalist fear of communism with a rejection of Islam. The result is a commitment to destroy Islam, particularly when it challenges the West's access to oil. To remain silent in this situation or to allow myself to be used by others to fuel this crusade would go against all that I believe."

PHOTO ACKNOWLEDGEMENT: *Dimension*

# STANLEY MOGOBA

*Committed to Peace*

Bishop Mmutlanyane Stanley Mogoba speaks of the
Bisho massacre on 7 September 1992, when soldiers
of the Ciskei Bantustan fired.machine-guns at a
fleeing throng of unarmed protesters, as "a moment
of truth".

Together with several other members of the National Peace Committee, I was standing between the Ciskei soldiers and the protesters when virtually without warning the soldiers opened fire. We hit the ground and lay there until the shooting ended. When we got to our feet 28 people were dead and more than 200 injured. Only three months earlier there had been the massacre at Boipatong. "Where next?" I asked. Since then we have, of course, seen an escalation of violence in Natal, Tokoza, Katlehong and elsewhere. Violence has also been part of our struggle but we had hoped that things would improve as the negotiation process got underway. The opportunities for peace-making are running out.

Emerging from a prison cell on Robben Island in 1966, where he was imprisoned for furthering the aims of the banned Pan Africanist Congress (PAC), Mogoba would in time come to play a leading role in the Methodist Church of Southern Africa, the World Methodist Conference, the SA Institute of Race Relations, the Medical University of SA, the Boy Scouts of SA, and most recently the National Peace Committee — of which he is Vice- Chairperson.

A person of many talents, having taken on himself many different responsibilities, his major commitment is to peace:

> Peace-making is perhaps the primary task facing Christians in South Africa today. If we have no peace we will not have much left in this country worth fighting for. Our romantic dreams about what this country ought to be must continue to inspire us, but the priority is to stop the war. If this does not happen I fear a Beirut, Sarajeva or a Somalia-warlord kind of situation. No one party or leader can either impose peace or encourage all sides to lay down their arms. It is going to take a united effort by all political leaders and it is the task of the Church to facilitate this process.

> Despite continuing violence, this is slowly beginning to happen. Political groupings are making compromises and leaders are beginning to talk to one another. This is not to suggest that the fighting is over, but it does mean we are making progress. Those who are not yet part of the peace-making process need to be persuaded of the priority of peace. People are being killed every day and politicians must be forced to do whatever is necessary to see that this stops. Lives are more important than political ideals.

Mogoba's commitment to the preservation of human life has long motivated him in his efforts to establish dialogue between political leaders. Long before such dialogue was politically acceptable, Mogoba prevailed on Church and community leaders to meet with the government — being harshly criticised as too moderate and ready to co-operate with an illegal regime. He was also part of several delegations to Lusaka which met with liberation movements in exile. Together with Archbishop Desmond Tutu, he was instrumental in promoting the meeting between Nelson Mandela and Chief Buthelezi in June 1993. "I am tired of taking political sides. I want peace," he insists. "Precisely because of this, however, we cannot fail to take sides — not for or against one or another political grouping, but for justice and peace."

Asked whether he believes there is a Third Force behind the violence, he is adamant: "Yes there is. It is a mercenary force that strikes to cause confusion, and exploits the political and social divisions between people in order to prevent peace initiatives. The timing of specific acts of violence to coincide with decisive events in the political process does not pass unnoticed. Precisely who makes up this force is very difficult to say, although we have some ideas, but they seem to obey the command of a variety of different instigators. The tragedy is that once this Third Force has initiated the conflict there is enough suspicion and hatred in the community for others to take it further. We need to persuade people not to allow themselves to be provoked into violence. When the killing begins reason is, however, often the first casualty. It is sometimes a case of either being killed or killing the other person first. To then sit around and ask who fired the first shot is futile." Mogoba cites the peace process amongst the hostel dwellers on the Reef as an example of the kind of initiative that can bring about peace. "People like Mvume Dandala (a Methodist minister in the area) managed to get the hostel leaders together, enabling them to see the extent to which the situation had been manipulated by outside agencies to foster enmity. He posed simple questions, encouraging the hostel dwellers to consider when the fighting began, what sparked it off, and whose interests it was ultimately serving. In this way he was able to empower people to take control of their lives; to be proactive rather than simply to react to the agenda of others. The outcome has been an amazing decline in the extent of violence between residents of some of the most notorious hostels on the Reef. This is a small but very important beginning. We need a thousand such initiatives all around the country."

For Mogoba, his involvement in the National Peace Accord is nothing more than a practical expression of what he sees as the work of the Church. Modest at times to the point of self-effacement, Bishop Mogoba plays a key role in facilitating dialogue between competing political interests. He does this not because he believes that all parties are equally right, but because having risen above his personal suffering at the hands of the apartheid system, he is able to ask others to rise above their suspicions and fears in the pursuit of peace. "Only then can we sort out the rights and wrongs," he insists. "Let's say I am less idealistic than I once was. I also realise, however, that unless the wrongs are dealt with there can be no lasting peace. But right now my priority is to stop the killing."

## Prison and the Ministry

"I'm a typical country boy," suggests Mogoba with a smile. The youngest of five children, he was born on 29 March 1933 in Sekhukhuniland in the Northern Transvaal. He left home at the age of 13 when he enrolled as a scholar at Kilnerton. "Until then I had never left my village. The only white people I had seen were doctors and government officials who entered the village where I lived. The first time I saw a train was when I boarded one at Stofberg station to make my way to Pretoria." Despite initially being considered too small for admission to Kilnerton, he was accepted after a medical examination. "In those days the only professions open to blacks were teaching or nursing. Very few of our people became doctors, lawyers or business people. The other option was to become a priest — but at the time that had not entered my mind."

Asked to speak of his involvement in the PAC, Mogoba comments: "I didn't deliberately choose to join the PAC as opposed to the ANC. It was just that in those days, depending on where you were living, you became active in either the ANC or in the PAC. Once drawn into one or the other organisation you somehow began to promote its ideals. I have never been opposed to the ANC. Both are obviously legitimate liberation movements, with more in common than is often realised." Although no longer a member of the PAC he has maintained his relationship with the organisation. "When I speak," suggests Mogoba, "I like to think they at least give me a hearing. A good example of this is when I met several PAC negotiators at the airport after they had walked out of the Codesa meeting. I suggested to them that they had made their point and should return to the meeting. They initially rejected my advice but in time they returned." Had he spoken with PAC leaders about APLA (the Azanian People's Liberation Army) in the wake of their armed strikes on civilians? "I certainly have," he replies. "They understand my concern."

An attempt by Mogoba to give advice to the PAC in fact led to his arrest in 1963. "The major evidence against me at my trial was that I had advised certain youths to burn a Dutch Reformed Church. The truth is I had strongly advised them against this action — and they listened to me. So, I actually went to gaol for having saved a Dutch Reformed Church building!" Readily acknowledging the debt he owes to his experience on Robben Island, Mogoba argues that while imprisonment was a complete disruption to his life, it was also "the start of a journey that is not yet complete". This, he says is "a journey that must continue until our people learn to live together".

He recounts his experience in solitary confinement while on Robben Island, a penalty for having attempted to send a letter off the island to the *Cape Times*, protesting about prison living conditions:

> I had been put in isolation before in Pretoria. During that time I was told that my daughter had died. The prison authorities allowed the principal of the local high school to accompany my wife to tell me this, but refused permission for us to discuss the matter in any detail. This was the lowest moment of my life. I thought of that experience when I was again placed in an isolation cell on Robben Island. Everything was taken away from me except for two pairs of khaki shorts and a filthy blanket. I did not even have a Bible to read. One morning Dennis Brutus was cleaning the passage outside my cell, and managed to give me a book called *The Human Christ*. This is the book that brought about my conversion and my call to the ministry. It tells the story of the rich young man who wanted to know from Jesus what he had to do to inherit eternal life. Jesus told him to sell all he had. The story somehow made a deep impression on me despite my poverty. I didn't even have clothes. But there was something about my imposed poverty which forced me to realise that there was more to life than possessions. At about midnight I went on my knees and dedicated my life to the service of God. I still, after all these years, don't fully understand what happened that night.

Soon after being released from prison Mogoba entered the ministry. A few months later his wife, Eunica Matsie, died in childbirth. "My life seemed to comprise one tragedy after another," he recalls. Sent by the Methodist Church to Roodepoort, where he began his pastoral training, he was endorsed out of the area by the Labour Bureau as 'an undesirable alien' five weeks after his arrival. No amount of Church intervention helped and the Church leadership transferred him to Middelburg. Mogoba recalls the irony of the rejection that followed. "This time it was the young black minister whom I was to replace who refused to leave and decided to call the influx control authorities.

191

They decided that I was not welcome and I was not even allowed to unpack my bags. I eventually began my ministry in Sekhukhuniland, in the place of my birth."

## A Scholar and a Poet

Mogoba returned home as a probationer minister and his mother, Reneilwe Mogoba, provided the environment necessary for her battered son to recover. Her name for him was Mmutlanyane, SeSotho for 'little rabbit'. In African folklore the rabbit is the little one who cleverly outwits those who are bigger, and especially those who believe their size gives them superiority. Mmutlanyane Mogoba was to become one who encapsulated the rabbit's propensity for overcoming obstacles. Unassuming, and impatient with the petty preoccupations of status, Mogoba soon rose above the limitations of his situation.

He earned a BA degree from the University of South Africa and a Teacher's Diploma from the Bantu National College in Pretoria. He later obtained a Licentiate in Theology from UNISA in 1967, graduated as an Associate of the Federal Theological Seminary in 1972, and in 1978 gained a Master of Arts from the University of Bristol with a thesis entitled "Christianity in Africa". In June 1989 he became the first black person to receive a Doctor of Laws degree (Honoris Causa) from the University of Cape Town. In his acceptance speech Mogoba described the degree as a "significant milestone in our journey to a new society in our land". Seeing the honour as a symbol of reconciliation and the promise of an emerging national unity he stated: "I have come a long way from the other educational institution which I attended in all its notoriety, Robben Island, to this elevated platform today. I accept this honour on behalf of millions in our land, who although not with us today, stand with me this moment."

In October 1991 he was elected Chancellor of the Medical University of South Africa, and twelve days later awarded an Honorary Fellowship at Westminster College in Oxford. He has published in academic journals and his Northern Sotho drama, Nnang, is prescribed reading for schools. There is also a poetic side to his nature: "Poetry, like theology, is best written in situations of stress. I have had only three poems published, all of which I wrote while on Robben Island. I wrote one about Table Mountain. It is a description of Table Mountain as seen from the quarry at the island. Another was written in the cell when I saw the moon for the first time through the prison

192

bars. A third is entitled "Concrete", written during my time in the
isolation cell." This is a poem that reveals the imagination and life
reaching beyond the isolation of his cell:

An unprecedented abundance of cement
Below, above and all around
A notorious capacity to retain cold
Without an equal facility to retain warmth

Inside is captured a column of air
And a solid mass of human substance
A pertinent question poses itself
Which loses heat to which?

As complete an enclosure as possible
Throwing its presence all around
Until recognised by all five senses
Achieving the results of refrigeration.

Hovering relentlessly is the stubborn stillness
Permeating both solid and gas
A free play of winged imagination
And the inevitable introspection
Stretch themselves painfully over
The reluctant minutes of the marathon day.[1]

## Theology and Struggle

Mogoba looks back to the years he spent at the Federal Theological
Seminary as the most important period of his theological formation.
He began his studies as a seminarian at Alice in an institution
established to combat apartheid education. After his ordination he
remained at the seminary as a lecturer, where his thinking was
shaped by the constant struggle of black students to overcome the
disadvantages of class, culture, and race.

Mogoba speaks of the trauma which he lived through when the state
expropriated the seminary property. "Confronted with angry young
students who looked to me to lead them in their defiance of the action
by the state, I was obliged to look beyond the present moment to the
long-term interests of theological education. I tried to persuade them
to concede this battle. Well, students do not take easily to that kind of

---

1. In Tim Couzens and Essop Patel (eds) The Return of the Amasi Bird; Black South
   African Poetry, 1891–1981 (Johannesburg, Ravan 1982,) p.220

*193*

counsel! I had discovered that struggle sometimes requires strategic concessions. Sometimes there is little to be gained through direct confrontation. I also discovered that the teaching of theology in South Africa is located in struggle."

Mogoba became Chairperson of the Black Methodist Consultation, established to promote black thinking and leadership in a Church dominated at the time by whites. "Having committed myself to this process I was asked to become Secretary of the Methodist Conference. I had no option but to accept." In 1988 he became Presiding Bishop of the Methodist Church. It is a position which he still holds.

A cautious and non-confrontational person by nature, Mogoba has throughout his life been prepared to speak the uncomfortable word at the right time. "In prison I stood for what I believed in and was brutalised. Since then I have had to make some hard decisions as a minister. Frequently the criticism against me has come from the ranks of those who have regarded me as a liberal. I have often walked a lonely road. Christian leadership is not about popularity. It is about trying to do the right thing. Political leaders are required to win votes and get the masses behind them. I recognise this and thank God for the moral calibre of some of our political leaders. Religious leaders have a different function which is to speak the truth in a direct and forthright manner, while trying to look beyond immediate issues in order to see the greater picture."

## Learning to be Human

"South Africa is made up of a range of people who have hitherto been largely excluded from contributing to the character and moral identity of the nation. We need to learn from one another what it means to be human. This, of course, presents a huge challenge to the religious communities of the country." Mogoba's views on the interface between African religion and Christianity as well as what he has to say about inter-faith dialogue and co-operation provide an insight into his thinking which is as creative as it is controversial in the eyes of many evangelical Christians. "I accept that this is a side of my thinking that I have not spoken a great deal about from the pulpit. I am beginning, however, to feel that the time has come."

"The Gospel is about enabling people to realise their full humanity, and we need to recognise that the cultural location of people significantly determines how they attain this humanity. The Church, as the major religious institution in this country has imposed its ideas of humanity and perceptions of God's ways with the world on everyone else. We often narrow our understanding of mission into a rather bigoted form of proselytism." Mogoba calls for the rediscovery of those African traditional beliefs which used to enrich people's lives. "*Ubuntu* is an African understanding of humanity that this country will do well to rediscover. While in Christian terms we refer to people as being made in the image of God, in the African tradition we speak of ubuntu, which means living as a complete human being. It has to do with realising one's full potential as a person. This is an affirmation of a way of life that embodies the qualities of decency, honesty, integrity and respect for others. It means that when somebody behaves in an untrustworthy way, that person is in danger of losing his or her humanity. Wherever people are struggling to regain their humanity or to promote the human cause, I believe that God is at work."

Stressing that this humanising activity is not the exclusive task of the Church, Mogoba speaks of religious people of different persuasions needing to live in community with one another:

> We share life. We share the oxygen, the rains that fall upon the earth and the land that our people work. In other words, we are thrown together to be neighbours, whether we like it or not. The Christian teaching on what it means to be a neighbour is very important in this regard. It teaches us that an authentic religion is one that integrates people into community. In South Africa this means we need to be in community with people who belong to religions like Islam and Hinduism, Judaism, and the African traditional religions.

> Any African will tell you that to be in community means to share and to influence one another. This is not to suggest that the different religions should be blended or syncretised into one another. It does mean that the different religious traditions will influence one another — which is the story of the inter-related history of religions. Christianity has been influenced by probably every religion and culture it has encountered during its two thousand year history. There is no such thing as a pure religion. Some would, in fact, go further and say that the Church has acquired its dominant status in the West precisely because it has incorporated the ideas of alternative religions and ideas.

Referring to the relationship between Christianity and African traditional belief, Mogoba emphatically rejects what he terms the 'missionary approach' of requiring people to turn away from their African culture.

The African Christians have not lost their Africanness, even though they have been reluctant to give expression to it in public. They still silently return to their traditional homes to present their new-born child to the ancestors, consult the *Sangomas* and regularly pour beer on the floor for the ancestors at family gatherings. Well, I think we are going to see these practices done far more openly in the future. People like myself who are in positions of Church leadership are the first generation of Christian leaders in South Africa not to condemn these practices. I do not see a fundamental contradiction between African religions and Christianity. Instead of allowing an unconscious syncretism between African traditional religions and Christianity, we should promote open and rational dialogue between these traditions. Not all African traditional practices are necessarily acceptable in terms of the teaching of the New Testament, but then there are many cultural accretions of the Christian faith which we would do well to reassess. The individualism, exclusivism, pride and materialism of contemporary Christian culture are but a few examples of the excess baggage of the Church. The kind of dialogue and internal critique for which I am asking can only lead to the enrichment of Christianity in Africa and to the humanity of our people. It also constitutes an exercise in taking the incarnation seriously, which requires that the 'Word become flesh' in the context where it is spoken.

Perhaps the greatest failure of the mainline Churches in this country, including those in our townships, is their refusal to divest themselves of missionary-imposed Western cultural acquisitions.

Bishop Mogoba suggests that an African world view has much to contribute to the resolving of problems central to contemporary Christian theological debate. "The Western mind with its Greek background tends to emphasise the transcendence of God: a consequence of which is a notion of God which leaves the world and the things of the world remote and isolated from the presence of God. Influenced by the notion of the extended family, the traditional African Christian tends rather to focus on the fatherhood or parenthood of God. For us God is to be understood within the context of belonging, within the context of family, and within the context of community."

Mogoba explains this sense of belonging to have important consequences for an understanding of life after death.

The idea of family contains an eternal quality. Death cannot destroy a family because a family exists beyond the limitations of

196

time. Individuals face death, but are not destroyed by it because they belong to the family. This concept enriches the Christian understanding of life after death. The departed person in Africa is not dead and removed from this life, but rather continues to be consciously affirmed in the family as the values, wisdom and example of that person are reincorporated into the family. The African is thus able to understand the Bible in a manner that westernised people never will. We understand the importance of remembering the heroes of the faith such as Abraham and Sarah, Isaac, Jacob, Rebecca and Rachel. We understand the reality of a person being surrounded by a great cloud of witnesses who have lived and departed this world. We understand how Paul can talk of Christ living within him. As my grandparents are part of me and my family, so Jesus is also part of the Christian. He is an elder brother. To be more theological: As the Second Adam, he is the quintessence of what it means to be human. To be fully human is therefore to affirm Christ within me.

For me, Jesus is the supreme ancestor. There are other ancestors, but from a Christian perspective I must regard Jesus as the greatest of the ancestors. And because African religions locate all ancestors under God, the perplexing question concerning the relationship between Jesus and God on the one hand and Jesus and humankind on the other is as much an African problem as it is a Christian problem. Africans, however, understand the role of mediators between God and humankind in a manner that certainly Protestant Christians do not. Africans further understand the importance of the family unit and the community as a space within which the ancestors communicate the presence of God. In brief, African Christianity speaks of God being experienced through Jesus who is, in turn, mediated through the family and community. This is actually a rather biblical view of things.

Mogoba is adamant: "Renewal in South Africa is impossible without the rediscovery of what it means to be a human being and that is only possible within the context of community." He sees this as essentially a spiritual activity. "This is what Christianity is all about. Ultimately, it is what all religions are about, and this is where the sphere of co-operation and dialogue between religions is to be found." Committed to peace, he argues that this is also the basis of peace-making.

PHOTO ACKNOWLEDGEMENT: Diana Russell and Mayibuye Centre, UWC

# RUTH MOMPATI

*A Mother and a Daughter of Africa*

Ruth Mompati was born in Ganyesa, a small
northwestern Cape village 80km north of Vryburg.
She moved with her parents at an early age to
Huhudi, the African township on the outskirts of
Vryburg. She returned home in 1990 having gone
into exile 27 years earlier.

"There were tears when she spoke to us — her tears and ours," a petrol attendant told me when I asked for directions to her home. To most people in the area she is Ma Rute or Mama Ruth. To some she is Aunty Ruth. She is a woman with a huge capacity to love. "Every young person who comes from home seems to be her son or daughter," a young UCT student who made the long trek to ANC headquarters in Lusaka in 1985 observed.

"I have a deep love for children," Ruth Mompati tells me. "Most mothers, especially those mothers who are also daughters of Africa, will understand when I say that all children are my children. The years that I spent in exile, without my children, drew me to everyone's children. In relating to them I missed my own children in a manner that perhaps only a mother can understand. I tried to be a mother to every child whom I felt needed a mother. My years in exile gave me the capacity to understand the grief of other mothers who were without their children. I recall, for example, meeting a white South African woman while I was still in Lusaka. She was extremely angry because two of her sons had been killed in Angola. I understood her grief. I met with Mrs Moloise in Harare after her son, Benjamin Moloise, was executed in Pretoria Central Prison for his part in guerilla activities. She told me of his final words to her: 'Mother,' he said, 'it's all right, it's what I expected. My death will contribute to the freedom of our people.' His mother told me how proud she was of her son. Beyond her words I understood her pain."

## Euphoria and Reality

Ruth Mompati recalls her return to the place where she grew up. "Shortly after returning to South Africa I left Johannesburg, early one morning, in a hired Volkswagen Golf. I arrived in Vryburg four hours later. Thousands of people were there to receive me. (A newspaper report suggested 20 000.) I was made to sit in the back of a huge Mercedes Benz. People lined the streets leading to the township, workers lifted shovels and picks in salute. When I arrived at what was my home in Pholoholo Street in Huhudi, I got out of the car, threw my clenched fists into the air and almost broke down with emotion but I restrained myself and greeted the crowd in Setswana, a language that I had spoken in exile in order to keep my link with home."

The next day she drove to the house in the village where she had lived with her parents, now occupied by her sister and brother-in-law. Again there were people to receive her. "I paused outside. I remembered my grandparents and my parents. I thought of the dung floors which I helped care for. Again I had to deal with my emotions."

Ma Ruth speaks of her euphoria and the reality of the place to which she had returned:

> There was the unbelievable joy of being home, of meeting friends and family. There was the loyalty of people who had suffered. There was also the reality of Huhudi, the one hundred-year-old township which now has a population of 25 000 people, its two paved roads, bucket toilets and swirling dust. I later visited what used to be Dithakwaneng, where I held my first teaching post. I remembered the spring at the top of the village which flowed into a stream that divided the village in two. There were vegetables and fruit of every kind. The season started with apricots and ended with quinces. It was later declared a black spot. Today the area is absorbed into white-owned farms and the people have been resettled on an arid stretch of land. Over-populated, there is scarcely a tree, the ground is barren and the people are suffering.

> This is the reality of the home to which I have returned. A place of expectation, filled with moments of euphoria. A place of sadness. A place displaying the wounds of apartheid. . . I was visiting my sister again when Chris (Hani) was shot. "My God," I said, "is this what we have come home for?"

A woman whose roots are deeply planted in the northwestern Cape, Ruth Mompati is adamant. "I am ready to do what may be required of me for a few more years, but I shall then return to this place to be buried with those who have died before me."

## Deep Roots

Conscious of her ancestral roots, Ruth Mompati speaks at length of her forebears. Her paternal grandmother, who was over a 100 years old when she died, used to enthrall her with stories of her family history.

> My grandfather's family were Christians but my grandmother's family saw no apparent reason to convert to the religion which the missionaries brought to the area. My grandmother's family was part of a well-established African community whose cultural and political infrastucture was still largely intact. This meant they felt less pressure to adopt the norms and customs of the colonisers and missionaries. Christianity had nothing to offer which they did not already have. The family therefore felt it was their right to avail themselves of such external resources as education and hospitalisation which the missionaries offered, without adopting their religious views.

> My grandmother's family referred to my grandfather's people as *makgoa*, which means white, in the sense of having adopted the

religion of whites. They nevertheless approved of the social and moral standing of his people. The marriage took place so the necessary *labola* or brideprice was presumably acceptable — although in our culture this is not a major concern. My grandparents were married twice: Once according to traditional culture and thereafter by Christian rites at the Kuruman Mission, I think by Rev Moffat.

Ma Ruth is proud of what she calls her 'double heritage'. Her father, although himself a Christian, carried this double heritage in himself. This, together with the presence of her grandmother in their home, instilled the importance of religious tolerance and open acceptance of Christian and traditional practices in the young Ruth and her siblings. "Unlike some Africans who practise Christianity and African beliefs separately, sometimes not wanting the Church to know of their engagement in traditional rituals, I came from a home where no real contradiction was seen between the two. Both religions were seen to affirm the same ends in life, the worship of God and the affirmation of decent, moral living. I grew up with a religion that stressed the importance of being a warm human being, hospitable, generous, concerned with the welfare of others and dedicated to caring for outcastes, the weak and the desolate. We went to church, but never felt that it was the major ingredient of being religious."

Concerned about the loss of religious and cultural identity as a centre around which families and communities are built, Ma Ruth blames apartheid for undermining the African sense of belonging to one another. "You cannot tear communities apart, destroy property and undermine cultural values without eroding the sense of self-esteem and commitment to compassion and tolerance which characterised the community from which I came. The distant memory of these values is, however, still part of the African collective past. It must be brought back into the present in a manner that enables us to cope with the challenges of our times." She speaks of the emphasis on competitiveness, individualism and aggression in contemporary society as needing to be tempered with the traditional values of Africa — communality, co-operation and tolerance. "I am hoping that in the emerging new society, African ideals and values, that have been thrust aside under the impact of industrialisation and western culture, will again be given a chance to be evaluated. There is something within African culture that needs to be rediscovered. It is in the souls of African people. It is part of our roots. It can be resurrected. It can help save the nation. I truly believe that all people in our country can be better people by drawing into themselves some

202

of the values of Africa. It is a very important thing for me to be African. I never forgot that I was a daughter of Africa. It is what saw me through the darkest days of exile."

Deeply attached to her father, Gaonyatse Seichoko, Ruth Mompati sees in him a symbol of true humanity. An uneducated man who taught himself to read and write, he spent part of his life as a peasant farmer, tilling the land and caring for his cattle. He interrupted these activities to be a contract labourer on the diamond mines and, in later life, he worked for a dairy in Vryburg. "He was a very simple man, with a very big heart. The humanity within him extended to everyone he met. He lived his religion. In many ways it was his example that enabled me to believe that there is something worthwhile in Christianity. The Church virtually turned its back on the plight of our people by directing their attention heavenward, while they continued to suffer on earth." Her mother, Sally Seichoko, was barely literate. She cared for the family and worked on the fields to help feed the family. "My father died when I was 14 years old. It was a devastating moment in my life. I remember him asking my mother before he died to ensure that my two sisters and I were given an education. All of my brothers died at an early age, one of TB, one of dysentery and a third as an infant. My mother died while I was in exile. I told myself that I would go home one day, visit her grave and say, 'Rest in peace Mama. I could not come to bury you, but I am here now, forever'."

## Leaving Home

"My father's wish that I receive an education was not easily realised. My mother's resources were limited and my eldest sister was already at school. I got a job with a Mr and Mrs Visser in Vryburg, caring for their little girl Pamela. They paid me 12 shillings and six pence a month (R1,25), for which I washed and ironed, cared for Pamela and, when she was asleep, cleaned the house. They were kind enough to me but could see no point in allowing me to take time off to attend school. By the end of the first year I knew my father was right and I was determined to get an education. The Vissers are both dead today, but I still want to trace Pamela. We were good friends, but our paths separated and we lost all contact. I hope she still remembers me." ·

Ma Ruth returns to her story. "I spoke to my mother and she arranged for me to stay with a family at the Tigerkloof Mission, an educational centre of the London Missionary Society (LMS). The next year my sister left school and I was able to move into the hostel until I had completed high school. From there I went to the Teachers' Training College at

Tigerkoof and eventually graduated and got a teaching post."

A new phase in Ruth Mompati's politicisation was about to begin. "It is important to know, of course, that it is not possible in South African society for black people to be politically unaware," she stresses. "You learn from an early age that whites regard themselves as superior to blacks. You ask yourself why this is the case, and with that the political drama unfolds before you. I grew up with the indignity of hearing my grandparents being called 'John' and 'Annie' by whites who were young enough to be their children. I listened to shopkeepers abusing black customers. As a school teacher I watched kids dying of the measles, whooping cough, the flu and other curable diseases. It was not necessary to be instructed in politics to know that something was wrong. I have never been able to cope very well with the suffering of children. My protective instinct immediately comes to the fore." Ruth Mompati joined the Northwestern Cape Teachers' Union and soon became active in fighting for improved teachers' working conditions and a better education for the children. The Teachers' Union was asked to give evidence before the Tomlinson Commission, appointed to enquire into black education. It was still working on its submission when the Commission filed its final report, leading to the Bantu Education Act of 1953.

## Johannesburg

A year before the passing of this Act, Ruth Mompati got married and moved to Johannesburg. "The marriage was a disaster, I prefer not to talk about it."

Disillusioned by the impending consequences of Bantu Education, she did a course in shorthand and typing. This led to her obtaining employment in the lawyers' firm of Nelson Mandela and Oliver Tambo. "Nelson Mandela and Oliver Tambo had emerged as political leaders at the time, and they were also extremely good lawyers. They further had a remarkable capacity to be available to ordinary people. No concern was too small for them to handle. Well, the outcome was an office crowded with people from early morning until late at night." Deeply involved in the Defiance Campaign in the fifties, she became further involved in organising people in support of the treason trialists in 1956. She escaped arrest on several occasions during the State of Emergency (declared in the wake of the Sharpeville Massacre) and was drawn into the underground structures of the ANC after it was banned in 1960.

"Those were my politically formative years. They were times of enormous pressure which prepared me for what was to come. I was a mother and wanted to be with my children, but could not turn away from the political demands." Ruth Mompati had worked closely with the two lawyers and felt there was no way out; she was obliged to do what they asked of her. Mandela was in jail and Tambo in exile, so she helped close down their practice. Later she was asked to travel to Tanganyika (Tanzania) to assist in setting up the ANC in exile. "I left my children, aged six and two, with my mother. Not being able to risk making my real intentions known to anyone, I told her I was going to study abroad. She was so proud of me! I was supposed to have been gone for a year, but the arrests of our leaders in Rivonia was the writing on the wall. I would have been arrested the moment I re-entered the country. I was too involved and knew too much to risk being tortured for information. I was instructed to remain in exile."

## Exile

"Those were very difficult years. Above all I missed my children. I could not be in contact with them or with my mother because I knew that my communications would be monitored. My biggest fear was that my children would be kidnapped. I asked myself what I would do if forced to choose between my children and the movement."

Cautiously sending messages through third parties, after ten years she asked the children whether they would like to join her in Botswana. "They came. One boy was sixteen and the other twelve. How was I as a mother to relate to two children whom I did not know? How were they to relate to me? It was difficult, but we made it."

She held many different offices in the ANC, including Chief Representative of the ANC in Britain. She served as head of the ANC board on religion and was the ANC Women's League representative on the secretariat of the Women's International Democratic Federation in Berlin. Later she returned to Lusaka to be Oliver Tambo's secretary. A senior member of the National Executive Committee of the ANC, she was a widely respected member of the Political and Military Council.

"I filled many different positions in the ANC. You do what needs to be done. Throughout my time in exile I also tried to care for people. Many of our young people came out of the country to be trained as soldiers. Many of them we sent to school. I took it on myself to help those young men and women, and to give them someone to turn to when they needed a mother. They thought they were soldiers, but many were still children looking for love."

# Religion

Ma Ruth has sustained others. What has sustained her? She speaks of the struggle for justice. "Nothing can get in your way when you know that the cause for which you are fighting is just and honourable." She speaks of human dignity, justice and democracy, recalling her childhood and the home of her parents.

> There I learned that each of us is endowed with an inner energy. In Tswana we called it *Seriti*. In Xhosa it is *Isithunzi*. Seriti means dignity or personality, coming from the word *moruti* which means shadow or shade. This force or presence within us has its origin in *Modimo* or God. Driven by this divine force, human beings who are awakened to this presence within them, cannot rest until the divine dignity of humankind is manifest in the entire community and society around them. It has to do with us ultimately not being able to deny being human. And to be human is to belong to the community as a whole. It is to have a responsibility to the entire community. All you need is something to get you going. The encounter between African traditional religion and Christianity, which I first experienced in my parents' home, started the process. My experiences as a teacher and my involvement in the ANC took it further. Now there is no turning back.

> I belong to the United Congregational Church which has its roots in the LMS and the Kuruman Mission. On Mother's Day I heard a wonderful sermon preached there about the struggle of women to realise their full humanity. In reality it was about the struggle of *Seriti*, the divine energy within women, coming to expression. To deny anybody the full expression of who he/she is, is to deny God. I realised that my grandmother was right. There is no fundamental contradiction between African traditional religion and Christianity. For me, religion is connected with what we do with our lives. It involves giving expression to the spirit of God within us.

# Women

Ruth Mompati is a veteran of the women's marches of the 1950s. A founding member of the Federation of South African Women, together with Helen Joseph and Lillian Ngoyi, she was at the forefront of marches to protest against women having to carry passes. For years she was the only female member of the National Executive Committee of the ANC and at the first meeting between the government and the ANC at Groote Schuur in 1990 she was one of two women present — the other being Cheryl Carolus. (See interview)

Outspoken on women's issues, Ruth Mompati insists on equal

opportunity for women and men. She has fought for this all her life and the positions she has held highlight both her skills and her successes in this regard. She offers two related comments on women's rights:

> We cannot separate women's liberation from national liberation. It is wrong for women to focus on their rights in some individual, bourgeois sense, as if this can be separated from the national question. This, I am afraid, is what some feminists seem to do. They pay lip service to the anti-apartheid struggle but do not address the issues of racism with the same urgency as they do sexism. This has undermined credibility and made the task of feminists who are concerned about racism and apartheid that much more difficult. To have equal rights in the ANC, or any other organisation, and to continue to be a victim of apartheid does not really help black women. For me, national liberation is a prerequisite for women's liberation. If I am to choose which should come first there is positively no doubt in my mind that I will choose national liberation. To suggest that a black woman can see things otherwise is simply not true. Does this mean that I am not an advocate of the women's struggle? Of course not. I fought against male prejudice wherever and whenever I encountered it long before it became a fashionable thing to do. I say to women who talk to me about sexual discrimination: "I understand your concern, fight it, but never in isolation from the many other issues we face in this country. So, roll your sleeves up and get involved. Prove your worth. There is space for you to do that." I undoubtedly favour more women's participation in the affairs of the country. Women must take the initiative in demanding this right, and this is precisely what is happening. For me liberation is, however, total liberation. Women's liberation is only one aspect of that totality.

## The Future

How does she see the future? Is she optimistic? "All kinds of things can go wrong. A new society cannot be built overnight. The violence terrifies me. It must become a national priority for us to bring it to an end. A time comes, however, when birth can no longer be delayed without irreparable harm to the child. That moment has come. I only hope that the perpetrators of violence, who oppose our liberation, realise this. There are difficult days ahead, but with enough goodwill and by God's grace we will make it. A negotiated settlement is the only realistic option we have. I like to think that in their better moments both the right-wing and extreme left-wing groups actually know that. I urge all South Africans to work together for a just and peaceful future for our children."

PHOTO ACKNOWLEDGEMENT: Mokgadi Pela, *Sowetan*

# ITUMELENG MOSALA

*A Black Theologian*

Itumeleng Mosala wears many caps in life. He is President of the Azanian People's Organisation (Azapo), an ordained Methodist minister, an academic and a social activist.

Primarily I am a black theologian. I am a believer, a socialist and materialist. For me the three go together in as much as I see religion as a cultural practice — a material practice — while both traditional African belief and Christianity are carriers of a socialist vision.

Given my background and lived experience I have no option but to believe. That is the nature of my world. It is impossible for me not to be religious. Although when socialism comes, when the material goals to which my religion has committed me are realised, it won't be necessary to be religious. The dawning of a new age will render religion, at least as we know it today, obsolete.

Suggesting that he is adopting a classical Marxist position on religion, Mosala responds: "Yes, although one which is tempered by a sense of the pervasiveness of the weakness or sinfulness of humankind. Marx was more optimistic than I am."

"There have been three great influences in my life," says Mosala. "These are Jesus, Marx and Steve Biko. When I wanted to give up being a Christian, I read Marx's *German Ideology* and that kept me in the Church. When, as students, some of us were in direct confrontation with the Church, Steve Biko told us to return to the seminary and work from within its structures." Concerned to integrate intellectual struggle with political engagement, Mosala's theology reveals strands of biblical insight, Marxian analysis and black consciousness. "I think it is important to maintain theoretical and ideological clarity in our struggle. Activism devoid of intellectual rigour can be a dangerous thing," Mosala observes.

## Growing Up Religious

Mosala speaks of his parents as being "very religious", even though they were not church-goers during the time that he was growing up. "My father, Montlaletsi Mosala, went to church occasionally. A petrol-pump attendant, he also had a heavy-duty driver's licence and was frequently away from home delivering goods to various parts of the country. My mother, Mosai Mosala, was a domestic worker. She liked to attend church, but her work and family responsibilities made this difficult. We, nevertheless, always said prayers in our home. There was a vibrant religious atmosphere at our table, with my father engaging my sisters, brothers and myself in long conversations on religious issues, the nature of morality and the history of our people. Looking back I realise that the values which I hold today can be traced back to my parents' home. While neither was educated nor particularly political, they taught me two very important theological and political lessons early in my life: One, that God is more than organised religion or the institutional Church, which means that I should never allow myself to be distracted by the compromises and contradictions of the Church. Two, that religion is about struggle, about fighting for the material manifestation of what you believe to be right."

Mosala went to school in Thaba Nchu and later attended Strydom College where he trained to become a teacher. He linked up with the local Methodist Church, because his friends were there, and came under the influence of the Rev Seth Mokitimi, who was Superintendent Minister of the Bloemfontein African Circuit. He had earlier (1964) been elected the first African President of the Methodist Church of Southern Africa.

"Mokitimi was a huge influence in my life," Mosala observes. "I actually become quite annoyed when the Church tries to claim this man as a product of itself. In reality his greatness was a contradiction of a Church that resolutely sought to maintain leadership in the hands of white ministers. Blacks were taught dependency. Mokitimi was Deputy Chairman of the Kimberley and Bloemfontein District of the Methodist Church — that ironic way in which the Church tried to show itself to be non-racial. The chairmen in the various districts were white and the deputy chairmen black. When eventually elected President, amidst the threat of some whites to resign, Mokitimi became *ex officio* Chairman of the District but in administration he deferred to the former chairman — who again resumed his position as chairman as soon as Mokitimi had served his year of office. By today's standards this was the worst form of tokenism."

Deeply appreciative of the influence of Mokitimi on his life Mosala continues: "Mokitimi was not a radical. In that sense he was a product of the Church. He did, however, manifest a kind of spiritual radicality. He believed in the dignity of black people, even though he was not ready to fight to give expression to this, either in the courts of the Church or the nation as a whole. He had enormous self-confidence and humility, and always enabled others to commit themselves to a more radical programme than he ever adopted. When some regarded us as arrogant, irresponsible and unfaithful to the gospel, Mokitimi supported us, counselled us and encouraged us to pursue our goals. Had it not been for Mokitimi I would probably never have entered the ministry." Mosala laughs as he observes, "I suppose some regard the old man as having rendered the Church a grave disservice in this regard!"

# Black Consciousness

Mosala arrived at the Federal Theological Seminary (FEDSEM), then located adjacent to Fort Hare University in Alice, when the Black Consciousness Movement (BCM) was at its height. Barney Pityana had just left Fort Hare, Steve Biko was under house-arrest in King William's Town (in close proximity) and the South African Student Organisation (SASO) had recently been banned from operating on all black university campuses. Without the restraints of direct state control, FEDSEM became one of the major centres of student political activity for the entire country. Stanley Mogoba (see interview) was on the teaching staff, as was Neville Ncube, also a Methodist minister, who had just been released from Robben Island for his PAC activities. (Neville Ncube was killed in a motor car accident in 1974.)

> My thinking became influenced by Ncube and I continue to be haunted by his insights. Very much a nationalist, Ncube saw no contradiction between African nationalism and non-racism. He repeatedly reminded us that ultimately blacks and whites need to live together in a new society. The contextual demands of the time were, however, such that the focus was on the need to stand on our own feet as black people and fight the fight that was before us. We did not have much time to think about non-racism. Maybe we should have given more heed to Ncube's dialectic. I certainly think we should have kept a more sustained dialogue with white people in the way which Neville (Ncube) saw it, while continuing to focus our primary energies on black people as Steve Biko encouraged us to do. That way Azapo and the Black Consciousness Movement would have focused on black politics, without being open to deliberate misinterpretation by outsiders.

For black seminary students a major concern was how to integrate their Christian faith with the experience of being black in South Africa. "I felt I needed either to resolve this or get out of the Church," Mosala observes. "I've still not resolved it and I am still in the Church!" A crisis point for us was the expropriation of the property of FEDSEM by the state, allegedly in order to meet the demands for more space by Fort Hare. "Students were incensed by the submission of the Church to the demand that it leave Alice. We tried to prevent the vacating of the campus by blockading the removal trucks. As a result some of us were locked up in the chapel but the removal went ahead and the seminary was relocated in Umtata (in the Transkei)."

Shortly after this relocation some students and black staff organised a Heroes' Day Service, which resulted in Kaiser Matanzima (Chief Minister of the Transkei at the time) insisting that those responsible

212

for organising the service be expelled by the seminary. While disciplinary hearings were still underway Matanzima took further action, demanding that the seminary leave the Transkei. "This," Mosala explains, "led to a major confrontation between BCM students and the seminary staff and Church leadership, who decided to comply with Matanzima's demands. In protest against their submissiveness and in sheer disgust we removed ourselves from the seminary, threatening to expose what we saw as the Church's cowardice both in Alice and now in Umtata." Things were about to reach a climax when Steve Biko appeared one night at great risk to his own safety. Explaining that he understood the point which students were making, and agreeing with their assessment of the situation, he asked them to return to the seminary. Mosala recalls Biko's counsel:

> He told us that black consciousness was more important than any of us, arguing that short-term victories needed to be weighed against long-term goals. He demanded that for the sake of the Black Consciousness Movement we were to go back to the campus, and not alienate the others on the campus merely because we thought we were right.
>
> I used Biko's argument recently in a presidential speech I delivered at the special Congress of Azapo which was meeting to consider its position on multi-party talks as a means of negotiating the future of South Africa. I failed where Steve succeeded.

"Biko taught us that the struggle is a long one and that strategy sometimes requires us to do what we would much rather not do," Mosala continues. "Our task, as ministers in training at the time, was to discover how to promote black consciousness within the Church and more importantly within the life blood of the Church, which is theology. It was here that black theology was born."

## Black Theology

Mosala sees black theology, which emerged as a direct result of the imposition of apartheid, as nothing less than a struggle for the very integrity of the Christian gospel in South Africa. He argues that strictly speaking, in South Africa, black theology could not have started before the institution of apartheid in 1948. Earlier, black people had suffered under English colonialism and the racism of the United Party and its allies. However, according to Mosala, this was qualitatively different to the suffering experienced under apartheid which deliberately defined blacks as less than human while defending itself in the name of Christian theology. Within this situation the question emerged as to whether it was possible to be both Christian and black. For Mosala it is a question not yet adequately answered.

In identifying two sources of black theology, Mosala provides a definition of black theology which challenges the identity of all theology:

> Black theology is parasitical on the Christian religious tradition to the extent that it operates within the framework of missionary theology. This makes the Bible and Christian tradition an important source of black theology. Black theologians seek to understand what a religion, first brought to the continent by Christian missionaries, means within a situation of black exploitation. As such, black theology takes the good news of liberation of which the Bible speaks, more seriously than the missionaries, the institutional Church or the dominant theology have ever done. It argues that for the claims of the gospel to be true for people living under the whip of racial and economic oppression in South Africa, the gospel must offer liberation from the burdens of apartheid which reduce the lives of black people to hell on earth.

> This leads to a second source of black theology, which is the totality of the black experience. It includes the history of black ideas and culture, but more importantly the black political experience under apartheid. Black theology refuses to see blacks as a pristine people frozen in pre-colonial culture. This is where African and black theology part company. Black theology is interested in the present black experience, which constitutes a vitally important ingredient in my theology.

> Black theology is written at the interface between the Christian tradition, as it has been handed down to us, and the realities of black experience in South Africa today. As a black theologian I assess, test and weigh the black experience against Scripture. I also test and verify Scripture against the black experience. To refuse to engage in this dynamic is to undermine the very process that has enabled the Christian faith to prosper and address the changing needs of each new context within which it has found itself. The alternative is to reduce the Christian message to commentary on past struggles. At worst it becomes a weapon of reactionary warfare.

Arguing that the agenda of black theology is the restoration of the humanity of black people, Mosala suggests that it is premature to deliver a final verdict on its success or failure as an intellectual and spiritual exercise in liberation. "Suffice to say," he argues, "at present things do not look too promising. Black theology has abandoned its origins located within the movement of resistance present in the grassroots black community. It has become alienated from this

214

community, to be housed in seminaries and religious studies departments. It has become the subject of dissertations and academic papers rather than a weapon of struggle. It has lost the creativity that it once had in generating cultural metaphors and religious symbols capable of arousing the masses. Today, black activists are driven by a different ideology. Black theologians have failed to keep in touch with the grassroots people and have not succeeded in adapting the message of black theology to address the changing needs of the community. Black theology no longer takes the demands and needs of the community as its point of departure. Quite frankly I do not know whether we will be able to re-establish the link."

Mosala is unhappy about what he perceives as an anti-intellectualism in politics. "I continue to believe in the importance of organic intellectuals in the struggle; people with their feet firmly planted in the grassroots political struggle who are able and willing to do some serious theorising and reflection. Unthought activism can be a dangerous thing because it is inclined merely to respond to the whims of those with the biggest political organisation. The size of the organisation is, in turn, often only what it is because of the money it manages to raise and the favours shown to it by the ruling classes of various nations. Careful analysis, rigorous critique and thoughtful proposals are urgently required in the creation of a new social order in South Africa, not least in a situation where the danger exists that the aspirations of the people may be sacrificed on the altar of negotiations. The life of the mind is as important as the life of the feet. We desperately need politicians who provide both."

## The Politics of Azapo

Is Azapo providing this kind of service to the nation? How does it both render the intellectual leadership suggested and appeal to the aspirations of the underclasses whose demands Azapo claims to represent? "The short answer has to do with giving expression to what people are instinctively feeling, while seeking a solution to these needs," suggests Mosala.

Responding to the criticism that Azapo has marginalised itself from current political developments by refusing to engage in the negotiation process, by excluding itself from opposition alliances, which today include whites, and by failing to provide the necessary flexibility required for a political settlement, Mosala observes:

Negotiations must not be allowed to emerge as the only available

215

strategy facing the liberation movements. There are other areas where the fight is to be fought — among the working-class, the youth and other alienated sectors of society. We see it as our task to articulate the fears and aspirations of these constituencies.

Concerning negotiations: There are in Azapo as elsewhere a variety of perspectives. My own view is that Azapo was right to stay out of negotiations. I still do not believe that negotiations can deliver freedom or liberation for our people. That was the point Azapo has been making. And in that we have been successful. The fundamental weakness of a negotiated settlement has been exposed to many black people by Azapo. We have placed the Constituent Assembly squarely on the agenda of the talks; we have changed general consciousness on the importance of international mediation; we have driven home the question of the need for the liberation movements to act together and negotiate together on all issues, especially on the issue of stopping violence; we have insisted that the land question must be on the constitutional agenda. We have won on these issues. The question now facing Azapo is whether there is still any strategic value in continuing to make the same points. I think not. I think that our organisation must begin to take seriously the importance of strategic re-posturing in relation to negotiations. And at its recent Congress Azapo did that. We decided to negotiate, but not at the multi-party forum. We shall negotiate with the liberation movements on the one hand, and with the South African regime in a neutral venue, under neutral chairpersonship. We are not prepared to give credence to all the enemies of our people who form the other parties at the multi-party talks. We are not prepared to make a mockery of the liberation movement in allowing it to be rendered ineffective by the sheer numbers of parties of the status quo.

Dismissing any suggestion that the continued refusal of Azapo to participate in the multi-party negotiation forum will effectively prevent them from influencing the outcome of negotiations, Mosala insists that they may well have more influence outside of this forum than within it. The conversation shifts to non-racial politics and Mosala comments:

Non-racialism stands embarrassingly present in black consciousness policy from the time of Biko and in Azapo's own policy documents. I say embarrassingly, because our praxis has not given expression to this. We are, however, committed without reserve, to the liberation of black people, and it is racist to suggest that whites cannot be committed to black politics. We have no reason to speak of non-racism simply to make whites feel a little more at home. The reason for our birth as an organisation was to

216

enable black people to cast off dependency and to liberate themselves. My own view is that we have made a lot of progress in this regard. In keeping the organisation totally black we have perhaps held onto our original tactic for too long. The present context requires that we review this.

Politics is about compromise and flexibility. To sacrifice key principles is, however, a short-sighted activity. Our major concern is to ensure that when settlement comes, people presently excluded from the political and economic structures of the country are included.

## An Ordained Minister

Itumeleng Mosala has travelled a long way since entering the Methodist ministry. I ask him to speak about his understanding of God. "I started off egotistically thinking that God was a personal being who ought to have been ready to meet my every need. I later preferred to speak of God as praxis. Today, I see God as a sacred space," he notes. "God is a reality which is beyond my comprehension. Yet I find myself continually drawn to that space, although I am unable to enter it. It is always beyond me, drawing me forward, demanding more than I can at any one point offer. I find it very difficult to speak of God in personal terms, partly because of Nazi Germany, partly because of apartheid. We cried to God in our hour of need and God did not answer. I still believe but I cannot understand."

Mosala speaks about sin. "I am a Marxist, but Marx was simply too optimistic. There is something about human nature which is captured in the biblical understanding of sin. It concerns humanity failing to realise its full potential, falling short of its own goals, failing to rise to the occasion. But I live in hope that good will ultimately triumph over evil. If I did not, there would be nothing worth fighting for. This is what makes the biblical myth of the pending rule of God, such an important political and moral incentive."

Mosala sees the Bible as being full of such motivations. "It is a powerful weapon in our struggle. It is a text with a complexity of practices, struggles and ideological experiences which continually reproduces the stuff of humanity. It is a powerful cultural weapon — and there is no law against us carrying it!"

217

PHOTO ACKNOWLEDGEMENT: Beyers and Ilse Naudé

# BEYERS NAUDÉ

*An Afrikaner of Afrikaners*

Driven out of the white Nederduitse Gereformeerde
Kerk (Dutch Reformed Church) in 1963, Beyers
Naudé had resigned from the Afrikaner
Broederbond long before it was popular or
expedient to do so.

Banned for seven years, he continued to be at the forefront of resistance. No sooner was his banning order lifted, and just when most people would have been ready to retire, he was elected General Secretary of the South African Council of Churches (SACC). When he retired from the SACC he formed the Ecumenical Advice Bureau. "When the old man will ever sit down I do not know," observed his life's companion Ilse Naudé.

> What really annoyed the leaders of Afrikaner nationalism when I broke ranks was that I was every bit as much a white Afrikaner as they were. I think I reminded them of that side of Afrikanerdom which they have never been able to tame. It is an Afrikaner willingness to cross frontiers — relating the Afrikaner experience of exploitation, poverty and struggle to others who face similar experiences. Afrikaner history has its fair share of such people. I think of people like the early trade unionist Betty du Toit, Braam Fischer, Breyten Breytenbach and others. The irony is that Afrikaners who are today the most rabid capitalists, oppressors and racists, forget that they were once socialists, economically exploited and the victims of racism. Thank God some Afrikaners are today seeing the folly of their ways. But too many still live in the past — imagining they can impose their will on blacks in the manner of their forbears. Maybe like the Israelites of old they will wander in the wilderness for their forty years before they enter the new society. When I see what the Afrikaner Weerstand Beweging and other like-minded groups are up to I fear the worst. They would rather destroy everything than accept social reality. This kind of aggressive bigotry is a blot on the Afrikaner people that continues to eat away at my soul. The romantics in right-wing organisations wallow in the memories of the past. "Never Again!" they say. In the process they court the very danger which they vow to evade.

## Heritage

Naudé is a white Afrikaner of white Afrikaners. "I can identify with St Paul who once observed that if anyone could boast in his Jewishness it was he. Well, if anyone should be so foolish as to want to boast about Afrikaner identity in this day and age, then it is me. My roots are strong and my heritage pure." Naudé was born within a Nederduitse Gereformeerde Kerk (NGK) parsonage, of conservative Voortrekker and Dutch stock. His father was a chaplain during the Anglo-Boer War, and a founder member of the Afrikaner Broederbond.

Baptised Christiaan Frederick Beyers, the name of a rebel Afrikaner general who drowned in the Vaal river trying to evade arrest by government forces, Beyers Naudé is a graduate of Stellenbosch University. He was a member of the elitist Afrikaner Broederbond and moderator of the NGK in the Transvaal. He was eventually rejected by the leaders of the same Afrikaner nationalism that gave him birth.

It is this heritage and identity that make Beyers Naudé such an enigma to so many — as if racism were the prerogative of Afrikaners alone. The racism of English-speaking South Africans is witnessed in their confused and ambivalent response to the message of people like Naudé. Naudé's challenge reaches beyond the confines of being an Afrikaner to strike also at the heart of English-speaking South African and indeed Western values. He challenges racism, greed and cultural chauvinism wherever they are to be found. Prophets require more than admiration from a distance.

Suggesting that conservatives and reactionaries might understand the essence of his message better than the liberals, he suggests: "That is perhaps why I find myself continuing to be concerned about my Afrikaner compatriots. Once you convince an Afrikaner of the error of his or her ways, you have a committed convert. Somehow liberals don't fully appreciate the extent of the change that is being required of them in South Africa. White privilege is something that cannot endure forever. When this is pointed out to whites they either rebel, as in the case of the right-wing, or they try to curtail the change process to their own benefit, as is the case with so many liberals. Few whites are prepared to face the full implications of what is required of them and to respond accordingly." It is this realism that makes Naudé the troublesome patron and irascible doyen of what he calls white liberation in South Africa. "Whites need liberating. It can only come through black liberation and a willingness on the part of whites to accept blacks as their unqualified equals."

## The Contours of Human Identity

How did Naudé emerge from the ghetto of a narrow and exclusive brand of Afrikanerdom to become an Afrikaner with a broad ecumenical vision and inclusive understanding of human existence? It is a risky business to delve into the dark recesses of the human psyche or the social maze of character formation. "When Jeremiah

221

was asked how he managed to become the troublesome person he was, he said it was the way he came out of his mother's womb," Naudé comments. "One's identity is formed as much by the social forces and experiences to which one is exposed in life as by one's response to those forces. Some turn and run when faced with realities that challenge their presuppositions, others enter the eye of the storm and find themselves changed by these forces. Exactly why some flee and others adapt no-one knows. Perhaps Jeremiah was right, it has something to do with the way in which God has made us."

His father, Jozua Francois Naudé, was a determined and zealous nationalist with an uncompromising sense of divine mission. He was committed to instructing his eight children, above all his two sons, in his understanding of the promises of God to the Afrikaner nation. He instilled within them the stories of British military aggression and their flagrant disregard for the human rights of the Afrikaner people. He persuaded the young Beyers of the just nature of the Afrikaner struggle against a foreign aggressor, and enshrined within his memory the stories of the conditions under which the Afrikaner forces waged their guerrilla war, the suffering of Afrikaner women and children in concentration camps, the social effects of the scorched earth policy, and the imperialist motivation behind the British war effort. He fostered in his children an evangelical zeal through the stories he told them of his mission work among black people in Soutpansberg, while serving under the command of General Beyers in the Anglo-Boer war. "It never occurred to my father, nor to me at the time, that the real victims of the white man's (sic) war were among the indigenous population. It was as though blacks did not even feature in the struggle. I was persuaded that the Afrikaners were the oppressed and that their struggle was sanctioned by a God who was the God of the oppressed," Naudé reports.

His mother, Adriana Johanna Zondagh van Huyssteen, had a strong personality. She was deeply religious. "She had strong views on the way in which her children should be raised. We were required to be well-educated, religious and obedient to our parents. She showed an unbending prejudice against the British and never questioned the rightness of the Afrikaner cause or their goal of eventual political dominance. It was not until later that I questioned her values or the control she exercised over my life," says Naudé.

From his parents Naudé inherited a sense of religious piety, a

222

captivity to certain imposed moral norms and a sense of social and political justice, with a bias in favour of the Afrikaner. This clear synthesis of moral and theological principles would eventually cause Naudé to question the very nationalism it was intended to undergird. Exposed to a different context these values came to receive a new content. "Those very instruments that had been such a mighty weapon in the Afrikaners' fight for existence and liberation, became the basis for my commitment to the liberation of others — namely to blacks in South Africa."

During his time at Stellenbosch University Naudé slowly began to question the alliance of theology and nationalism which formed the basis of his parents' home. These were questions which, however, remained at a preliminary and latent level in his early life. He identifies three people, in relation to whom he began to question his own politics and theology: Johan du Plessis, who had been tried for heresy and dismissed from the NGK Seminary shortly before Naudé's arrival on the campus; H. F. Verwoerd, who lectured Naudé in sociology and who eventually became Prime Minister; and B. B. Keet, his seminary Professor of Ethics.

There is today still a certain animation in Naudé's voice when he speaks of what he calls the pettiness, the corruption and the narrow-minded attitude of the NGK with regard to du Plessis' heresy trial. The Supreme Court eventually ruled in du Plessis' favour, but the Church refused to allow him to lecture, although they were compelled by the court to pay him his full salary for the rest of his working years.

He remembers Verwoerd as a brilliant, coherent, well-prepared and disciplined lecturer: "Verwoerd would enter the class precisely on time, read his lectures, close his books, and walk out. There was no discussion, no personal contact with students, and in the lectures which I attended he was quite apolitical. There was a certain logic in what Verwoerd taught and what he demanded from students that made a lasting impression on me." Was he surprised when Verwoerd's grand scheme of apartheid later emerged? "Yes, I was surprised at first, but as time passed and I thought back to the man I knew, I began to realise that it was a consequence of his ruthless logic. Segregation was the acceptable order of the time. Most whites saw it as the most natural way of relating to blacks. Verwoerd's rigidity and logical precision demanded total separation. It was a consequence of the man's mindset. I have been afraid of grand and inflexible schemes ever since."

Then there was Professor Keet, or Bennie, as Naudé calls him. "He was the only theology professor who made any real impression on me. A man of enormous compassion and absolute honesty, he soon found himself politically isolated by the other professors." Naudé established a firm friendship with him, which later resulted in deep theological and political solidarity between the two men. "Years after I had left the seminary he continued to be my mentor and confidant." In 1961, shortly before his death, Keet wrote an essay on the South African crisis, entitled "The Bell Has Already Tolled". For Naudé it was decisive: "It was a prophetic statement that the Church refused to hear, but one that convinced me that I was on the right track when I prepared myself psychologically for the break with the NGK."

> The seeds of my theological dissent were sown during my time at Stellenbosch, primarily by Bennie Keet. I nevertheless had a deep hankering to remain part of the Afrikaner community. It is not an easy thing to leave the warmth of the Afrikaner family within which conformity brings rewards, acclamation and support. Once the moral and theological questions were posed, however, it was difficult to accept all that one was expected to condone to remain within the inner circle. I've been 'gone' many years, but I still feel the pull of the family. I cannot go back, but every time I see another Afrikaner breaking rank my heart is warmed. I live with a constant desire and sense of obligation to persuade my people to become part of the broader South Africa. Some criticise me for this, suggesting I should leave them to their own devices, that I am still too tribalised! I can only be who I am.

## NG Predikant

Beyers Naudé began his ministry as a *hulpprediker* (assistant minister) in Wellington in 1939. "Although driven by numerous questions, I was a loyal member of the National Party and vigorously opposed South Africa's engagement in the war, believing that Britain was fulfilling her usual aggressive policy in confronting Hitler." A few years later Naudé became *predikant* to the Laxton congregation in the Karoo, and eventually moved to Pretoria East.

"A few years later I read Ben Marais' *Kleur Krisis en die Weste* (*The Colour Crisis and the West*) (published in 1952)," he recalls. "Ben

Marais wrote the book after visiting the offices of the World Council of Churches. All it did was to question the biblical justification of apartheid, and by today's standards the book is patronising and even reactionary, but at the time it was enough to create a storm within the Afrikaner community. I thought his argument was essentially sound but never got too involved in the affair. It was a decade later before I confronted the Church and almost four decades before the NGK would be forced to face the full implications of Oom Ben's (Marais') cautious question."

In 1953 Naudé undertook his first journey abroad as a member of the NG *Kerkjeugvereniging* (NG Church Youth Association), an event that marked the beginning of his ecumenical exposure. It was, however, his years spent in Potchefstroom from 1955 to 1959 that he regards as most formative. He attended some of the sessions of the Reformed Ecumenical Synod which met in that town, and he soon realised that the Reformed family of churches in other parts of the world was at theological loggerheads with the white Dutch Reformed Churches in South Africa. This confirmed his innermost doubts and questions. It was also while in Potchefstroom that he was visited for the first time by a group of young white ministers who were serving black, coloured and Indian congregations. These experiences exposed him to the effects of Group Areas and apartheid legislation on black people, and gradually enabled him to begin to move beyond the limits of the white exclusivity within which he was ensconced. He visited their congregations, he saw and he grieved.

During this time he made contact with the theologically conservative Gereformeerde (or *Dopper*) Kerk. "I attended their Bible Study groups and gained a decisively new existential understanding of the Word of God. I began to understand what people meant when they said they were confronted by the Word of God to act in a certain way. This was the beginning of my contextual theology, although my context was still white. I realised in a rather superficial sense that God was calling me to challenge the situation in South Africa. My direct engagement in the struggle against apartheid can be traced back to the double experience of firsthand exposure to black suffering and the discovery of a theology grounded in relating Scripture to lived experience."

In November 1959 he accepted a call to the Aasvoëlkop congregation in Johannesburg. "I had only been in my new congregation for four months when the police shot and killed 69 black people (in March 1960) who had reported to the Sharpeville police station to hand in their passbooks and invite arrest. This presented me with a new crisis of faith." The resultant unrest was quelled, individuals and organisations banned, and white dominance re-established. Before the year was out, however, a WCC delegation responded to the crisis by meeting with South African member churches (including the Transvaal and Cape synods of the NGK as well as the Nederduitsch Hervormde Kerk) at Cottesloe in Johannesburg.

## Cottesloe

The Cottesloe Consultation produced a statement of far-reaching symbolic value. The delegates from the Nederduitsch Hervormde Kerk (NHK) rejected the Consultation Statement out of hand, while the majority of the NGK delegates supported it — at least initially.

The statement was regarded as self-evident by most Christians around the world, yet in South Africa it created an unprecedented storm. It rejected the biblical and theological justification of apartheid. "This rejection aside, the statement was not exactly radical, even by the standards of the time. It was, however, seen by the Prime Minister, Hendrik Verwoerd, ever the logician, as warranting his intervention," Naudé recalls. "Verwoerd sensed danger and called the NGK delegates to order. Insisting that they had allowed themselves to be influenced by the liberal views of the WCC, he told them that they had a duty to the Afrikaner people and the state to maintain white supremacy. Verwoerd was an intimidating and ruthless man. His status was enough to get virtually every one of the delegates effectively to withdraw their support for the statement." He required them to recant, and recant they did — except for Beyers Naudé. He stood alone. "It was the beginning of loneliness and isolation, something that I would experience again and again in the years ahead." The night before the Transvaal synod made its final decision on the Cottesloe Statement, Naudé wrestled with his conscience:

> I had to decide. Would I submit to the political pressures which I was experiencing or would I stand by my convictions — which were by this time rooted in years of theological struggle? I discovered that night just how firm and holy those convictions were. I simply had to make a stand. I put my position to the synod with all the respect I still had for the highest assembly of my

226

Church. In obedience to God and my conscience I told the synod that I could not see my way clear to giving way on a single one of the resolutions that came out of Cottesloe. I was convinced that they were in accordance with the truth of the gospel.

Was he surprised that he alone ultimately defended the carefully considered Cottesloe resolutions which his fellow NGK delegates had earlier found to be firmly grounded in the Scriptures? "I was not only surprised, but deeply shocked," he replies. "I knew some would not be able to withstand the pressure, but the capitulation of others who had played such an important and creative role, both in organising the Cottesloe Consultation and in the actual writing of the statement, came as a hammer blow. Some spoke of their surrender as a strategy on the basis of which to work 'from within' the Church to bring about change. Some 'phoned me to apologise for their lack of courage. Others simply held their silence. Some to this day will tell you they did not capitulate. But they became silent. That, as far as I am concerned, is capitulation." The NGK, like the NHK, withdrew from the WCC and set up a commission to investigate the teaching of the Bible on questions of race. The outcome was the well-known study entitled *Ras, Volk en Nasie en Volkereverhoudinge in die Lig van die Skrif* (*Human Relations in the Light of Scripture*) which contributed directly to the decision of the World Alliance of Reformed Churches to declare apartheid a heresy in 1982. Naudé points out that several documents have come from the white Church since 1982 and in them one can discern a change of attitude. "They have theologically adjusted their position — but carefully and cautiously so as not to offend too many within their ranks who continue for one reason or another to imagine that God shows special favour towards the Afrikaner. The truth of the matter is that the ghost of Cottesloe continues to haunt the NGK. At its General Synod in 1994 it will have to decide whether to unite with the black and coloured Churches to form the Uniting Reformed Church. This will be the opportunity to put the ghost of Cottesloe to rest for once and for all." For Naudé, the Cottesloe event of more than thirty years ago, is "an event where the NGK allowed the voice of blood, passion and nationalism to override the voice of God. With this the NGK has not yet fully got to grips".

## Obeying God

History moved fast for Naudé after Cottesloe, but not without a moment of unexpected irony. He was elected moderator of the

Transvaal synod two years after it had voted to reject the Cottesloe findings, and a mere two months after his widely publicised, recriminatory resignation from the Broederbond. "The agony of my decision to resign from the Afrikaner Broederbond was grounded in a realisation that it would be seen by Afrikaner nationalists as a betrayal. I knew that reprisals would come sooner or later. This is what made my election as moderator so surprising. I was quite overwhelmed and stunned," he notes with a sense of amazement that lingers after all these years. "Some told me it was the will of God. Quite frankly I did not know what to make of it. Then things began to fall into place. The first request the synod made of me was that I resign my position as editor of *Pro Veritate* (a journal of theological critique), which I had established the previous year." For Naudé this was an intensely difficult moment for he saw it as an attempt to establish a *quid pro quo*. The Church would *affirm* his integrity and insights. He, in turn, would be expected to back off on his critique of the NGK. "When colleagues and adversaries are being pleasant and conciliatory it is not easy to stand by one's convictions," he observes. "Again I agonised, but simply had to refuse the request." This was in April 1963. In August of that year he founded the Christian Institute, and applied to his Church for permission to retain his clerical status, while serving as Director of the Institute. Permission was denied and he resigned as moderator of the synod. His farewell sermon, preached to his Aasvoëlkop congregation, was appropriately entitled, "Obey God Rather than Man".

His inaugural lecture as director of the Christian Institute was significantly entitled "Versoening" (Reconciliation), and it was delivered at the Central Methodist Church in Johannesburg, then under the pastoral care of one of the great patriarchal figures of Methodism, the Rev Dr J. B. Webb. "At a personal level it was people like Ds Tema, E. E. Mahabane, Seth Mokitimi, J. B. Webb and Joe Wing who supported me at the time. Beyond that there was a measure of support from some colleagues in the NGK, but this soon gave way to alienation. The cost of rejection by the Afrikaner community is perhaps something that only an Afrikaner who breaks rank with his own can understand. This was nevertheless a time of liberation for me. It was the beginning of a new solidarity with a different community — an ecumenical community of people in resistance. More than that it was a time of acceptance by the black community.

Today I am a member of the NGK in Afrika (the black NGK) where I worship and minister. I have learned from personal experience that the black community is very accepting and ready to receive those who wish to become part of the greater South Africa. There is a lesson here for white South Africans who fear the future."

## Christian Institute

From the founding of the Christian Institute until the time of its banning, together with the banning of its leaders, in October 1977, the life and person of Naudé was inextricably bound up with the fortunes and tragedies which constituted that organisation. The story of the Institute is in many ways the story of Naudé's remarkable propensity for change. Many people catch glimpses of a different world 'out there', some even test the climate of that world, but most, to a greater or lesser degree do not venture boldly beyond the warmth and security of home. This is what makes Naudé different.

With an insatiable, and at times reckless, quest to free himself from what he perceives as contextually imposed presuppositions, Naudé has relentlessly sought to cross frontier after frontier. It is this that drew him out of his captivity within a narrow nationalism, and this that throughout the days of the Christian Institute enabled him to show a remarkable flexibility in responding to new insights and needs. The Christian Institute that initially bore the marks of Naudé's white, Reformed and scholarly theology, became increasingly open to the cross-currents of ecumenical thought and above all to black thinking and critique. As the Institute became increasingly black, so Naudé's personal identity underwent further change. Naudé speaks again of the sense of rejection that occurred as many withdrew from this cauldron of encounter between races, ideologies and theologies. "I discovered," he states, "that one's quest for life and liberation is an enduring journey. There are repeated barriers to cross and each time there are those who refuse to make the crossing with you. Well that's just the way it is. All we can do is take people as far as they are prepared to go. It is never easy to travel alone. But then there are always a few who are already on the road. It's merely a case of linking up and travelling on together."

Beyers Naudé's fame spread far and wide during the fourteen years that the Institute existed. He received enormous international ac-

229

claim, while at home he was the victim of persecution and rejection by the white community. The events of crisis and splendour surrounding his life were extensive: harassment by the security police, right-wing terrorism, libel suits, arrests and trials, honorary doctorates, awards and recognition, numerous speeches and lectures, visits abroad, involvement in every major political event of the time, countless engagements with both the exalted and lowest members of society. Finally there was a five-year banning order served on him in October 1977 and renewed in 1982 for a further three years. Quite suddenly it was lifted on Wednesday 26 September 1984.

In the past he has spoken of his bannings as his "seven lean years". "I suppose they were both lean and fat," he says looking back. In one way the banning order ensured that he was not able to influence society at large. From the point of view of the authorities, he also became embarrassingly visible. Church leaders, politicians, overseas visitors, concerned citizens, black and white people, the young and the old all beat a path to the door of the Naudés' Greenside home.

## After the Banning Order

Beyers Naudé was quickly drawn back into the mainstream structures of the ecumenical Church after the lifting of his banning order. As General Secretary of the SACC and through the height of the Church's involvement in resistance, Naudé was a major player in extra-parliamentary politics. When political organisations were unbanned in 1990 and the first ANC delegation was appointed to meet the government in the historic Groote Schuur event, Naudé was appointed as part of the ANC team. "I told Madiba (Nelson Mandela) that I was deeply honoured, while pointing out that I had not actually joined the ANC," he recalls. "This didn't seen to bother him." The media picked up the story and veteran ANC politician Walter Sisulu was reported as saying: "He has always been part of us."

## Hopes and Fears

Naudé has always dreamed big dreams. "If politics is about what is possible, religion is about the quest for what is not immediately possible," he suggests. What then of the future? "Once again the Afrikaners, and more particularly right-wing Afrikaners, are going to be a factor in the future. Although right-wing Afrikaners constitute a

*230*

small group within the greater Afrikaner community, they are capable of evoking emotions and fears well beyond the confines of their own followers and even beyond the Afrikaner community. Some will opt for guerilla warfare and there will be desperadoes and racists from around the world ready to support their cause. I fear bloodshed for years to come. This having been said, I do not believe they can either win or survive forever. My counsel to my fellow Afrikaners and to all whites is: Face reality, deal rationally with your fears, commit yourselves to building a united non-racial South Africa and you will be surprised to discover how ready blacks are to understand your fears and to accept you — together with your culture, language and religion."

PHOTO ACKNOWLEDGEMENT: *South*

# EBRAHIM RASOOL

*Bridging the Two Worlds of Islam*

Ebrahim Rasool regards himself as a typical
younger generation Muslim — with a commitment
to the modernisation project.

Classified as coloured by apartheid law, he was raised within the coloured community. He sees this as an essential ingredient of his identity. Ebrahim was born in District Six (near the city-centre of Cape Town) but Group Areas legislation, in the early 1970s, forced his family to move to Primrose Park, a suburb adjacent to Manenberg. His story has an authentic Western Cape ring to it:

> Having attended *Madressa* (Muslim religious instruction classes) from my pre-school days, I was exposed to the machinations of the Mosque and all the internal wranglings of *Kaapse politiek* (Western Cape politics) for as long as I can remember, having gained my religious and political education in Kombuis (kitchen) Afrikaans. I am emotionally attached to this community; the mosques of the Western Cape are my home. I am, at the same time, deeply committed to enabling Islam to come to grips with the impact of modern critical thinking.

> The vast majority of Muslims live in two isolated or compartmentalised worlds — the world of traditional Islam and the secular world of business, critical thinking and western education. This is dramatically symbolised in the Muslim woman who leaves her home in the morning with a scarf over her head. She removes it at the bus stop, places it in her bag and puts it on again in the evenings when she arrives back at the bus stop. Men, in turn, leave their secular selves at the door of the mosque as they take off their shoes and enter in order to say their prayers. They then, all too often, leave the religio-ethical values of Islam aside as they go about their daily business. Outside of the mosque they remember their religion only in the practice of a particular ritual or in order to defend some aspect of Muslim dogma that may emerge in the course of their day. The rational and secular on the one hand and the religious on the other seldom meet in significant dialogue.

Struggling to integrate these two worlds in his own life, Rasool recognises that this kind of talk does not endear him to the conservative *ulama* (clergy). "I seek to show empathy with those who have for generations been locked into the two isolated worlds of Islam; I can, however, do no other than give expression to the quest for my own integration as a person. There are a vast number of Muslims who feel as I do. A moment of truth will sooner or later dawn for Islam in South Africa. Without the apparatus of state on its side, as is the case in Muslim countries, it will need to either adapt or find itself thrust into social irrelevance as an increasing number of its younger members simply drift further into secularism. Islam is obliged to find an authentic identity in the modern world. If it does, a

234

surge of spiritual energy will empower the Muslim community, enabling it to make a profound moral contribution to the emerging South African nation."

Will this divide the Muslim community, already plagued (like all other religions) with internal divisions? "I suppose it will," concedes Rasool. "New birth is always painful. We have defended our identity and practices for generations, persuading people to conform to outdated custom and belief. We should not, therefore, be surprised when they resist change."

## The Route Travelled

"If to be coloured means to have 'mixed blood', then I have all the mix that is required. My maternal grandfather was a fourth generation Englishman, whose ancestor came to South Africa with the colonial troops at the beginning of the last century. My maternal grandmother's forbears arrived in Cape Town as Javanese slaves. My grandmother on my father's side, was a Dutch woman — evoking speculation that Thys Lourens, the former Northern Transvaal rugby captain, is my father's cousin — and my paternal grandfather was an Indian indentured labourer who arrived in Natal as a sugar-cane cutter in the last century."

Ebrahim Rasool speaks of being raised in a home without any serious ideological leaning. It nevertheless harboured "the usual political memories which face the coloured community". His father's mother was reclassified coloured and the family was driven out of District Six when Ebrahim was in standard two. "My mother brought a certain Muslim piety into our home, with Sheikh Nazeem Mohamed (President of the Muslim Judicial Council) being regarded as our family's spiritual leader. My father was always more of a free-thinker. He bought the *Cape Times* and the *Argus* everyday, bringing the 'outside' world into our Muslim home, encouraging us to discuss the events that were happening around us. He helped instill a culture of reading in me from the time that I was very young. So from the word 'go' I lived at the nexus of Muslim traditionalism and secular free-thinking. I am still trying to integrate the two."

The next important stage in Rasool's upbringing came when he attended Livingstone High. The principal of the school was

*235*

R. O. Dudley, a strong New Unity Movement person; currently its President. "In my matric year (1980) I was Secretary of the Student Representative Council (SRC) and on the Committee of 81, which had overall responsibility for co-ordinating the school boycott in the Western Cape. I spent hours in Dudley's office, discussing the political correctness or incorrectness of the boycotts. . . When a pupil was sent to afternoon detention for one or another reason and Dudley was on duty, the event invariably turned into a political lesson. I studied German as a subject and soon found that the passages which I was given to translate would carry an appropriate level of leftist teaching. A favourite author in German literature was Bertolt Brecht, the independent Marxist dramatist and poet. Livingstone was great on independent thinking — although always within the ambits of leftist thought."

Appreciative of political insights that he gained during this period of his life, Rasool also recalls the sense of frustration he experienced at the time.

> New Unity Movement politics has to do with the 'struggle of the mind' — an exercise in weighing alternative arguments, seeking to strip away the different layers of debate and argument in order to reveal the essential principles involved, ever vigilant not to act on a principle considered politically incorrect, opportunistic or unclear in any way. This internal rigour is a discipline from which one can only benefit. It can, at the same time, have a paralysing effect at the level of political action. Taught to wait for the right moment and to act on the right principle, I began to feel that Unity Movement people were in danger of losing out on a crucial opportunity to take the fight against apartheid an important step forward. It was a case of the quest for the best political option becoming the enemy of what was, in effect, an important step ahead. In time I began to question their notion of correctness and what is best, but never without a deep respect for the essential ideas within the movement.

Arriving at the University of Cape Town in 1981, Rasool was still a convinced advocate of Unity Movement politics. "I took a principled stand on a number of issues. Studying there as a black person under permit, my commitment was to get what I could out of the place and not to participate in the various sport, extra-mural and other activities. When I graduated with a BA and later with a teacher's diploma, I did so in absentia. My Unity days convinced me that

236

participation was opportunism and a sure recipe for absorption into the bourgeois milieu of liberalism."

Rasool was at this time about to undergo a further important development in his life. "I began to discover a new religious dimension to my life. Although always consciously religious, towards the end of my standard nine year I was excused from attending *Madressa* in order to have more time to study. I simply loved the freedom not to pray. It was a new found liberation, and I began to oppose what I saw as an unprincipled practice among some Muslims to take time off school to go to the *Jumah* (Friday prayers). I viewed this as mere conformism, rather than thoughtful religious practice. The fundamentalists saw me as trying to undermine the faith, and with this the stage was set for me to seek to understand precisely what it meant to be a Muslim. Without ever doubting my religious affiliation or questioning my commitment to Islam, I began a quest for religious authenticity. It would prove to be a long quest, and one that would include several shifts in focus and direction."

Rasool joined both the Azanian Students Organisation (AZASO) and the Muslim Students Association (MSA). Again he found himself confronted with two worlds that needed to be reconciled. "Through AZASO I encountered Mama Sisulu and other ANC people, discovering a brand of politics that was more colourful, less cerebral and more broadly inclusive. Through the MSA I encountered a religion that was related to the political struggle in which I was engaged. Slowly my religious and political personae were coming together. Farid Esack assisted me in this quest in a significant manner and later, through my involvement in the Call of Islam, the integration was taken a step further." Rasool explains the religious renewal he experienced both in relation to the growing influence of Muslim fundamentalism in the wake of the Iranian revolution, and a perceived need to identify the essential moral principles on the basis of which to respond to the influences that were drawing him deeper into organised politics.

> I saw a need for both a spiritual journey inwards, in an attempt to understand my own identity, as well as a need to reach out to a community of people committed to the values that constitute my identity. The fascinating thing for me was that this community included Muslims as well as Christians, Hindus, Jews, atheists, historical materialists and others. Muslim fundamentalism was

237

not satisfying my inner yearnings for answers to the questions I was posing — the answers were too trite, too dogmatic and quite unrelated to the world of questions, struggle and political realism of which I had become a part. The fundamentalist revival did, however, evoke in me a certain longing for spiritual fulfilment and religious integrity. The mere formalism of my past religion was no longer sufficient to satisfy my new found spiritual quest.

My first three years at UCT were the most religious years of my life. From the end of 1981 through to 1983 I prided myself in not having missed a single prayer. I prayed five times a day. I was involved in the *Halqa* (study groups) and often participated in *gadat* (spiritual exercise groups).

This inward journey was accompanied by increased political engagement. Invited (in 1983) as a member of the AZASO Executive to attend the United Democratic Front (UDF) launch in the Western Cape, he arrived late — having been instructed by his father to weed the lawn before he went. He nevertheless unexpectedly found himself elected to the Regional Executive. The following year he helped form the Call of Islam, an organisation committed to drawing Muslims into the political struggle. In January 1985 he started teaching at Spine Road High School in Mitchell's Plain, a school deeply involved in the student protests and the school boycott. Detained for three months at the end of 1985, on his release he was served with a banning order. His involvement in the UDF had nevertheless increased and he went into semi-hiding, deciding not to announce his involvement in meetings ahead of time and not to sleep at home. This enabled him to remain out of prison until June 1987 when he was again arrested and imprisoned for thirteen months. After his release he was again restricted, but together with others in a similar situation, he chose later to 'unban' himself. During this time he and Rashida were married. "We had a traumatic courtship which survived the political storms of the eighties, my imprisonment and an intense struggle, in which both of us shared in a quest to make sense of what it means to be Muslim and yet part of the modern world. In many ways Rashida was more ready to integrate the two worlds than I was," he observes with appreciation. "We have walked the journey together every step of the way."

The Rasools lived in ambiguity, between Ebrahim's self-claimed freedom and the threat of imprisonment until the unbanning of political organisations in February 1990. Their political involvement was then directly through the ANC. Ebrahim Rasool was elected Treasurer of the Western Cape region in 1991.

## Religious Reconstruction

Rasool sees religion as both a journey into past tradition and a quest for contemporary relevance. "To neglect the former is to cut oneself off from a history of struggle and quest that can only condemn one to a shallowness of pursuit that by definition leaves one unable to answer the complex questions of life. In a word, I realise that our struggle is not essentially unique. It is a contemporary manifestation of an ancient and enduring quest to be human and to live in community with other people. Religion teaches us a number of lessons on how to cope with that journey — things like prayer, fasting, the place of festivals and so on. Simply practised out of habit or obligation they remain unrelated to the contemporary struggle. Once they are related to, and made part of, contemporary living, they become more than religion; more than a practice adjacent to the rest of our lives, they became part of life itself."

Equally important in this quest, argues Rasool, is a sense of belonging. His early years of religious instruction provided him with the symbols, stories, memories and practices which welded him into the Muslim community.

> This sense of community, of being a Muslim, going to the mosque, sharing in the fasts and celebrations and practising Muslim tradition is a vital part of who I am. This is where I belong. It is here that I draw on my roots for sustenance. I am part of a Muslim culture, which is the interweaving of things like Malay choirs, weddings, funerals, certain kinds of food, the singing of spiritual songs, gatherings at the mosque and so on. So, when I speak of my quest for religious identity, it is within this broader context. I am part of Islam in the Western Cape. Even when I am critical of it, I am dependent on it. I find myself trying to separate those things within Islam that are residual of past cultures and practices from what is essential to the religion itself — but find it almost impossible to do so. This having been said, there are dimensions of this tradition to which I cling, understanding them to be indispensable to life itself. I am, however, becoming increasingly aware that they are covered in layers of custom and prejudice that obscure the very reality to which I want to cling.

Pushed to define this reality, Rasool resorts to traditional religious

239

language. "It is a God consciousness." And who is this God? "I really don't know," comes the immediate response. "The Qur'an speaks of Allah as an all-encompassing presence, a dimension to life itself, but a personal presence, a reality that evokes in me a sense of worship and submission. Yet, to leave a Qur'anic understanding of Allah there, is to make Islam into a fatalistic religion of submission to what prevails at any particular time and place in history. The Qur'anic God calls me to reach the full potential of the person who I was created to be, thoughtful, self-critical, understanding, given to justice, and ready to serve the purposes of God in the world. Prayer, worship and fasting, all key ingredients of Islam, enable me to do this. When, however, I am simply held captive by such practices, oppressed by them through habitual submission rather than thoughtful participation, they are no longer the channels through which my God-given potential is realised. They then become oppressive. They prevent me from worshipping God in an intelligent and worthy manner. Religion is about an innate awareness of God as the One who is the source of my being, and whose will and purpose I seek to serve in life. Prayer and fasting are only important to the extent that they serve this end. To the extent that they hinder this, they stand in need of reform and reconstruction."

## Politics and Human Values

Religion, for Rasool, is about the worship of God, without which he believes we fall short of our full potential as human beings — of the realisation of our true selves. He, in turn, sees politics as the expression of one's true self in the world. "Politics," he suggests, "ought to be the extension of your essential self, requiring it to be a disciplined, value-oriented exercise." This, he argues, is not however what shapes the behaviour of most political players.

> The truth of the matter is that one's adherence to moral values can be an impediment to one's political advancement in life. Many of us once thought that liberation politics was inherently moral; some of us are discovering that this is not the case.

> We are living in a time of negotiation and alliance politics which necessitates compromises and certain political deals, carefully balanced *quid pro quos* and a willingness to live with policies and practices that we never thought we would be prepared to accept. Perhaps this is the nature of the politics of transition. Maybe there is no other way out of the dilemma of South African politics, so I

240

am not unduly critical of certain compromises. It does, however, raise the question as to what happens to the values which form our essential selves and for which we have been fighting all these years.

There are two options: The one is to forget about values, and many people are finding themselves pushed in this direction, as the jockeying for positions in the constituent assembly and other bodies takes place. The outcome is a politics of sterility, a mere functionalism that makes little contribution to the resolution of the very contradictions of society that have forced the alliances and deals in the first place. The alternative is for some individuals to hold to such values that have given the fight against apartheid a level of ethical dignity and respect. The question is who is going to do this? Who will be the carrier of these values?

This is where Rasool believes religion can make its biggest contribution. Religion should inspire people to do the right thing, whether or not it is expedient or in their self-interest to do so. "To the extent that religion deals with ultimate things, things worth dying for, it is at least one of the carriers of human and liberatory values. For all the failures of the major religions of this country, when the struggle was at its height, Mosque and Church alike were obliged to concede that the things that activists were dying for were the values that formed the bedrock of their religious beliefs. It is these same values — love, justice, decency, human rights, democracy, honesty, a decent education, housing, concern for the poor and so on, that stand central to the Muslim religion, as they do to other religions." Rasool argues that the integration of religion and politics, which was beginning to emerge in the 1980s in response to the intensity of the evil of apartheid, has given way to the old kind of religious formalism that separates religion into a realm of its own.

"It is in the interest of the liberation struggle as a whole," he continues, "that the religious conscience of the nation be kept alive as a basis for ensuring the survival of the very values that have sustained the struggle over many years. I am not suggesting that it is only the religious community that can do this. I have too much respect for the moral integrity of some non-religious people who share this concern for values. Some are Marxists, some are humanists, and many are simply decent people who are not too sure what they are. . . There is, however, a moral incentive at the centre of the great religious traditions of South Africa that, if released at a time when a new nation is in the process of being born, can make a far-reaching

241

impact on the future. Values that are born now, entrenched in a constitution and become part of a democratic culture in this formative period of our history, will be crucial for the future identity of the nation. On the other hand, if the politics of the emerging nation simply functions at the level of 'business as usual', the new South Africa might not be so new at all."

## An Optimist

Rasool explains the relationship between his understanding of the dominant idea of the present age and the continuing struggle for values. He feels we need a sense of perpetual dissidence or ongoing struggle within the dominant movement for change.

> Each epoch produces its own dominant movement for renewal, in opposition to the prevailing structures of oppression in any situation. Nelson Mandela symbolises that movement in South Africa today. This is not to suggest that the movement represents all that either he or we have been struggling for. It is not an egalitarian movement and it is not a movement which represents the aspirations of the nation as a whole. South African political reality is such that compromise is inevitable. It is, however, a movement whose history is such that it can be no other than open to the ethical ideals for which we are continuing to struggle. So, my concern is not primarily that all that we had hoped for is not present in this movement, it is rather that there are elements within it that are today questioning the veracity of these values.

> These values are nevertheless deeply entrenched in our struggle and I believe they will win through. People have suffered and died for them. They constitute an important part of our identity as a people, and will not be easily forfeited. These values are also a part of the *religious* identity of our people. Religious organisations have a special obligation to share in the process of keeping these values alive.

Rasool also speaks about these values in relation to a special kind of democratic vision, which he sees operative in the Western Cape in particular. "We have a long history of political diversity in the Western Cape," he observes. "Sometimes it is ridiculed by ANC officials and people from other regions. Provided these 'troublesome democrats' who are responsible for this brand of politics remain in solidarity with the major forces for democracy, they actually constitute an important source of perpetual dissidence. This is no bad element to have in any nation. It is, above all, an important ingredient in a nation like ours, which is struggling to define its emerging new character in the face of the demand for compromise which emerges from the vast social and political diversity of South Africa."

"As it is in the interest of a democratic government to allow the visionary dimensions of religion to continue to disturb the less than ideal compromises that it is forced to make," Rasool continues, "so it is also in the interest of that government to encourage the kind of 'loyal dissent' that characterises Western Cape politics."

## Religion Again

The conversation turns back to religion. Arguing that religious institutions have a mission to serve a purpose which is greater than themselves, Rasool again stresses the need for these organisations to be transformed in order to render this service.

> My concern for religious reform is not grounded in some sort of personal need to turn the Mosque upside down. It is based on the belief that the Mosque, together with the institutions of the other religious traditions in South Africa, has an important role to play in the South African struggle, by helping to keep the values which it holds dear. For this to happen Islam itself needs to be re-formed. . . The problem is that it cannot contribute to democracy because its history is marred by the institutional support it has given to caliphates, tyrants, authoritarian leaders and one-party dictatorships. Some even supported Saddam, merely because he claims to be a Muslim. There are simply no grounds for that sort of religious opportunism and chauvinism in a liberation struggle. We have for too long, in too many places around the world, provided theological legitimation for the very kind of inequality between rich and poor that is now being rebelled against in South Africa.

> Islam needs to rediscover the basis of its identity, asking to what extent suggestions that Allah provides for all of us in different degrees and that we should be satisfied with our lot in life, are really little more than ruling class ideology imposed on the poor in the name of Allah. That kind of religion is no more than the opiate of which Marx spoke. There is, on the other hand, an ethical incentive in the Qur'an that needs to be rediscovered and related to the world in which we live. For this to happen, however, Islam is obliged to look critically at its own soul. It is a process that is beginning to happen despite the desperate attempts by some within our ranks to suppress all forms of dissent.

Rasool believes the liberating incentive at work in South Africa knows no limits and no restrictions. "Muslims cannot be part of a political struggle for renewal and expect that struggle not to reach into their own structures," he argues. "The ANC and other political groupings that favour renewal need, in turn, to understand that there are no short cuts to mobilising the Muslim constituency for change. To simply fraternise with a few Sheikhs and Imams is not enough. The ANC needs to engage the Muslim community in dialogue, challenging fears, racism and other hang-ups, while allowing itself to be challenged by the legitimate concerns of the Muslim tradition."

## Women

Rasool sees no contradiction between being both pro-Muslim and being in favour of women's rights. He is in agreement with Ali Mazrui, the renowned Islamic and African scholar, in speaking of an "interrupted Islamic revolution on women's rights" which needs to be reactivated. Mazrui describes pre-Islamic Arabia as fostering one of the most sexist societies of the ancient world. Women were regarded so lowly that infanticide among female babies was widespread. Polygamy was without restriction and men could divorce their wives virtually at will, while it was near-impossible for women to divorce their husbands.

"Within a generation," suggests Rasool, "Islam had stopped the practice of infanticide, restricted polygamy and expanded women's property rights. Islam teaches that 'paradise is at the feet of mothers', opening up huge theological possibilities concerning the rights of women." This possibility was interrupted essentially by two developments in Muslim history. The rise of royalist Islam after the death of the Prophet Muhammad and the later termination of the *Ijtihad* (independent judicial review by individuals) which located legal authority in the hands of religious leaders. The outcome was eventually the emergence of Muslim royal dynasties which gave rise to the institution of harems and separation of the sexes. The closing of the gates of the *Ijtihad* in the seventh century, in turn, took away the right of individual interpretation of the Qur'an and the Sunna (Islamic tradition). "The outcome," says Rasool, "was the aborting of a progressive thrust inherent in early Islam."

"Let me leave it there," he continues. "I have already been too critical of Islam which I love, which gives me identity and which I will affirm until my dying day. It is enough to observe that the teaching of Islam

244

on women leaves a great deal to be desired." Widely known as a person committed to equality between the sexes, I ask Rasool whether he practises this equality in his own home. "At the risk of sounding arrogant, I am probably one of the very few Muslims around who tries to live a totally non-sexist life. From the time that Rashida and I were married, we have shared all responsibilities in life from cooking, to caring for the baby and cleaning the house."

The Rasools have named their daughter Tahrir Thandeka, Arabic and African names which mean respectively 'to be free' and 'to be loved'. "She is a symbol of our commitment to Islam, to Africa and to social justice."

PHOTO ACKNOWLEDGEMENT: Diana Russell and Mayibuye Centre, UWC

# ALBERTINA SISULU

*A Woman of the Soil*

Albertina Nontsikelelo Sisulu is a person of
enormous dignity and presence. She has been a
sustaining wife to a husband who was in prison for
26 years and a sacrificing mother to five children.
She has also emerged as a leader and symbol of
struggle in South Africa.

The mother of a nation not yet born, she has lived through the birthpangs and trauma of struggle. 'Mama', as she is affectionately known, is a name that can scarcely be denied her. Imprisoned on many occasions and banned from 1964 to 1983 (which included ten years of house arrest), her 90 days of detention under the Suppression of Communism Act in 1963 stand out most vividly in her memory. She recalls a policeman coming into her cell late one night:

> He told me my four-year-old child was in the intensive care unit of Baragwanath Hospital, suffering from pneumonia. "Tell us where your husband is and you are free to go," he told me. Shattered by the news I also realised that for the sake of both my husband and my child I could not betray the struggle. I told the policeman this. His eyes were hard and determined. "Then you will die in this cell and rot in the ground. You will not see your husband nor your children again." I looked at him and found myself saying: "I was born of the soil. I can only become part of it again." I was determined that even if I were to die in that cell I would die without selling out the nation. I prayed that God would give me the strength to do what I knew was right and not to allow that policeman to know my inner fear.

Mama speaks of another occasion when she realised that if she were to die, six members of her family would not be able to bury her. Her husband was serving a life imprisonment on Robben Island, two of her children were in exile, another was in jail, an adopted son was serving a five year sentence on Robben Island and her seventeen-year-old grandson had just been arrested. "Those were dark days," she recalls. "The struggle has demanded a high price from many of us."

## The Man in the Bedroom

I ask Mama to speak about what sustained her during those dark days, what kept her going through decades of struggle. "Well, it is difficult to convince some people who ask me that question," she replies. "Hopefully you as a minister will understand. I believed in God, and repeatedly reminded myself that nothing is without an end. I had an inner God-given assurance that one day we would be free. I've always known this to be the will and purpose of God for all people." She offers to give me a concrete example of her trust in God.

> My husband was terribly worried, especially during the earlier part of his imprisonment, as to whether I was able to cope financially and otherwise. I told him not to concern himself because there was a man in the house who assisted me. He was

taken aback and asked, "A man?" I explained that I was talking about the Almighty God.

God was like a father to me, and still is. I used to look up into the corner of my bedroom and speak to him as though I could see him. He seemed to answer me and guide me through many a very difficult time.

Since Mama Sisulu refers to God as a man and as a father, I ask how she feels about feminist notions of God as a mother. Is it not important to find more inclusive notions of God? "Well, for me God is a father," she replies. "I find it difficult to conceive of God in any other way - perhaps because of the positive relationship I always had with my father, and later with Walter (Sisulu). The males with whom I have enjoyed the closest relationships in life have never tried to dominate or oppress me. They have given me a dignity that has enabled me to realise my potential as a person — as a woman in my own right. My sons have similarly always shown me respect. She recalls her early relationship with her father:

I was fifteen years old when my father died. He was only forty-eight years old, dying from what I think must have been some kind of miners' disease, because he worked on the mines for many years. Shortly before he died, he called the children to his bedside, explaining that he was going to leave us soon. He appealed to us to look after one another and then turned to me: "Nontsikelelo," he said, "if you were my eldest son it would have been a natural thing for me to ask you to take responsibility for your sisters and brothers, but you are not. You are, however, strong and you are able to do what I am asking you, which is to take responsibility for your brothers and sisters." It could not have been easy for my elder brother who was standing next to me, but I resolved that day that I would honour my father's trust in me.

This was a formative moment in my life. My father, who had loved me and cared for me, now gave me the responsibility of being a person in my own right. He did not require me simply to fit into the traditional male-dominated hierarchy of responsibility.

Mama resolved not to marry, to become a professional person and to care for her brothers and sisters. "It was for me as though my father's wish was a God-given vocation. Well, as you know I did marry. I met Walter when he was already an active member of the African National Congress Youth League. We married in 1944. I was fortunate, in that I encountered a man who treated me as an equal, as a person who could be trusted to meet the challenges of life with him."

Mama argues that perceptions of the divine may emerge out of one's lived experience. "Males have played positive, creative and supportive roles in my life, so I personally do not have any difficulty in referring to God as a man or as a father." Conceding that some others have not had these positive gender relations, she is ready to allow that the pursuit of an alternative understanding of God or metaphor for the divine is a legitimate exercise. Her reflections become quite philosophical:

> Perhaps we all create God in our image or understanding of life. . . The point is, we don't really know who or what God is like, we therefore tend to see God in relation to an experience that is central to our existence. I suppose I have done this with my father, as someone who always believed in me and was ready to come to my assistance. He enabled me to deal with the challenges of life. I at the same time accept that for others God is a mother. It all depends on one's own personal experiences.

> Different people have different names for God. The missionaries gave our people names for God, but we knew that God long before they came. We called him Modimo, Unkulunkulu and Modiri. So I accept that the struggle for names continues and this is important. . . It is helpful to remember that in so doing we are influenced by life's experiences. This frees us to allow people to relate to God in terms of their own reality. When we do so we realise that most of us are seeking to give expression to a common reality or dimension of life.

Having said this, Mama again stresses the importance of the personal dimension of her religion. "For me God has always been a father and I suppose he always will be. Maybe I am too old to change. I simply ask people to accept that this understanding of God has got me through some very difficult times in life."

## African and Christian

Religion for Mama Sisulu is, however, more than *talk* about God, it has to do with living a life of responsibility and liberation. She sees this as grounded in both Christian and traditional African beliefs. "My notion of God as a father is grounded in me being affirmed and entrusted as a woman to take responsibility for life. Religion is about taking that responsibility." At this point Mama again resorts to normative church language in order to make her point.

> God demonstrated his expectations of the Church by sending his only son, Jesus Christ. Christians are, in turn, called to care for those for whom Jesus died — that is, for all people. This means that the Church should be in the forefront of the struggle for the

250

liberation of the oppressed people. They are the special responsibility of the Church.

This essential belief makes her critical of the Church. "The Church has not fulfilled this responsibility," she continues. "People are dying, while too many Christians are content to remain inside their churches, read their bibles and say their prayers. One cannot claim to be a Christian without leaving the security of the Church and participating in the struggles of the oppressed. If Jesus could go to the cross to defy the unjust laws of his time, so must the Church. This is what God expects of us. It is part of our responsibility."

Mama Sisulu's understanding of the task of the Church in South Africa is rooted in biblical teaching. It reflects a traditional African understanding of life. She sees her religious experience as Christian, while giving expression to a belief in African notions of belonging, of extended family and community. It is the latter which she believes needs greater emphasis in contemporary society, to ensure that the greed and aggression that are so prevalent among people, but quite foreign to traditional African culture, are overcome. Although western ideas have contributed a great deal to contemporary African culture, her concern is that the loss of many traditional values has undermined our common struggle. She sees African togetherness, the sense of being an individual in relation to others and the need to care for one another, as something we need to carry from our past with us into the future. In traditional African society, religion plays an important role in this regard. Her observations are succinct:

> For the traditional African, the divine is at the centre of the community. God binds the community together in common struggle. Religion teaches us to care for one another, to bear one another's burdens and to rejoice in one another's successes.

Mama Sisulu laments the loss of what she calls the 'African way'. It is this loss, fuelled by the aggression of people in their fight against apartheid, that she sees as having contributed to the breakdown in communication between the youth and their parents in African society.

> In former generations one would never respond to a person of one's parents' age in the kind of way in which many young people do today. Old people were treated with respect. That is how I grew up and that is the kind of behaviour I would like to see among our children today. We need to rediscover a sense of family belonging and mutual support for one another. When I say this I know some think that I am just an old woman; one who is unable to accept

change. My response is to ask whether the collapse of such traditional values has made for a better world or not. I think the answer is clear.

Arguing that the recovery of this traditional value system is an important dimension of the solution to South Africa's problems, she continues, "It is only when people begin to show consideration and respect for one another that South Africa will be able to enter a new age of peace and democracy. I am suggesting that in African traditional culture we have the outlines of a system of social behaviour that can assist us in the reconstruction of society".

## A Social Vision

Continuing to speak of traditional African life, Mama Sisulu relates this observation to the contemporary discussion on economics:

> Our great-grandparents used to be seasonal wanderers. In the winter they would move to warmer areas and in the summer to cooler regions. The men would hunt for animals and the women would take responsibility for agriculture and cooking. The work was done communally and what was produced was shared among the entire community. Today this sense of community has been lost. It is probably gone forever.

> We must in some way preserve the sense of working together and create a system of economic life that ensures that we all share in the profits. This sense of sharing cannot, however, be imposed on people. It can only emerge from our living as a family, from within a compassionate community that has a sense of belonging. Our first task in this regard is the creation of a sense of being one people, a united country and an integrated nation. In the absence of this unity, I have some concern about those who speak as if we can force people to share. The South African Communist Party (SACP), for example, speaks of a common destiny and economic socialism. This is fine. My question is how to create a common sense of belonging that makes this possible. Maybe we never will. Maybe society is simply too complex today for the communal ideas that are part of our African tradition to be reproduced.

Aware of the hard work and perseverance that are necessary to ensure that there is progress at the social and economic level, Mama is sceptical about some of the suggested solutions to prevailing problems. "My concern," she observes, "is that socialism does not always encourage responsible living. It sometimes discourages self-initiative and hard work. Somehow we have got to create a system that encourages hard work, personal initiative and responsibility. This is the appeal of capitalism, it provides an incentive. However, I feel

252

strongly that people must learn to care for one another — for the weak and less able. This is the appeal of socialism." Insisting that her understanding of economics is insufficient to suggest how to create an economy that promotes both an incentive to work and a willingness to share, she sees no reason why we should not demand that both capitalists and socialists give their attention to this in a way they have not done before.

> The SACP was the first to fight against social and economic injustice in this country and therefore I instinctively support the Party. The communists have not, however, convinced me that it is possible to translate their economic vision into reality, but neither have the capitalists convinced me that their system will take care of the poor. Perhaps it is only as we continue to share our ideas, and workers and business people take seriously the challenge facing the country, that a new economic system will emerge — a system that addresses the need for a dynamic and growing economy as well as ensuring a fair distribution of wealth. It will certainly need to be different to the form of socialism that we have seen in Eastern Europe and different to the capitalism of the West, which leaves a few people rich and the masses impoverished.

## Remembering the Past

Responsibility, perseverance and dedication are important elements in Mama's vision for a new society. They reflect her own journey through life, which functions for her as a model of what others can do and how the nation can be rebuilt.

The second eldest of five children, she was born in the Transkei in the district of Tsomo. By the time she was 15 her parents were both dead. She had to leave school to care for her six-month-old sister because her grandparents, with whom they lived, were too old and frail to do so. From this early age Mama Sisulu had a sense of commitment to her brothers and sisters, stemming back to her father's dying request that she care for them. She was at the same time determined to complete her schooling.

> After my parents died I missed two years of school. When I started school again I soon made good progress and was given the opportunity, together with other students in the district, to write an aptitude test designed to identify the three top students who would qualify for a bursary to attend high school. I won second place, but when they discovered my age they disqualified me. I was distraught, thinking that I had lost my chance of gaining an education. A local priest intervened and spoke to my grand-

253

parents who decided to use their meagre resources to pay for my education. I knew what it cost them and I was determined to work hard.

She initially wanted to become a teacher, but circumstances did not allow this. She thought seriously about becoming a nun, but realised that this would require her to dedicate herself to the Church which would not enable her to care for her brothers and sisters, so she went to Johannesburg where she trained to become a nurse. "Soon I was able to send money home to assist with the care of my sisters and brothers and to repay the school fees which my grandparents had paid. I felt I was beginning to fulfil the commitment which I had made to my father and to meet my responsibility to my brothers and sisters. This did me as much good as I hope it did them! I was learning that it is possible to meet one's obligations in life and that hard work and dedication can enable one to rise above many challenges."

It was at the Johannesburg General Hospital that the young Albertina faced the harshness of apartheid for the first time. "At home I had known poverty but never the full impact of racial discrimination. Employed in what was then known as the Johannesburg Non-European Hospital, I experienced the reality of white *baasskap* (domination). Even after I had worked my way up to be the senior nurse, in the absence of the sister-in-charge a junior white nurse would be called in to take charge of the ward in which I worked. I faced what black people have lived with daily in South Africa, which is the knowledge that colour is more important than skills! It is prejudice that has persuaded some of our young people that there is no point in acquiring skills at school or anywhere else. This is but one instance of the way in which apartheid has undermined the culture of learning. I also saw the aggression of whites against blacks and the contrast between white wealth and black poverty." During this time she was introduced to the ANC by Walter Sisulu, her future husband. She joined the movement almost immediately. Married in 1944, her initial hopes of a quiet married life were soon shattered. "I had hoped for a normal family life, providing for my husband and children the stability of a home that I never had, but that was not to be."

The participation of the Sisulus in the struggle against apartheid made them the victims of sustained state intimidation and persecution. Mama Sisulu was first arrested in 1958 for participating in an anti-pass protest, and imprisoned for four weeks. In 1963 she was again arrested and held in solitary confinement, under the Suppression of Communism Act, for three months. On her release she was banned first for five years, and then on several occasions after that. Walter Sisulu who had, in turn, been imprisoned and detained on several occasions, was during this time convicted of furthering the aims of a banned organisation and organising a national stay away. Released on bail, pending an appeal, he was under 24-hour house arrest. On 20 April 1963 he went underground to join Umkhonto we Sizwe. Three months later he was arrested in a police raid on the secret headquarters of the ANC at Lilliesleaf Farm. Found guilty of high treason he was imprisoned for life on Robben Island. With this, a new chapter of pain and hardship began for the Sisulus, removing any possibility for a normal family life.

> I was left alone to care for our children and battled financially. I wanted to give my children a good education, and feared that I would not have the money to do so. When they were able to go to school I was unable to visit their teachers as my banning order prevented me from entering any educational institution. I was very concerned about my children. These were bad times, but the community did a lot to help me. The importance of community, of belonging and of caring for one another , was again made real to me.

The pain of those years seems to resurface as Mama Sisulu recounts the events. Deeply attached to her husband, she recalls the pain of being separated from him.

"The worst part of my banning was that I could not visit Walter very easily on Robben Island. I had to apply for special permission and sometimes this was only granted the day before the expected visit or even the day after. This sometimes meant the cancellation of a visit for which I had waited for months. I never got used to having to deal with that kind of uncertainty. On several occasions I was obliged to forfeit my visits as I did not have enough money to fly to Cape Town and the train took too long." The few days she was allowed to be out of Johannesburg was simply insufficient to travel by train.

"Even when I did manage to get to Robben Island, the visits were very strained experiences, especially in the early days. They caused a number of happy and yet depressing emotions within me. At first only one visit of thirty minutes was granted a year. And, on some occasions it was cut short because we mentioned the name of someone whose name did not appear on the prison authorities' list of family members. The rule was that we were only allowed to talk about family affairs and family members. One one occasion the visit was terminated after 15 minutes."

In 1983 Mama herself was again arrested. Charged with furthering the aims of the ANC at a funeral by singing ANC songs, handing out pamphlets and draping an ANC flag over the coffin, she was sentenced to four years imprisonment. Her conviction was, however, set aside on appeal. In 1985 she, together with 15 others, was charged with high treason, but the charges against her and 11 of the other accused were withdrawn. In 1988 she was again served a restriction order, preventing her from travelling outside of the Johannesburg area. "I never really got accustomed to the many restrictions and arrests that I suffered," she observes in response to the obvious question. "I never quite got used to it. Each time my nerves played-up all over again. The anxiety and the concern resurfaced. But I knew that this could not go on forever. I never doubted that we would win. God gave me this assurance."

## Women

I ask Mama to speak specifically about the place of women in the struggle. "There is certainly sexism in all structures of society, including the struggle for democracy and the ANC," she observes. "It is a woman's right and obligation to fight against this discrimination. There are, however, different ways of doing this. I have already spoken about the positive relationships which I experienced with my father and my husband. I have also spoken of other women who have not enjoyed this kind of positive encounter with men. Our different experiences probably affect the way in which we respond to institutional and other forms of sexism. I am concerned about the kind of feminism which is rooted in the aggression of a past experience, which is then directed against all men. I am also concerned about the kind of narrow individualism that is sometimes isolated from other aspects of our struggle — in trade unions, among the youth and the unemployed. Women's concerns must be located within and in relation to the entire struggle. It is an inherent part of the total struggle. I do not accept the promotion of a kind of feminism that ignores the need to change the essential structures of society." Concerned to promote the cause of women within this broader context, she speaks of her place in women's organisations.

In 1944 I joined the ANC Women's League, which was formed to ensure that women's issues could be discussed and acted on. It recognised the fact that men did not understand the problems that affected women directly such as children, maternity grants, education, cost of living and so on. Because some women were

256

afraid to associate with the ANC but wanted to promote these kinds of concerns, I joined with other women to form the Federation of South African Women (FEDSAW). One of our first major campaigns was the anti-pass protest, resulting in the massive women's march on the Union Buildings in Pretoria. The men were elated because of the number of women we were able to mobilise, but less happy when we promoted specific issues concerning the rights of women in relation to men.

Expressing an understanding for the position of some (notably men), that the issue of women's rights should not be allowed to detract from the broader struggle, Mama is at the same time adamant that specific women's rights be given the fullest attention within the context of the other issues being addressed in the struggle for democracy. "We must strive for a truly non-racist, non-sexist and democratic South Africa. This has major implications for existing relations between women and men just as it does for relations between races. It is very difficult for some men to understand this." But she is optimistic about future rights for women, precisely because of the important role women have played in the struggle over the years.

Women have suffered as much, and probably more, than men over the years. A women is often a mother, and it is a painful thing, perhaps the most painful thing in the world, for a mother to see her child suffer — to see her child being killed. Throughout our struggle men, women and children have died alongside each other. Yet, in more recent years our children have paid a price far in excess of anything that any mother can reasonably accept. No black mother who witnessed the madness of people shooting children in the 1976 Soweto school uprisings and elsewhere has been unaffected by this. It radicalised black women in a manner that perhaps no other event has ever done. It drew women into the struggle at every level — in order to demand an end to the slaughter of our children. As mothers, we were compelled to demand: "Kill us if you must, but in God's name leave our children alone."

It is now our obligation to participate in the next phase of struggle, which is the fight for the rights of our children and the rights of women, together with the rights of all human beings in the new South Africa. We cannot leave this to men. There are certain things we can actually do better than they can.

Quietly, and with great confidence she concludes: "There is a general awareness of sexism beginning to emerge, at least in some sectors of society, in South Africa. This is making an increasing number of women stand up and demand their rights. There is also a small but significant number of men who understand this and support it. We have along way to go yet, but women's rights are on the agenda and we must keep them there."

## Children

Mama Sisulu's concern is for the future welfare of children. She knows that the effects of apartheid will be experienced at every level of existence for generations to come. "No child," she argues, "should ever again be asked to pay the price that our children paid. In the process of helping destroy apartheid, they have in many instances destroyed their own chance to share in the future society in a meaningful manner. People often talk about these children as a lost generation. Maybe they are. I would like to think not. We have got to help restore them to their rightful place in life." Concerned about the loss of vision and hope that has come to characterise the attitudes of many children, her question is a pertinent one: "How can we build a next generation that has hope and a sense of responsibility, if we do not redeem these children?" Asked where we begin, her response is immediate: "By ensuring that the children return to school. There is perhaps no single greater task facing the nation than education," she insists. "Education is often a long way and difficult journey, especially for those who are not well equipped to undertake the journey. It is, however, the only means of self-improvement."

"Some people seem to imagine that after the first democratic government is installed, the inequality and suffering of apartheid will be over. Such thoughts are not only wrong, they are extremely dangerous. We need to teach people that they are the ones who will build the future, that they need to be equipped to do so and that this requires education, training, fortitude and hard work." Mama Sisulu believes there is no easy walk or short-cut to success. While apartheid has denied black children a space within which to succeed, it is the obligation of the entire community to ensure that a new culture emerges within which children will recognise their *obligation* to succeed for the sake of the entire nation. "Either they must grab this opportunity with both hands or else the noble-minded dreams of our struggle could be reduced to nothing. New values have got to be injected into every aspect of society. It is the obligation of families, Churches and religious organisations, community organisations and government to promote the desire to know, to teach and to learn."

Albertina Sisulu's journey from the soil of her village in the Transkei has been a long and difficult one. She speaks with the dignity and assurance of one who has gained wisdom and insight from the suffering and hardship endured. Like everyone else whose story is included in this volume, she is grounded in her own context and experience. "We are each required to walk our own road — and then stop, assess what we have learned and share it with others. It is only in this way that the next generation can learn from those who have walked before them, so that they can take the journey forward after we can no longer continue. We can do no more that tell our story. They must make of it what they will." These are the words of one who is, indeed, the mother of a nation that is waiting to be born.

# JOE SLOVO

*A Believing Unbeliever*

Joe Slovo, South African Communist Party chief,
shatters the preconceptions of the anti-communist
media. In many ways he is an uncle-like figure.
However, his vast knowledge of politics, worker
struggles and Marxist debate leaves one in no doubt
where Slovo is ideologically located.

"When I first met Comrade Joe I thought he should be called Oom Joe," observed a young Cape Flats activist shortly after Slovo returned to South Africa from 27 years in exile. "But then as we spoke," continued the youth, "I realised he is *Comrade* Joe — although not just an ordinary one!" A grey-haired lady who was briefly greeted by Slovo at the event where the youthful comrade encountered his uncle and comrade, was heard to comment: "He's such a nice man, I only wish he wasn't a communist!"

Quiet spoken, Joe Slovo is a warm person, generous with his time. Obviously thoughtful, he is able and willing to speak at length on a number of subjects. Concerned about questions of morality and the source of ethical behaviour, he philosophically discusses the nature of good with all who are willing. As a good Marxist he is keen to stress that the point is not merely to think about the world or even to understand it, but to change it. Convinced that it is possible to have a social order which is kinder and more gentle than that which he has witnessed in the Soviet Union, Eastern Europe or the West, he speaks of the need for a new set of values and ideals in relation to which a better society needs to be built. He has a keen interest in religion and the origins of religious belief, while being eager to explain his secular humanism and materialist understanding of life. As a theologian I was left with the feeling that, despite some differences between us, I was in dialogue with a kindred spirit.

Much of what Slovo says sounds a bit like theology in secular dress. Yet clearly he is operating from a different premise. He has what he calls "a bent for a scientific approach to reality". His case is simply stated: "I cannot present a scientific argument for the non-existence of God, but then neither can I prove the existence of God." Having listened to his views on life, his socialist vision and understanding of religion, I suggest he might be "a kind of believing unbeliever". Thinking for a moment, he responds, "In the sense that I believe in the roots of faith and understand its driving energy, I think that is a pretty neat way of describing me." He shares the vision of communal goodness found in most (all) great religions, while having rejected the metaphysics that constitutes part of the dominant religions of the West.

## A Journey Away From Religion

Slovo believes that we are all born atheists. The socialising process does the rest. Raised a Jew in a Lithuanian village ghetto, he was educated in a school run by the local rabbi. "I had the Bible drummed into my head over and over again." Not sure that he ever fully grasped what the rabbi was getting at, religion provided him with a sense of belonging and self-identity in the face of the anti-Semitism of the time. "This is ultimately what religion is all about," he tells us. "It helps us belong. It gives us a sense of identity. It constitutes a way of dealing with the vicissitudes of life — either by way of *escape*, as a result of which we systematically destroy the inner resources we have at our disposal to cope with the challenges of life, or by way of *encounter* through which we develop these resources.

Slovo's mother died shortly after he emigrated to South Africa with his family at the age of nine. He recalls going through the ritual of saying prayers for the dead — the *kaddish*. Twice a day he prayed in the synagogue in Bellevue, a suburb in Johannesburg, without ever understanding the purpose of these prayers. Slowly, he says, a sense of religious doubt and rebellion began to rise within him. "While other boys were playing football, I harboured an irrational sense of obligation to repeat the same prayers over and over again, while wanting to get on with life by joining the other boys on the sports field. That, I think, is where my religious doubts began. At the time I could not explain my uneasiness about having to pray for the soul of my dead mother, but looking back it was the beginning of the realisation that belief in the afterlife is rooted in a sense of human powerlessness. It is grounded in a simple refusal to accept that life actually ends."

Religion, for Slovo, is a human creation, intended to explain and legitimise humanity's inability to deal with suffering and defeat. This is a theme to which we return. Obviously ready to acknowledge the reality of human limitations, he feels that religion too often reinforces and legitimises human failure, persuading us to capitulate in the face of life's difficulties. Concerned to unleash the more creative and heroic resources within the human psyche which cause us to rebel against evil, triumph over defeat and shape our own future, it is clear that Slovo was forced from an early age to develop these resources in order to enjoy any measure of success in life. Indeed, there is a sense in which Slovo's philosophy of life is a reflection of his own grappling with the meaning of life.

Slovo's father was a truck driver, often unemployed. Compelled to leave school at the age of thirteen the young Joe found employment as a dispatch clerk for a chemist, and soon became drawn into the labour movement. He joined the Communist Party of South Africa in the 1940s. He later graduated with a BA and an LLB degree from the University of the Witwatersrand, fought in World War ll and became active as a defence lawyer in a number of political trials. He married Ruth First in 1949, and their lives were dominated by the political struggle. He covertly shared in drafting the Freedom Charter although in 1953, under the Suppression of Communism Act, he was banned from attending all gatherings. He remembers the Congress of the People at Kliptown which he observed through a pair of binoculars from the top of a tin roof about a hundred metres away from the square where the meeting took place. In 1956 he was accused of treason — the charges were dropped two years later. He was detained for four months in 1960, became one of the earliest members of Umkhonto we Sizwe (the military wing of the African National Congress) and left the country on a special assignment in June 1963; shortly before the raid on Lilliesleaf Farm in Rivonia near Johannesburg, where other members of the military high command were arrested and jailed for the next 27 years.

A particularly sorrowful memory for Slovo is the price he and Ruth First required their children to pay for the political activities of their parents. "Black children often know massive material deprivation, while white children of parents engaged in resistance," he points out, "experience a different kind of suffering. Black children whose parents rebel against apartheid are regarded as heroes by schoolfriends and neighbours. White kids are shunned. Shaun, Gillian and Robyn (the Slovo children) were told that Ruth and I were traitors, communist filth and liars." He pauses. "Only in recent years have we as a family come to grips with all that happened."

What is the source of his endurance in crisis? Slovo explains that it comes from immersing himself in working for the goals he has set himself. "There will always be suffering in the world," he concedes. Then, seeming to challenge his own observation, he continues: "My goal is to ensure that a society will one day emerge within which hurt will be kept to an absolute minimum and the kind of unnecessary suffering which our children had to face is eradicated from the face of this earth." I ask him about the assassination of his wife who was killed by a parcel bomb explosion in Mozambique in 1982. "The depth of that wound is still with me. I was particularly angry that violence of this kind should be extended to someone who had never been involved in the military." Feeling that there ought to be "a kind of morality even in war", for a long time he lived with "a great deal of deep, deep sorrow and a degree of bitterness" while being determined not to allow this to shape what he believed his task to be.

I didn't feel that getting the bastards responsible for my wife's death would solve the problem, although I would obviously not have grieved had they been apprehended and dealt with appropriately.

My rational response was to work even harder to ensure that this kind of thing would never happen again. The violence against Ruth was not an isolated case. She was not the only victim of a violent society. I was convinced that the best way to deal with evil was to prevent it from recurring.

Four years later a British court awarded Slovo £25 000 damages against *The Star* newspaper in Johannesburg for reporting that he had orchestrated the murder of his wife. "This kind of personal attack is what I've found perhaps most painful in life," he allows. Responding to the rumour that he was a colonel in the KGB, his words are decisive: "That is total nonsense. It's an absurd proposition."

My interview with Slovo takes place shortly after his initial treatment for cancer. He speaks of the reality of death. "I am not experiencing any anxiety or grief at present," he says. "I rise to challenges and don't easily quit. If necessary I shall fight the disease. I've still a lot of work to do." He is silent for a while. "I understand from my doctors that my life is probably not going to end too quickly. . . I have had a wonderful life, despite the wounds, suffering and deprivations — and that life must end sooner or later." He insists that the reality of death has not influenced his views on religion.

Is there a Slovo apart from politics? "I am not a single-minded person. I read widely, listen to classical music, enjoy the company of friends and play a bit of poker. The problem with life is that it has a way of setting one's priorities." For him the priorities are clear: Thoughtful political engagement in the South African struggle.

## In Quest of the Moral Life

He explains that the reflective life (necessary for creative political work) involves dealing with the competing forces within us. Allowing that morality has to do with integrating the plurality of desires and interests, memories and experiences that constitute one's history, he stresses the need to forge a set of values and principles in relation to which we can work out our response to life. As he sees it, the crises and events of life continually modify these principles. "There is no ethical absolute or set of ethical rules," he argues, "to which we are simply required to adhere — except the obligation to create a more humane society within which people are taken seriously. And this means firstly a society within which the hungry eat, the naked are clothed and the homeless have houses." He emphasises the importance of recognising that no one tradition, whether religious or secular, has a monopoly on this humanising process. His appeal is for an open society within which we learn to understand and respect the various traditions from which people draw their moral inspiration and values. "When it comes to ethics we need all the help we can get. Instead of trying to impose our values and the source of those values on others, we need to encourage them to give expression to moral beliefs and ideals — then, as we talk together, I am convinced that we will find that the major ethical and religious traditions have more in common than we realise." Arguing that public moral debate in South Africa has been too narrow and parochial, he pleads for a broad-based participation in the creation of a more tolerant and pluralistic culture. "Everyone has the right to share in the quest for a new morality."

He tells the story of his encounter with ds Johan Heyns, the former moderator of the Dutch Reformed Church, at the Peace Conference called in September 1991, in an attempt to put an end to the violence sweeping across the country. "If you do not believe, if you do not have faith, if you have no God hypothesis, what is the source of your morality?" he reports Heyns as asking. Slovo's response was that the most cursory survey of history shows that religion has never been a guarantee of morality or compassion. There were the crusades, the conquest of the Americas by the Conquistadors, Kaiser Wilhelm's troops who marched into World War 1 with "Gott Mit Uns" emblazoned on their buttons, tyrants who have ruled in the name of Yahweh, Allah and Christ, and apartheid that has been legitimised by Christian Churches.

While insisting that religion is simply not a working hypothesis in his life, he is at the same time ready to concede that the religious memories of his youth have influenced his present ethic (positively and negatively), and that religion as a social phenomenon continues to be a source of interest and stimulation in his ethical reflection. He believes that correctly understood and implemented, the major religions of the world can and ought to play a constructive role in society.

## Not the Opiate of the People

Slovo rejects as unMarxian the notion that religion is the opiate of the people. When elevated to the status of a general statement on all religion, the slogan is "unMarxist, because it is undialectical and unscientific," says Slovo. He insists that the anti-religious stance of Marxism on religion emerged as a critique of the specific crimes, committed in the name of a specific kind of religion, which undergirded economic greed and political exploitation. "To the extent," he continues, "that religion distracts the attention of the poor away from the causes of their oppression, by directing their attention to a future reward in heaven, religion is the opium of the people. Marx was correct, religion of this kind is a deadly disease which would better be eradicated from the face of the earth." Slovo is quick to point out, however, that not all religion serves this end. "The majority of the people in South Africa have deep religious roots and the new Constitution must guarantee the fundamental right to believe and practise religion. This must, however, include the right not to believe — without prejudice, suspicion or fear of retribution."

This has implications for the relationship between Church, Mosque, Synagogue and Temple on the one hand and the State on the other. It has special implications for the public promotion and practice of religion, leading Slovo to argue that the compulsory teaching of a specific religion in state schools is as undemocratic a violation of basic human rights, as was the prohibition of religious tuition in schools in Eastern bloc countries. "If religion is taught it must be taught in a non-sectarian manner, designed to expose our children to different religions as well as the various philosophies behind atheism," he says. "In this way mutual understanding and the freedom of choice can thoughtfully be promoted. Freedom is grounded in the availability of information and free discourse." Asked whether he would prefer religion not to be taught in schools, he responds, "I support the teaching of religion comparatively, which means that religious, atheist and agnostic ideas must receive equal attention." This approach to the teaching of religion can, he believes, make an important contribution to a new South Africa.

## Many Different Gods

"There are many different religions and gods," Slovo insists. "The God of Trevor Huddleston, Archbishop Tutu, Frank Chikane and others, but also the God of Verwoerd and his cohorts — as well as the

Gods of an array of religionists who use other more subtle ways of subverting the struggle of the oppressed." Showing a particular fascination with the religion of Jesus, Slovo's challenge to the Church is that it return to its origins, relocating itself, like Jesus, on the side of the poor and the marginalised in society. He suggests there is no obvious evidence that Jesus formed a close friendship with any rich person, and that when he addressed himself to the rich it was to inform them that if they wanted to enter the kingdom of heaven they should share their wealth with the poor. "From my perspective," he continues, "the Sermon on the Mount comes very close to a socialist manifesto."

He sees Jesus as a liberation leader in every sense of the term, who resorted to such tactics of struggle as the situation required. Reflecting on the New Testament story, he points out that: "When Jesus' disciples faced danger he advised them to sell their cloaks and buy swords. When hunted by the state Jesus withdrew underground. When entering Jerusalem shortly before his arrest he sought the protection of the masses." Slovo is quite sure: "The religion of Jesus is not an opiate." With a wry smile he adds: "I am no theologian, but wonder whether Jesus would not at least have understood Operation Vula (a covert military contingency plan instituted at the time of the initial talks between the government and the African National Congress) as something demanded by our context."

## An Unrehabilitated Utopian

Moving on from Slovo's exegetical forays into the New Testament, his understanding of the human quest for fulfilment is tough but not uncompromising. "Religion teaches us that God made people in His or Her image. That notion needs to be stood on its feet. I believe it is rather the human collective that made God in its image."

He argues that humanity has projected 'into the heavens' what it has not been able to accomplish on earth. The notion of a perfect God and a world to come within which poverty and tyranny are defeated, is for Slovo a manifestation of the sense of human powerlessness that has emerged over the millenniums.

> What Marxism has done is take the human longing for the perfect society and incorporate it into a socialist vision. It turns an otherworldy, religious notion into a political programme. Sure there are weaknesses, sometimes called sinful dimensions, to the

human character such as greed and the lust for power. That is partly why democracy is so important. It is an important antidote against tyranny, a dangerous possibility that lies deep within the human spirit. But I also believe in the greatness of the human spirit, the ability of humanity to build a paradise on earth, at least in the sense of putting together a society that is a vast improvement on what is seen in either the capitalist world or the former socialist countries of Eastern Europe and the Soviet Union. *I am an unrehabilitated utopian, and intend remaining one until the day I die.*

If the human race is to conquer the dehumanising aspects of life, a utopian or eschatological vision of what society can and must become is imperative. I reject the metaphysics associated with religious belief, while recognising that the vision of an impending kingdom as described in the Bible and the Qur'an can make an important contribution to politics. Believers must, however, accept the responsibility to translate this vision into political action.

He points to the coalescence of the social visions of true Christians, Jews, Muslims and socialists. "Of course we have all fallen short in translating our visions into practice, but that does not invalidate these visions." He believes that there is a need for religious people to rediscover the moral vision that constitutes the roots of all great religions. Similarly, it is the task of socialists to acknowledge the failure of socialist countries, to return to basics, and ask what the socialist dream means in present historical circumstances. "Without a socialist vision," he argues, "I believe the world will be a poorer place. I say this conscious that the destruction of this vision constitutes the undermining of an important part of what the religious traditions found in South Africa are all about." He concedes that the Eastern European model of socialism has failed. His booklet entitled *Has Socialism Failed?* indicates that the SACP must commit itself to a multi-party democracy, freedom of speech, thought, the press, movement, residence, conscience, religion and organisation. "To argue," says the unwearying (and provoking) Slovo, "that the socialist vision per se is dead is for the Christian to concede too much. It is to concede that the social vision of the gospel is dead."

## I was Wrong

Slovo was an early critic of the attempted coup against Gorbachev in mid-1991. Why did he take so long to come to the point where he openly condemned the Stalinist practices in the Soviet Union and Eastern Europe? What is his response to those who suggest that his earlier silence was a simple matter of political expediency and co-option? "That's not an easy one to answer. I was wrong." He repeats the question. "Why was I silent?"

I was part of a tradition within the SACP which was historically closely tied to the Comintern (the Communist International in Moscow). . . My engagement, together with that of many others, in the South African struggle included an uncritical 'religious adoration' for the so-called achievements of the socialist world. Today I marvel at the romanticism that characterised that period of my life. There *were* positive achievements in the Eastern European socialist countries, but the obvious cracks in the system were already beginning to appear. . .

My first uneasiness about Stalinism came when Krushchev revealed a number of atrocities in 1956. . . At the same time I questioned to what extent these crimes were being exaggerated by the imperialist world seeking to destroy what I had convinced myself was a successful workers' state. Then when I and others went into exile in 1963, the Soviet Union and Eastern bloc countries provided us with the only international base from which to pursue our national struggle. That created a natural bias against believing all that was reported in the western media. Living in the Soviet Union also made it extremely difficult, if not impossible to get at the truth behind Krushchev's claims. . . I was also preoccupied with the South African struggle. This was virtually all that mattered to me at the time.

I asked questions, but regarded my energy best spent solely in relation to our own struggle. This was wrong. The level of questioning nevertheless intensified and our party, earlier than most communist parties, began to move away from the basic totalitarian propositions which formed the foundation of the negative features of Stalinism.

Ideological and political isolationism and entrapment is a deadly thing. No one is immune to it. That is why democracy is an essential ingredient of a free society. South African society does not have many democratic, cultural and political memories and/ or resources to draw on in this regard. We all need to work hard at this. We dare not again drift into the habits of the past.

## Perhaps an Agnostic

What is the source of Slovo's restlessness? Where does his vision and strength to keep striving come from? Explaining my interest (as a theologian) in the transcendent dimension of history, I ask what draws him forward to what has not been realised in history. Does he have a sense of a transcendent reality in life? His reply is to distinguish between a sense of a transcendent *agent* and transcendence as a human and historical ideal. "I have a sense of human transcendence. I am driven by the incompleteness of myself and society as a whole. I have a vision of what society can and ought to become, which functions as a lure, continually drawing me into social engagement." Understanding that a believer might personify this dimension of reality as God, Slovo, the non-believer, prefers to leave this reality unnamed. For him this reality occurs as part of a human reality, to be unravelled and explained socially and psychologically. "Above all," he says, "it is a reality which simply must be taken into account in the pursuit of a more complete and better world."

As a historical materialist he is down to earth and practical in talking about what it means to be human. There is at the same time a poetic dimension to Slovo as he speaks about humanity and history. "We are driven. To be human is to reach beyond ourselves to what we ought to become." He argues that there is a sense of incompleteness and a drive for fulfilment within all human beings who take the time to ask what it means to be human, and rejects any suggestion that his sense of vision and inner restlessness make him significantly different from other people. He rejects all talk of being some kind of martyr or hero. "Life," he explains, "is a two-way process. You get out of it what you put into it. To pursue a goal and to be driven by a cause is a glorious and fulfilling thing. When that goal and cause are recognised by global consensus to be right, noble and good, one can only be grateful to have been some small part of it." And what is the nature of that goal? "First and foremost it is a non-racial, non-sexist, democratic South Africa," is his unqualified reply. "The struggle for socialism is a longer-term project. This means that part of my life's vision is hopefully about to be realised, while the struggle for another part of it still lies ahead of me. That's what makes life so exciting and worth living!"

Why he is an atheist? "Because I fundamentally believe our fate is in our own hands rather than being determined by some mysterious force outside of history." I suggest to him that the biblical God is to be found *within* history — a spirit, a dynamic force; a presence that drives the human soul and history itself towards completion, emancipation and hope. Quick to respond, Slovo insists: "Well, that is pretty close to what I tried to say earlier. My concern is that the human drive for fulfilment be realised in an age of equality, in a situation where

*271*

morality and caring for one another are executed in a concrete and practical manner in this world; not in some distant world-to-come. There is, I believe, a certain drive to this kind of fulfilment which is part of the human soul — a notion which I employ in a non-religious sense! Maybe I need to say I am an agnostic rather than an atheist!"

Slovo judges religion, like any other philosophy of life, on the basis of its social function. Does it contribute to the social and political struggle for justice? "Religion in South Africa and elsewhere is today a more ambiguous phenomenon than the kind of religion which Marx knew when he wrote his critique of religion. My interest in religion is partly due to the liberating religious praxis of people whom I have come deeply to respect in the struggle."

"I understand why religious people pray," he says. "Prayer can be an extremely positive dimension in life. It can put people in touch with ideals and values of the humanising process, helping them to reach beyond their prejudices and fears, while enabling them to reach out to one another in the pursuit of goodness. To pray, from my perspective, is to reflect on the purpose and intent of one's engagement in life. Then, to the extent that it leads people to engage in concrete actions designed to further the ends for which they pray, prayer can be an important part of political praxis." Preferring not to get into debate about whether there is someone 'out there' waiting to answer prayer, Slovo is ready to respect the prayers of all people who are seeking to promote peace on earth.

## Let's Stop Arguing

Asked to comment on the challenge facing religious institutions in South Africa, his comment is a telling one: "It has something to do with reaffirming their roots. It is to replicate, in the contemporary context, the liberating dimensions which are at the foundation of religious aspirations." He argues that religious people have resented those who have questioned the legitimacy and relevance of religious belief which has deviated from its own most sacred origins, and persecuted those who dared to suggest an alternative approach to life. Marxists, he is equally ready to concede, are guilty of religious persecution that can only be condemned in the strongest terms. "Marxists and religious people owe one another a whole bunch of *mea culpas*. We actually have a hell of a lot in common."

Slovo is reminded of one of Lenin's more conciliatory comments on religion. "We must stop arguing about whether or not there is a paradise in heaven. Whatever we may believe about that matter, let's build a paradise on earth." "That's about where I am at," says Slovo. "And should I eventually discover that there is a paradise in heaven, that would be a bonus!"

PHOTO ACKNOWLEDGEMENT: South African Chapter, World Conference
on Religion and Peace

# DESMOND TUTU

*Obedience to God*

"It is easier to love the man than to agree with all
that he says. But to know him is undoubtedly to
love him."

These are the words of a life-long friend and admirer of Archbishop Desmond Tutu. Tutu disarmingly responds to suggestions of political unpredictability: "I have my idiosyncrasies the same as anyone else, and sometimes speak up when I should probably let things go. I try to think things through. I pray about matters. Obedience to God is very important for me. Perhaps it is my attempt to respond to the living, dynamic God that makes me appear unpredictable. Maybe this makes me ungovernable!" He laughs. "What I am suggesting is that the Church must sit a little loose to political ideology and never be too concerned about being politically correct. Our task is to be agents of the Kingdom of God, and this sometimes requires us to say unpopular things."

The Archbishop's theology is equally capable of suffering the charge of incorrectness. He has managed to upset some Christians by suggesting that God is not a Christian! "If you say God is a Christian, what happens to God's relationship with the Jews? What about devout Muslims? The Dalai Lama is a person of unquestionable holiness. I've experienced God in a Buddhist temple." An elderly parishioner observed that the Archbishop was correct but "the initial impact of what he says is sometimes a shock to the system".

Controversial at times; few will question the impact of Desmond Tutu on South African and international affairs.

## The Political Task of the Church

Nelson Mandela spent the first night of freedom at Bishopscourt, after twenty-seven years in prison. The next morning Tutu escorted Mandela to his car, prayed for him and sent him on his way. "I can now get on with the work of the Church," the Archbishop told reporters. Three years later his words still concern some Christians who struggle to discern the role of the Church in the present political situation. "Before we simply got out there and disrupted things . . . we made the place ungovernable," observed a young member of a township Church. "Now we are not sure what we ought to do."

I ask Tutu to revisit the February morning in 1990 when Mandela left Bishopscourt. "I hoped that the release would mark the normalisation of the political process in South Africa, and that I could take a far lower profile in the political arena," he observes. "Prior to February 1990 we often held political rallies under the guise of church services. Such actions were politically necessary and theologically correct.

276

Then, with the unbanning of political organisations and the release of Nelson Mandela, I believed the Church should render a different kind of service to the community. I hoped to leave the overtly political work to the politicians and to minister to the spiritual and material needs of people."

Tutu speaks of a practice he has followed for several years as a means of regaining his spiritual and physical strength:

> I often meet with a solitary in England. This wonderful person has for some time counselled me to become more contemplative and as I bade Mandela farewell, I thought that perhaps that moment had come. I wanted to have more time for meditation and more time to give to people who are hurting, to visit the so-called informal settlements and squatter camps on a more regular basis and to use my resources to renew the lives of the poor. I wanted to get out of the limelight and contribute, in a quiet and effective way, to the healing of the nation. I continue to believe that this is an area of ministry which the Church has neglected through the apartheid years. We need to empower people to rise above their circumstances, to reclaim their full humanity and to seize the moment in which we live in South Africa. Blacks and whites need to rise to the challenge which God is offering us.

He discusses the inter-relationship between faith and politics: "Faith is a highly political thing. At the centre of all that we believe as Christians is the incarnation — the participation of God in the affairs of this world. As followers of that God we too must be politically engaged. We need inner resources in order to face the political demands of our time." Returning to the hopes he attached to Mandela's release from prison, he continues:

> Well, things didn't quite work the way I had expected when Nelson Mandela was released from prison. I was hoping for too much. I soon discovered that the poor, to whom I sought to minister in a new way, were continuing to suffer because of the grandstanding and prima donna behaviour of some of our politicians. So, I once again visited homeland leaders, spoke with the leaders of the national liberation movements and with government representatives. In a polite but often forceful manner I have tried to knock their heads together, tried to persuade them to stop dilly-dallying and to get the democratic process under way. My fear is that if we do not get on with the process, the violence that is racking our country will escalate to the point of no return. To an extent I have found myself thrown back into the rough and tumble of the political arena, but playing a new role. Any political role

which I played earlier was of a caretaker kind. Our leaders were in prison, Church leaders were thrust into political roles. Today our role is to persuade politicians to get on with the job.

Stressing the importance of timing and process in politics, Tutu mentions the facilitating role he played, together with Bishop Stanley Mogoba, in arranging the meeting between Mandela and Buthelezi. "My role was that of a catalyst. The idea of the meeting had been in the air for some time. I had just celebrated a very beautiful Eucharist at the consecration of the Bishop of Zululand, Chief Buthelezi was present and the mood was correct. I put the question to him and he agreed. The opportunity to speak to Nelson Mandela was in an equally apt situation. We had participated in the Gandhi centenary celebrations and in the unveiling of the Gandhi statue. I put the question to him and he agreed. The role of the Church is not to be overtly political, but to facilitate the political process." Several years ago Tutu was asked to explain his persistent refusal to espouse political ambitions. "Archbishop Makarios, the Ayatolah Khomeini and Dr D. F. Malan," he replied.

The Archbishop's decision not to allow his priests to belong to political parties was regarded by some as an example of something he would have done well not to have turned into an issue. "Some clergy were very angry with me. We all have personal political persuasions, but as ordained clergy and representatives of the Church we have a special responsibility to make ourselves as approachable as possible to all political groupings. We are required to suspend our own personal political persuasions at the level of party membership in order to facilitate the political process at another level. Take Natal for instance. It would not only threaten the life of a priest if it were known that he or she was a member of this or that political party, it would also render the ministry of that priest virtually impossible in some rural and township parishes."

## Communism

We talk about communism. "Some suggest that I am anti-communist," Tutu observes. "That is not the case. My objection is essentially theological. Dialectic materialism, on which communism is based, is essentially an atheist philosophy." He accepts that there are those who see a space for God within this philosophy and that there are Christians who belong to the South African Communist Party. His concern is, however, that communism fails to locate God at the centre

278

of history. "Communism places too much trust and confidence in human beings. For people to be good and just, they need to be exposed to the grace and goodness of God. Dialectical materialism does not do this and that, in a nutshell, is my problem with communism."

Tutu adds that this does not mean he is not prepared to work with communists: "I have the greatest admiration for people like Joe Slovo and Chris Hani. I walk arm in arm with them. Communists and Christians have co-operated in the struggle against apartheid and I see no reason why we cannot work together for justice in the future."

What of his participation in Chris Hani's funeral? He was severely criticised for what some saw as his overly enthusiastic and spirited participation in this event. The Archbishop stated in his sermon: "For us Chris was a hero and a great leader, irrespective of whether he was a communist or not. We were oppressed by those who claimed to be Christian." To what does he ascribe the hostility from sections of his Church to his participation in the funeral? "White fear and confusion. How can I turn my back on a person like Hani? He has done more for justice than most Christians."

## The Challenge of Africa

As President of the All Africa Conference of Churches (AACC), Tutu has spoken about the loss of human values in Africa. He recalls his visit to the 25th anniversary of the AACC in Nairobi in 1988. "In my sermon I referred to the galling fact that there was often less freedom in the independent Africa of today than was found in the much-maligned colonial days, and that if detention without trial is evil in South Africa it must be evil everywhere else." The Voice of Kenya was present at the rally but Tutu's speech featured neither on TV nor on the radio. *The Standard* (a Nairobi daily) quoted the Kenyan Minister of Manpower Development and Employment, as saying that in Kenya detention was "constitutionally gazetted and part of development". Another minister observed that it was "sad and bad" for the Archbishop to make such remarks in Kenya. Having been welcomed to Kenya by President Arap Moi, Tutu's departure was less propitious. "President Moi was not happy with me. But he still allowed me to use the VIP lounge!"

At the Harare Assembly of the AACC in 1992 Tutu said Africans were disillusioned with politicians and tired of corruption and repression.

"Africa will not be the same again," he told delegates in his opening address. "The so-called ordinary people, God's favourites, are sick and tired of corruption, repression, injustice, poverty, disease and violation of their human rights."

Responding to President Robert Mugabe's opening remarks on the prophetic role of the Church in Africa, the Archbishop observed: "I assure you, Mr President, we will want to continue to keep governments on their toes as we seek to be the voice of the voiceless. It is the role of the Church to be the conscience of society." Despite this, the Archbishop reports that Mugabe responded warmly and positively towards him. "He insisted that it is right and proper that ministers of religion should speak out clearly regarding the moral and ethical implications of any policies and actions, placing the insights of the Church's social doctrine at the service of the wider community. The Church in Africa, as everywhere else in the world, must insist that government is honest and ensure that the cries of the poor are heard in the highest decision-making structures."

## A Prince of the Church

The character and person of Desmond Tutu is both a contradiction and a challenge to anyone trying to do justice to all that he is. He is at once both a prince of the Church and a very ordinary and humble person.

He has transformed Bishopscourt from a place of neglected former grandeur to all that it perhaps never was. He has given the office of the Archbishop of Cape Town a status that it has not had in generations. "His tenure will be an impossible act to follow," one of his priests observed. He has used his ecclesial dignity to confront presidents, prime ministers and ministers of state, while showing a deep pastoral concern to minister to those occupying high office. To the chagrin of some, he has on several occasions gone the extra mile, to consult with former officials of the apartheid regime — although other Church leaders had resolved not to do so. He has also dug in his heels with a resolve and outspokenness unequalled by others, former Prime Minister Vorster discovered when the Bishop terminated his talks with the government several years ago. P. W. Botha was reprimanded on more than one occasion and President F. W. de Klerk has experienced both the charm and the wrath of the Archbishop.

He carries the pomp, ceremony and lavishness associated with high church episcopacy with aplomb. Even a sense of regality. There is also another side to Tutu. He is a man of the people, a simple parish priest and a son of the soil of Africa. He can talk of things divine with all the solemnity and precision of an ecclesiastical teacher, and laugh, joke and taunt with all the eloquence of the Soweto and Johannesburg streets. A man for all occasions, he can speak to alienated black youth, to the most pious evangelicals, to white nationalist Afrikaners, and to the secular business community. A personable man, ready to make a 'phone call and write a personal note, he will step down from a stage in a crowded hall to greet a friend. Tutu observes: "I like to regard myself as primarily a priest, whose task it is to minister to people, leading them in the ways of the gospel. I am also a bishop whose task it is to be a minister and shepherd to priests and laity alike. I take this calling seriously." It is this sense of vocation that detracts from any sense of aloofness to which any lesser person could fall victim.

## Spirituality and Theology

Those who know Tutu best soon recognise that there are two over-riding dimensions to his character. He is a profoundly spiritual person and deeply theological in his understanding of life.

His spirituality is so profound that some regard it as simplistic. Regular in prayer, meditation and fasting, he administers the sacrament to himself in airflights across the Atlantic. Most meetings which take place in his office commence with prayer and many hardened reporters have been told to close their eyes and pray.

On one occasion the Archbishop withdrew from a conference held at St Peter's Conference Centre at Hammanskraal, after delegates had been struggling all day to agree on a particular statement. He later returned and, announcing that he had been alone before God, shared the insight he had gained. His sincerity earned the response of a delegate who obviously disagreed with his counsel: "You put me at a disadvantage Father, I would dare to argue with you but not with God."

A subtle form of manipulation, some have suggested. Few who know Tutu, whether or not themselves religious, doubt his sincerity. He insists:

> It is extremely difficult to know and discern the will of God. It involves thoughtfulness, a willingness to search the scriptures, an ability to plumb the depths of the Christian tradition, and consultation. God's will has to do with what is healing of the

wounds of society — right, just and decent. To know what this means, we need to cleanse ourselves of our ourselves - of our fears, greed, ambitions and personal desires. This is where prayer, fasting, meditation and the sacraments come into the picture. Honest prayer and disciplined living are incredibly illuminating and revealing.

The Archbishop is a theologian. His books, articles in professional journals and conference presentations are enough to make the point. More than that, his thinking and everyday activity are theological. He locates theology at the centre of the political fray:

> Theology is among the most important and crucial disciplines in South Africa today. It reminds us of the worth and potential of people. It tells us that no-one is expendable and that the rights and dignity of all, even those whom society regards as insignificant, are to be treated with respect. Only when this lesson is learned will there be peace. Theology also teaches us that all people, including the most respected and unquestionably decent leaders, are mere mortals capable of succumbing to the temptations and blandishments of power. This means we should not become disillusioned or cynical if those who are oppressed should one day become the oppressors of tomorrow. Theology alerts us to this possibility, reminding us that sin is a stubborn, persistent dimension of the human character. We must be vigilant in ensuring that the good that is within all people triumphs over the evil that is also there. That briefly, is the task of the Church in South Africa and Africa today. We have an enormous responsibility. At a very simple level, we must commit ourselves to tell the truth. We must identify evil wherever we see it. South Africa is wallowing in lies which must end. We must never again tolerate a situation where a General can simply inform a Commission of Inquiry that he has lied and get away with it. There can be no justice and no peace where government and security force officials can tell lies with impunity. The problem is that such things are contagious. If we do not do something about it, we could end up as a nation of liars.

## Christianity and Other Faiths

Tutu has been a patron of the South African chapter of the World Conference on Religion and Peace since its inception. He talks about religious pluralism:

> For me, Jesus Christ is the revelation of God, but I am opposed to proselytism. Our task as Christians is simply to live attractive lives that are transparent with the gospel. We take ourselves far

too seriously when we think that God is relying on our evangelical campaigns to make everyone Christians, in order for them to enter into communion with God.

People sometimes ask me what I make of the fourth gospel which quotes Jesus as saying: "No one comes to the Father except by me." (John 14:6) The question is whether this means it is by the incarnate Christ or the preincarnate Logos that we enter into union with the divine. Surely it is through the eternal creative Word of God that this happens? There are many different manifestations of God's Word. If this is not the case, how do we account for the encounter between God and Abraham, Sarah or Moses? Jesus Christ had not yet appeared. I have encountered holiness, spiritual insight and the presence of God in people of many different religions. I cannot be so arrogant as to insist that these people become Christians.

Concerned that Christianity is too influenced by imperialist and racist ideas which reject all that does not fit into European and missionary world views, the Archbishop insists that we develop the freedom to use our own cultural metaphors to speak of God. "By encouraging people to do this, we enable them to discern the presence of God in their midst." This, of course, has major implications for the Church in Africa. Addressing the question of syncretism and fears about the loss of a Christian identity, Tutu comments: "For goodness sake, God was able to look after God long before we were around. It is not for us to decide who God is and where this God is to be found."

## Life's Journey

In his own unique way Desmond Tutu entertained and needled the Eloff Commission, appointed by the government in 1983 to investigate the activities of the South African Council of Churches, by explaining, with a touch of irony, how his father Zachariah Tutu, a school headmaster and a somewhat proud Fingo, inexplicably married Aletha Matlhare, a Motswana woman who washed clothes for a white family. "Am I Xhosa or Motswana?" He soon, together with his two sisters, learned to speak Xhosa and Tswana as well as English and Afrikaans. His roots are inherently African. He can be no other. He is intensely South African, and yet for many years travel documents declared his nationality to be "indeterminable at present". A man with a huge sense of humour, he laughs as he observes it would be no bad thing if a few more of us were less sure of our precise identity — "it might help us find a new common identity in South Africa".

Born on 7 October 1931 in the township outside of Klerksdorp in the Transvaal, Desmond Mpilo Tutu married Leah Nomalizo Shenxane, a school teacher, and former student of his father. Neither of them could have foreseen the prominence that would characterise their lives. Having earned a Teacher's Diploma from Pretoria Bantu Normal College in 1953 and a correspondence BA degree from the University of South Africa in 1954, he taught at Johannesburg Bantu High School and later at Munsieville High School in Krugersdorp. Called to the priesthood, he earned a Licentiate in Theology at St Peter's Theological College in Rosettenville, and was ordained priest in 1961. He earned his BD Hons and M Th degrees at Kings College, University of London. Returning to South Africa, he lectured at the Federal Theological Seminary in Alice, while serving as chaplain to students at Fort Hare University. From there he was appointed to the University of Botswana, Lesotho and Swaziland, where he taught on the Roma campus in Lesotho. Next came a four year appointment as Associate Director of the Theological Education Fund of the WCC, which again located him in England. On his return home he was appointed Dean of Johannesburg. He later became Bishop of Lesotho, vacating that position a few years later to become General Secretary of the South African Council of Churches. After serving the SACC in this capacity for several years, he became Bishop of Johannesburg. In 1986 he was enthroned as Archbishop of Cape Town.

His numerous honorary doctorates, international awards, medals and salutations are too numerous to mention. Among them was the Nobel Peace Prize, awarded to him in 1984. It was greeted with an official silence from the government. Even the staunchly pro-government newspaper, *Die Vaderland*, thought that while "the man says things that stick in one's craw and send blood rushing to one's head . . . formal congratulations by the state for one of its citizens who had gained international recognition, would decidedly have been in order". On the other hand Alan Paton, the doyen of liberal thought in South Africa at the time, thought that the Peace Prize should have gone to someone whose concern it was to feed the hungry and not one who calls for economic pressure which "could put a man out of a job and make his family go hungry so that some high moral principle could be upheld".

Awards have continued to flow. There is, however, a strange, although not an unpredictable irony, about his acclamations — not until 1993 did any South African university choose to recognise his achievements. The award of an Honorary Doctorate of Laws by the

284

University of Cape Town came belatedly. Asked to comment, he carefully observes: "In the eighties UCT gave honorary degrees to blacks who were acceptable to the white establishment, in a way that I was not. There was a time when I would have given it back and I don't need it now. But I've decided to accept it as an act of healing."

## Unstoppable

What does he fear most about the future? "Violence," he insists. "My greatest concern is how to break the cycle of endemic violence. I am concerned that there are political leaders who may refuse to accept the outcome of a democratic election. I fear the involvement of sinister neo-facist international organisations like the World Preservationist Movement."

"I, at the same time, believe in a great God," Tutu continues. "The violence, the resistance to change and the horrible things that we are presently experiencing must not be allowed to stop the inevitable. Peace will take a Promethean effort on our part, but ultimately it will come. I say this because I firmly believe that this is God's world, and God is a God of justice. This is what makes us unstoppable."

# AFTERWORD

## *The Future Is Now*

"A small miracle" — this was the response of President Nelson Mandela to South Africa's first democratic elections held from 27 to 29 April 1994. Thomas G. Karis, historian, author and veteran South Africa watcher — who was also kind enough to write a foreword to this book — states that "there appeared to be no precedent for the peaceful relinquishing of power to an oppressed racial majority by a militarily undefeated regime".[1]

When Mao Tse-tung was asked what he thought of the 1789 French Revolution he is alleged to have replied: "It's still too early to say". It's early days in the South African experiment. The South African edition of this book, published immediately prior to South Africa's historic election, is entitled *The Spirit of Hope*. The journey was still, at the time, towards the promised land. The promised land has been entered. The future is now. The milk and honey are not plentiful. Archbishop Desmond Tutu has, at the same time, suggested that the gravy train stopped just long enough for a new load of politicians to get on board! Of course things are more complex than that. The State President and the cabinet have agreed to take a salary cut. There is a fierce expectation that government be answerable to the people. There is talk of a national character radically different from that of the past. South Africa's first democratic Parliament has taken important steps towards creating more transparent procedures, while the task of creating a culture of openness, transparency and accountability continues to challenge the nation.

The nation-building process has begun. The title of this edition of the book, *The Spirit of Freedom*, seeks to capture this. Eric Foner, the Columbia University historian who delivered the thirty-fourth T. B. Davie Memorial Lecture at the University of Cape Town shortly after the South African election, reminded us that "freedom is not achieved in a day, or once and forever." Taking as his topic 'The Story

---

1. Thomas G. Karis, " 'A Small Miracle' Continues: South Africa, 1994–1999," *The Round Table: The Commonwealth Journal of International Affairs*, Apr. 1995.

of American Freedom', Foner quoted Eric Wolf, a previous T. B. Davie lecturer: "Freedom is a process that is forever unfinished".[2]

A journalist "who has spent many years covering South Africa" and who read the manuscript of this book for the University of California Press suggested that the book could be more relevant in years to come than what it is now. The implication is that the vision that inspires a revolution is rarely sustained under the demands of government. Scandals have already shaken the government. At the same time, South Africa has witnessed a level of moral outcry on the issues that was never allowed under the apartheid regime. At another level, a 'negotiated revolution' is even less likely to deliver on its promises. The interim constitution that emerged after a protracted period of intense negotiations, while demanding a high price from the majority party (which garnered 62.6 percent of the total vote), has nevertheless contributed significantly to the stability of the country. The new constitution that is likely to come out of the Constitutional Assembly is also likely to contain a number of political compromises. It may be that the duress and demand for constitutionally guaranteed open and moral government is just what is needed to entrench the nascent dynamism of the struggle for freedom. Opposition, political struggle and the sheer will to deliver in the face of critique, analytical scrutiny and healthy cynicism have rarely harmed the democratic process.

## Where Are They Now?

History is not only the creation of individuals. Great leaders and significant players have, nevertheless, always helped shape the texture and direction of the historical process of any nation. A nation's people (good and bad) give expression to the collective forces and values that shape a nation. Of course, the national character is shaped by more than 'great people'. This point was made in the Introduction to this volume. A reviewer of the book is correct: a companion volume on the 'ordinary people' (those whom someone once called the 'aristocracy of anonymity') would certainly be in order.

Where are those people interviewed for this book now? They fall readily into three categories: those who have entered government and organised politics, those who are in the structures of civil soci-

---

2. Eric Foner, "The Story of American Freedom," 34th T. B. Davie Memorial Lecture, 20 July 1994, University of Cape Town.

ety and those who are part of the *izithethe* (cultural tradition). They remind the nation of its origins and early aspirations.

Nelson Mandela is, of course, the first President of a democratic South Africa. Less than 2 percent of white South Africans voted for the African National Congress (ANC) in the election. Recent opinion polls show that almost 60 percent of the white population thinks Mandela is doing a good job as President. Coloureds and Indians, most of whom also voted against the ANC, show a similar appreciation of his leadership. As one individual said, "President Mandela is the single most important nation-building factor in the country". Govan Mbeki is Deputy President of the Senate, working side by side with Kobie Coetsee, who is the President of the Senate and a stalwart in F. W. de Klerk's National Party. Allister Sparks tells the story of Coetsee's formative role in persuading the former State President, P. W. Botha, to enter into negotiations with Nelson Mandela while Mandela was still serving a life sentence for his activities against the state.[3] Ela Gandhi, Ruth Mompati and Albertina Sisulu are among the one hundred women in the National Assembly (of a total of four hundred members). Ebrahim Rasool is Minister of Health and Social Welfare in the Western Cape Regional Assembly. Cheryl Carolus chose not to enter elected politics. She has since been elected Deputy Secretary-General of the ANC.

Neville Alexander continues to head the Workers' Organisation for Socialist Action (WOSA), while providing the single most articulate expression of South African left-wing political views. He is a leading voice behind the movement for the establishment of a Workers' Party. Franz Auerbach, retired as an educator, now works with the Jewish Board of Deputies and the World Conference of Religion and Peace. Frank Chikane has relinquished his position as General Secretary of the South African Council of Churches and is studying development economics at Harvard University. Sheena Duncan, veteran leader of the Black Sash, continues to·work with this organisation, giving leadership to the promotion of human rights. Nadine Gordimer continues to ply her trade as an internationally celebrated South African novelist. Fatima Meer is director of the Institute for Black Studies at the University of Natal and a member of the Board of the South African Broadcasting Corporation. Stanley Mogoba is

---

3. Allister Sparks, *Tomorrow is Another Country: The Inside Story of South Africa's Negotiated Revolution* (Sandton: Struik Publishers, 1994; New York, Hill and Wang, 1995).

head of the Methodist Church of Southern Africa. Itumeleng Mosala has relinquished his position as President of the Azanian People's Organisation (AZAPO). He is a professor in the Department of Religious Studies at the University of Cape Town. Beyers Naudé, who turns eighty in May 1996, continues, with Wolfram Kistner, to head the Ecumenical Advice Bureau in Johannesburg. Desmond Tutu retires as Archbishop of Cape Town in 1996.

The *izithethe* include many of those already named — Nelson Mandela, Govan Mbeki, Albertina Sisulu and Ruth Mompati. Others include Chris Hani, assassinated three months after I interviewed him. Joe Slovo died of cancer during the week that this afterword was written. Ray Alexander and Trevor Huddleston are both active in their retirement, promoting those values to which they dedicated their lives.

## Values

The notion of value-based politics — alternatively, the insistence that politics is more than the art of the possible — is a major theme of South African politics. But what is value? When Gill Marcus, a key figure in South African transitional politics, was asked to define 'value' she replied, "It is trying to live a life that has value"; it involves "making a contribution to others".[4]

The pursuit of ideological, religious and cultural value-based debate has always been part of the South African struggle. So fierce has this debate been in recent times that it threatened to militate against political compromise and peaceful settlement. The fear of a black majority government has been translated into a deep-seated ideological belief by most whites of the moral superiority of white culture. Blacks look askance at such claims. Some young Africans, whose only encounter with whites has resulted in exploitation and suffering, have internalised this in the slogan "one settler one bullet". Muslims in the Western Cape who have come to accept that male dominance in public and religious sectors of society is the will of Allah are not easily persuaded by the critique offered in this book by Fatima Meer and Ebrahim Rasool on the place of women in Islamic society. Examples are plentiful. Marxian ideas have fired the dispossessed masses. Doctrinaire notions of capitalist gain have been the staple diet of white, as well as bourgeois black, entrepreneurs

---

4. "'A Life of Value': Gill Marcus Talks to Todd Pitock," *Jewish Affairs* 48, no. 4 (Summer 1993), p. 25.

who have amassed their wealth through the maze of apartheid privilege and patronage. Ideological belief and value do not make for an easy road to compromise, political settlement and the creation of something new.

Some, on the other hand, saw the values debate as little more than a ruse for preserving the status quo. The axiomatic cry for "liberation before education", the disregard of moral persuasion and the support for armed struggle were often seen as the only basis for social change. Others interpreted ethical critique as a pretext for replacing the existing order of the time with the forces of darkness. Talk of human rights (South Africa did not subscribe to the 1948 Universal Declaration of Human Rights until 3 October 1994) was dismissed by the South African state as unnecessary outside interference in domestic affairs. Ethical critique of apartheid was regarded as Communist propaganda and anti-apartheid activists were jailed or killed as terrorists. The South African struggle that had for generations managed to avoid terrorist attacks on civilians, schools, restaurants, pubs and rural villages threatened, in the run up to the elections, to be engulfed in a spiral of indiscriminate violence and structural collapse.

This disregard for ethical standards and the absence of respect for human life were not confined to the political realm. Family feuds, marital violence, murder, rape, the abuse of children, alcoholism, corruption and exploitation became rampant at every level of society. I quote from an address by Barney Pityana to priests who had completed their pre-ordination training and were about to be appointed to their first parishes: "We live with the human and physical devastation caused by apartheid. All around us are the symbols of that fierce struggle. We can see it in the victims: the widows, the crippled and those mentally and physically affected by torture. We see it in the breakdown of discipline in schools and in the breakdown of family life. We see it in the prevalence of crime as a way of life in many of our communities. We see the moral breakdown so much that we no longer recognise it as such. It has become a way of life."[5]

The effects of the apartheid monster will continue to haunt South Africa for years to come. Apartheid's worst consequence is still to be faced — the dehumanisation of both blacks and whites. Designed to

---

5. Address at Awards Ceremony, College of Transfiguration, Grahamstown, 22 Feb. 1994. See also N. Barney Pityana's review article on my *Spirit of Hope, Journal of Theology for Southern Africa*, no. 88 (Sept. 1994), pp. 69–72.

promote the 'good life' for whites, apartheid sought to reduce blacks to a status within which they would be content with an existence devoid of human rights and social and material well-being. Many blacks could conclude nothing more than that their existence was located beyond the bounds of white compassion or reason. Whites, in turn, saw as their right the enjoyment of social privilege at the cost of black suffering. They demanded this privilege. They fought for it. As black rebellion and white repression intensified, ethical ideals and human values were thrust aside in pursuit of political and personal gain.

The South African story of reconstruction is as much moral as it is political. The accentuation of values — drawn from what Nadine Gordimer, in her interview in this book, argued is "part of the collective consciousness of humankind, gleaned from earlier generations and centuries of moral insight, wisdom and different ways of dealing with the mysteries of life"— continues to inspire political debate in South Africa. This is not to suggest that South Africa is more morally alert than some other countries. It is not to suggest that South Africa's politicians and national leaders are necessarily more principled than others. We used to say that South Africa (despite its 'irreligious' behaviour) was an intensely religious country. Theological debate broke out on the floor of Parliament; moralisms as well as ethical concern permeated the national milieu. Today, given the multicultural, ideologically diverse and religiously plural nature of the emerging South African debate, it is more accurate to talk of the value-based nature of South African debate. The boundaries between belief and non-belief are not always clear. The contours of value are shifting, and the ultimate shape of the national soul is yet to be decided. Religion is part of this quest, and religious symbols figure boldly in debate, as witnessed in the interviews with avowed atheists — Neville Alexander, Ray Alexander, Nadine Gordimer, Chris Hani, Govan Mbeki and Joe Slovo. There are also other sources of value. These include traditional African culture, Marxism and other secular belief systems, and the insights gained from generations of practical struggle.

Legislation providing for an established Human Rights Commission, a Truth and Reconciliation Commission to deal with past atrocities, a code of conduct for the police and armed forces, as well as legislation governing the treatment of prisoners, the application for bail and other matters pertaining to the due process of law, all point to a commitment to deal with matters of human rights and values after the revolution. The main protagonists in these developments are people given to the promotion of values. They are people committed to "making a contribution to others". Several are interviewed in this book.

## Difference

The energetic nature of cultural pluralism, for so long suppressed and manipulated to the benefit of apartheid belief, is only just beginning to realise its full dynamic. So dynamic is 'difference' that some fear that South Africa's explosive ethnic and cultural mix could drag the country into a Bosnia-Herzegovina type conflict. The KwaZulu/Natal region continues to seethe under the force of political, tribal and ethnic conflict. Some right-wing Afrikaners still demand an independent Boerestaat. Things can go wrong. There is, at the same time, a new realisation of the potential for living together on the basis of difference — a difference that ultimately unites.

It has been suggested that the inauguration of President Nelson Mandela constituted the first post-modern event of its kind in human history.[6] The religious traditions represented by the priests, the imam, the rabbi and the *imbongi* (African praise singer) who participated in the ceremony each contained their own particularity and integrity. On one level these religious incantations were contradictory — they constituted a discord of words and symbols. On another level one sensed that something new was being born. The incantations gave expression to a culture of difference within which there is no obvious synthesising unity. The unity is beyond and within the difference. Where it all ends is yet to be seen. This is what makes the process so interesting. Is the future essentially a polyglot? The present is a collage. It is a collection of particularities, existing in relation to one another. In the relationship is the total picture. It is more (and less) than an integrated mosaic.

The lack of creative dealing with the politics of difference among South Africans has, as a result of imposed separation under the apartheid regime, long plagued the nation. Although non-racism has popularly been associated with Charterist (ANC) politics, it is also the goal of the Pan Africanist Congress (PAC) and the Black

---

6. See John W. de Gruchy in *Christian Century*, 15–22 June, 1994.

Consciousness Movement (BCM).[7] The means of attaining this ideal, rather than the ideal itself, are what divides the different liberation movements in South Africa. It can be reasonably argued that the formula whereby people who have been forcibly separated by racist laws can live together in a common society constitutes the new *kairos* (a time pregnant with possibility) facing the nation.

The question is whether political universalism (the affirmation of individual rights under the banner of what Charles Taylor calls difference-blind liberalism) is ultimately undermined by the affirmation of cultural particularism.[8] Can we have both national unity and the celebration of diverse cultures, religions and ethnic identities? It is in relation to these questions that the future of South Africa is likely to be resolved.

Steve Biko's words stand as a warning against any notion of assimilation that makes passivity the conduit that leads from rejection to acceptance: "Blacks are tired of standing at the touchlines to witness a game that they should be playing. They want to do things for themselves."[9] Predictably accused of racism in liberal circles, he responded: "If by integration you understand a breakthrough into white society by blacks, an assimilation and acceptance into white society by blacks, an assimilation and acceptance of blacks into an already established set of norms and codes of behaviour set and maintained by whites, then YES I am against it."[10]

Western notions of multiculturalism do not solve this problem. They allow different cultures to exist side by side, without challenging the dominant culture of the ruling class. This centre remains Eurocentric, male and white. Differences, whether of religion or culture, are regarded as private matters to be 'separated' from the affairs of state and kept out of the public square.

Given the close link between culture, race and economic disparity in South Africa, the question must also be asked whether ethnic cate-

---

7. See Robin Petersen, "Towards a South African Theology of Non-Racism," *Journal of Theology for Southern Africa*, no. 77 (Dec. 1991), pp. 18–26. This notion is further developed in Charles Villa-Vicencio, "The Quest for a National Identity," *JTSA*, no. 86 (Mar. 1993).

8. Charles Taylor, *Multiculturalism and the Politics of Recognition* (Princeton: Princeton University Press, 1992), p. 62.

9. Steve Biko, *I Write What I Like* (London: Heinemann, 1987), p. 154.

10. Ibid., p. 24.

gories such as 'blackness' are in fact critical and radical enough to deal with the underlying divisions in South African society. Neville Alexander's discussion of black consciousness included in this volume must be taken into account in this regard. He argues that "any cultural product that enhances humanity, by weakening the perpetuation of the system which enables men [sic] to exploit others, is beautiful". His concern is, however, that like any other ideology, black consciousness can be co-opted by the very forces it seeks to overthrow. If its leaders are "bought off by the powerful and all-pervasive oligarchy to become satellite 'capitalists' or apologists for these, the Black Consciousness Movement will become another conformist attempt: it will become a consumerist movement providing the ideological basis of firms catering for Afro-styles. It will give the appearance of militant opposition while in reality constituting a necessary and even a vital aspect of the establishment". Alexander continues: "The Black Consciousness Movement correctly stresses the unity of the oppressed people of South Africa." His argument is that a critique of apartheid must necessarily go beyond colour. He shares black consciousness's rejection of white liberals, while suggesting it would be a mistake to believe that all liberals are white. "Liberalism," he declares, "is a greater danger in the long run to the struggle of the oppressed than Fascism."[11]

Although, for the foreseeable future, alienation and exploitation in South Africa are likely to continue to be accurately symbolised by categories such as 'black' and 'female', an increasing number of black males (at least) are likely to find themselves in privileged and socially unhindered positions in South African society. And, if human nature can be predicted, some will in turn defend the structures that make this possible. In brief, there is every indication that race, colour and ethnicity could become increasingly ambiguous social terms in South Africa. The challenge of non-racialism (by no means realised yet) is an extremely difficult thing for non–South Africans to understand. As an ideal that has long driven the South African struggle, its future is not yet assured. Nor is its content fully understood.

---

11. See "Black Consciousness: A Reactionary Tendency," first published in 1974. Reprinted together with a reassessment of this argument in Neville Alexander, "Black Consciousness: A Reactionary Tendency?" in N. Barney Pityana, Mamphela Ramphele, Malusi Mpumlwana and Lindy Wilson, *Bounds of Possibility: The Legacy of Steve Biko and Black Consciousness* (Cape Town: David Philip, 1991; New York and London: Zed Books, 1991) pp. 238–52.

There is a growing realisation in South Africa that cultural and political openness is the only basis for nation-building. This openness involves a willingness to allow everyone to participate in the shaping of the future, even those with the most rigid views on race, culture and future identity. T. S. Eliot has suggested that the greatest creativity occurs at the friction edge of cultures — where the old meets the new, where cultures fuse, where the growing edges of traditions are most vibrant and fragile. For societies in transition, where people are obliged to face that which is new, there is a disposition to discover options for living together that 'stable' societies never know. Empires that have not yet fallen and people who live as happily in the iron cage of intransigence usually regard adventure as unnecessary and stupid. It takes a certain kind of compulsion to embark like Abraham and Sarah, on a journey into "the unknown, not knowing where [we] are going."[12]

Gloria Anzaldua, in *Borderlands / La Frontera*, a story written from the perspective of a Chicana lesbian living in the United States, shows how the struggle for survival on the edges of society contains the potential for new forms of human understanding. "The new mestiza [person of mixed ancestry]," she says, "copes by developing a tolerance for contradictions, a tolerance for ambiguity. She learns to juggle cultures. She has a plural personality, she operates in a pluralistic mode — nothing is thrust out, the good, the bad and the ugly, nothing rejected, nothing abandoned. Not only does she sustain the contradictions, she turns the ambivalence into something else."[13] Renato Rosaldo comments: "In making herself into a complex persona, Anzaldua incorporates Mexican, Indian and Anglo elements at the same time that she discards the homophobia and patriarchy of Chicano culture. In rejecting the classic 'authenticity' of cultural purity, she seeks out the many-stranded possibilities of the borderlands." Rosaldo argues that because of their long-practiced art of cultural blending, Chicanos have become leaders in developing "new forms of polyglot cultural creativity."[14]

---

12. Quoted by Jerzy Smolicz in a dialogue with Neville Alexander in "The Quest for a Core Culture," *Bau* (a publication of the National Language Project) 8; no. 3 (Sept. 1993), p. 5.

13. Gloria Anzaldua, "Borderlands / La Frontera: The New Mestiza" (San Francisco: Spinsters / Aunt Lute, 1987), p. 79. Quoted in Renato Rosaldo, *Culture and Truth: The Remaking of Social Analysis* (Boston: Beacon Press, 1989), p. 216. Italics added.

14. Rosaldo, p. 216.

Anzaldua's story is repeated in Soweto and in the Cape Flats (a coloured resettlement area in Cape Town) every day. Migrant workers from Transkei, Venda, Zululand and Qwa Qwa encounter urbanised neighbours and unlawful immigrants from Zaire, Nigeria, Ghana and elsewhere. There are gangsters and thieves, frightened people and an emerging bourgeoisie. They speak English to enter the realm of employment. They speak Afrikaans to negotiate the still entrenched apartheid bureaucracy. They speak *tsotsi-taal* in the *shebeens* (township pubs), whereas on the mine compounds the lingua franca is *fanakalo*, a dialect which is ultimately non-language. The 1976 Soweto rebellion was followed sixteen years later by a hero's welcome for a Robben Island fugitive who was to become the first president of a democratic South Africa. This is all part of a dynamic Sowetan culture. It is an identity that is. It is a culture also en route. In its openness it anticipates the future.

The Cape Flats is not Soweto. It is Muslim, Christian, Hindu and atheist. It is Malay. It is coloured. It is black. It is communist, workerist and survivalist. It also provided the ('new') National Party, which imposed apartheid on a nation for forty-five years, with its only provincial victory in the country's first democratic election.

The interim constitution of the emerging South African nation is designed to bring different cultures — those that were, in terms of apartheid ideology, supposedly each sufficient unto themselves — into a unity. South Africa has always been a place of difference. Difference is palpable. Now, however, for the first time in a long history of struggle, difference is viewed positively. To have spoken of difference in many progressive circles prior to 1990 would have been to provoke anger. Apartheid-insulated difference was necessarily spurned. Today the *kairos* challenge is to discover how difference can be employed to build a nation.

Will the cultural collage, the numerous subaltern identities, eventually blend in difference and unity? How will Soweto, the Cape Flats, Kwa Zulu, the former Bantustans, Johannesburg, Potchefstroom, Pretoria and Cape Town (each with evolving cultures of their own) encounter one another? Alternatively, will Christians, Muslims, Hindus, Jews and atheists who fought a common struggle against apartheid — having been beaten by the same apartheid police, locked up in the same prisons and gone together into exile — be able to maintain the unity that forged unity in difference? Will the separate cultures co-exist side by side — 'separate but equal' (to use a bad phrase)? If so, from where will the social tissue come that binds the nation? Will the centre hold? Will everything collapse? It is too early to tell. There are, however, some tentative signals hidden in the journey travelled thus far. The interviews in this book provide some clues.

Reference has been made by several interviewees in this book to the traditional African understanding of *ubuntu*. The word affirms an organic wholeness of humanity. It bespeaks a sense of wholeness realised in and through other people. The notion is enshrined in the Xhosa proverb *umuntu ngumuntu ngabantu* (a person is a person through persons).[15] This is a belief that recognises within other people the presence of the divine through which a person attains full humanity. *Ubuntu* is the realisation that, like it or not, we are shaped for good and bad by a host of others with whom we share our lives. Meaningful relationships, whether by blood, by marriage or even by association, are cherished dearly in traditional African culture.[16] Such relationships constitute an organic identity that the Western world can comprehend only with difficulty. This identity primarily involves kinship within one's own clan, but such relations also emerge with 'personal strangers' — people among whom I grow in my humanity, whether through affirmation or conflict.[17] There is ample evidence in South African history of traditional Africans drawing others (whether missionaries or white settlers — some of whom later turned against the Africans) into kinship with themselves. In sum, an African sense of community includes and unites, and in so doing it changes.[18] The story of Soweto, with all its cultural assets and liabilities, makes the point. It also reminds us that neither African culture, nor any other culture, should be romanticised.[19]

---

15. See Gabriel Setiloane, *African Theology: An Introduction* (Johannesburg: Skotaville, 1986), pp. 13–16.

16. Ibid., p. 9.

17. See discussion on culture, ethnicity and group identity in Gerhard Maré, *Ethnicity and Politics in South Africa* (London: Zed Books, 1993), p. 12.

18. For further discussion see, *inter alia*, Leopold Senghor, *On African Socialism* (London: Pall Mall Press, 1964); Setiloane, *African Theology*; Leo Apostel, *African Philosophy: Myth or Reality* (Gent: E. Story-Scientia, 1982); Augustine Shutte, *Philosophy for Africa* (Cape Town: University of Cape Town Press, 1993).

19. See Archie Mafeje, "African Philosophical Projections and Prospects for the Indigenisation of Political and Intellectual Discourse," Seminar Paper Series no. 7 (Harare: Sapes Books, 1992), p. 27.

At the heart of Africa, despite its changing character, there is dialogue with one's own and with other people. This dialogue is a deep-seated anthropological and religious given. There is recognition that within the other, however different, there is humanity and the promise of an enriched life which makes social bonding possible. A common South African culture does not exist. But given the place of belonging, forging and uniting in African encounter, it might or might not eventually emerge. The celebration of African culture ensures that whatever the nature of future South African culture, at the centre of human encounter there must be mutual respect. If South Africa is to be one nation, there must be a nexus where the different cultures meet or at least where common values within these cultures enable some form of organic union.

Culture, language (there are eleven official languages in South Africa) and other identity-creating factors such as religion, memory, gender consciousness and social location can be neglected only at the cost of excluding people from the democratic process. Democracy is about the proliferation of stories, symbols, languages and religions. The exclusion of these is tantamount to the exclusion of people whose identity is constituted by them. In South Africa, however, the quest is for something to hold the nation together after generations of racial, ethnic, cultural and religious division.

This quest has something to do with discerning that which transcends what is immediately evident in any particular culture, religion or ethnic-based value system. It involves recognising the possibility of transcendence in every story. It involves the hope for something more than what is immediately before us. It has something to do with discerning universal meaning in one's own story and the stories of others. It is about discovering something greater than what immediately comes to expression in any particular story. It involves the glimpse of something radically new, yet grounded in the traditions of the past and the realities of the present.

A prerequisite for this quest is openness to others — and to the other. A commitment to openness involves creating socio-political and cultural structures that facilitate and promote encounter, dialogue and openness, without making any attempt to determine or prescribe the ultimate shape of the future.

It is appropriate to end this afterword to a book about great South Africans with a quotation from the recently published autobiography of Nelson Mandela:

I was not born with a hunger to be free. I was born free — free in every way that I could know. Free to run in the fields near my mother's hut, free to swim in the clear stream that ran through my village, free to roast mealies [corn] under the stars and ride the broad backs of slow-moving bulls. As long as I obeyed my father and abided by the customs of my tribe, I was not troubled by the laws of man or God.

It was only when I began to learn that my boyhood freedom was an illusion, when I discovered as a young man that my freedom had already been taken from me, that I began to hunger for it. . . .

But then I slowly saw that not only was I not free, but my brothers and sisters were not free. . . . It was this desire for the freedom of my people to live their lives with dignity and self-respect that animated my life, that transformed a frightened young man into a bold one, that drove a law-abiding attorney to become a criminal, that turned a family-loving husband into a man without a home, that forced a life-loving man to live like a monk. . . . Freedom is indivisible; the chains on any one of my people were the chains on all of them, the chains on all of my people were the chains on me.

It was during those long and lonely years that my hunger for the freedom of my own people became a hunger for the freedom of all people, white and black. I knew as well as I knew anything that the oppressor must be liberated just as surely as the oppressed. . . . When I walked out of prison, that was my mission, to liberate the oppressed and the oppressor both. Some say that has now been achieved. But I know that is not the case. The truth is we are not yet free; we have merely achieved the freedom to be free, the right not to be oppressed. We have not taken the final step of our journey, but the first step on a longer and more difficult road. For to be free is not merely to cast off one's chains, but to live in a way that respects and enhances the freedom of others. The true test of our devotion to freedom is just beginning.[20]

The spirit of freedom continues to brood among South Africans. Freedom is indeed a process that is forever unfinished. There is, however, every indication that with the correct constitutional safeguards, the right kind of political culture and a general sense of goodwill, the 'small miracle' will continue to unfold amidst the in-

20. Nelson Mandela, *Long Walk To Freedom* (Randburg: Macdonald Purnell, 1994; Boston: Little, Brown, 1994), pp. 616–17 (page citations for Macdonald Purnell edition).

evitable ups and downs of the political process. Add to this the importance of socio-economic growth and improvement of the lot of the poor and disinherited, and South Africa can make it. All this requires a lot of hard work.

— Charles Villa-Vicencio
31 March 1995
Human Rights Day
Cape Town, South Africa